OF HORSES AND MEN

Tales from a rural New Zealand farrier

FRANS JANSEN

www.wildsidepublishing.com

real stories. real hope.

Copyright ©2020 Frans Jansen

Published by Frans Jansen with Wild Side Publishing November 2020
Email: fransjansen@xtra.co.nz
www.wildsidepublishing.com

All rights reserved. No part of this publication may be reproduced, distributed, or transmitted in any form or by any means, including photocopying, recording, or other electronic or mechanical methods—without the prior written permission of the publisher, except with brief quotations embodied in reviews and certain other non-commercial uses permitted by copyright law.

Maps on page 6 are copyright ©Google.

The 'OF HORSES AND MEN' heading on the front cover is a real-life, handcrafted sign made from genuine horse shoes by Frans in his little blacksmith shop. In the winter, when there is not much demand for shoeing horses, he hides there recycling horseshoes, making signs, hangers, wine racks, gate numbers and all sorts of gadgets. **Please visit www.trademe.co.nz and look for member: 'realequine', or simply type in 'horse shoe products' and you will find it.**

Logo: The horse shoe with the heart (made from an old horse shoe) is made by Frans. He calls it: *'Lucky Love'* when he sells them, but to Frans it means: *'For the love of horse shoes.'*

Would you like to see how Frans puts a horseshoe on a horse?
Please visit www.youtube.com and search, 'Frans Jansen Farrier'.

Back cover photo: This is Sue's horse, a beautiful Percheron mare, probably bigger than a Clydesdale, with the biggest hooves Frans ever had to deal with.
"Sue and her husband owned a farm on the other side of Maungaturoto and on one occasion Sue came back on her motorbike after twenty minutes looking for her horse. She was rather upset and disappointed that she could not find her horse and asked if I would like to come back another day. Luckily the horse did turn up eventually."

Front cover photography: Sarahlee Cobb, Sarahlee Studio | sarahlee.c@hotmail.com
Cover design: Collaboration by Wild Side Publishing and Sarahlee Studio
Typesetting and layout: Janet Curle, Wild Side Publishing

National Library of New Zealand (Te Puna Matauranga o Aotearoa)
Title: Of Horses and Men: True tales from a rural New Zealand farrier

ISBN: 978-0-473-54243-6 (paperback)
        978-0-473-55692-1 (epub)

Subjects: Memoir, Pets/Horses, Nature/Horses, Equine, New Zealand Non-Fiction

First printing November 2020 New Zealand
International listing February 2021 www.ingramspark.com

OF HORSES AND MEN

Acknowledgements

Thanks to... Linda from down the road for setting up my laptop and guiding me along in the computer world. I felt like a dinosaur learning new tricks, but thanks to her patience I managed to learn even a little more than the basics.

Bob for showing me some more things this laptop can do, saving me heaps of time.

Andre for teaching me English—spelling and grammar, and for editing this book; a 'mammoth task' he called it.

Sarahlee from Sarahlee Studio in Whangarei, for designing the draft cover of this book, taking the front cover photo and for editing all the photos.

To all the customers who unknowingly became colourful characters in this book. There was something about them or their horses which compelled me to record it on paper so we will not forget them or forget what happened.

To Laurel for booking us on a cruise-ship to Vanuatu. Her reasoning, that there was absolutely nothing for me to do, worked well. A lot of the stories in this book have been written at seven o'clock in the morning on deck 13 next to the coffee shop. I thoroughly enjoyed it.

All my customers who kept on asking when this book, I had told them I was writing, was finally coming. It was a sure way to keep me motivated.

KAIPARA DISTRICT
Auckland
Tauranga
Hamilton
Wellington
New Zealand
Christchurch

NORTH ISLAND
Auckland
Hamilton
Tauranga
Rotorua
Taupo
New Plymouth
Napier
Hastings
Palmerston North
Wellington

Pipiwai
Hikurangi
Tutukaka
Ngunguru
Tutamoe
Donnellys Crossing
Ruatangata West
Pakotai
Aranga
Parakao
8
Whangarei
Titoki
Poroti
Pataua
Taiharuru
Parua Bay
Kaihu
Whangarei Heads
Mamaranui
Tangiteroria
Omamari
Tangowahine
Ruakaka
Omana
7
Awakino Point
Dargaville
Waiotira
Bream Bay
Baylys Beach
6
Waipu
Taipuha
9
Arapohue
Te Kopuru
Langs Beach
4
3
Mangawhai Heads
5
Paparoa
Maungaturoto
Matakohe
11
Mangawhai
Ruawai
Pahi
Kaiwaka
10
Hukatere
Tinopai
Kaipara Harbour
Te Arai
Tomarata
Te Hana
Port Albert
Wellsford
Whangaripo
Leigh
Pouto
12
Wharehine
Tapora
13
Matakana
Warkworth
Mangakura
Kaipara Flats
Snells Beach
Kawau Island
Glorit
Woodhill Forest
Makarau
Puhoi

Maps © Google

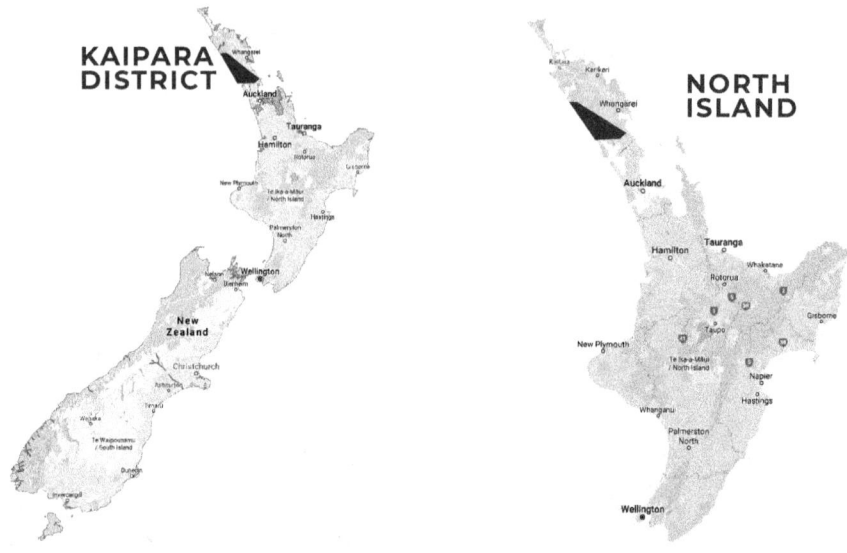

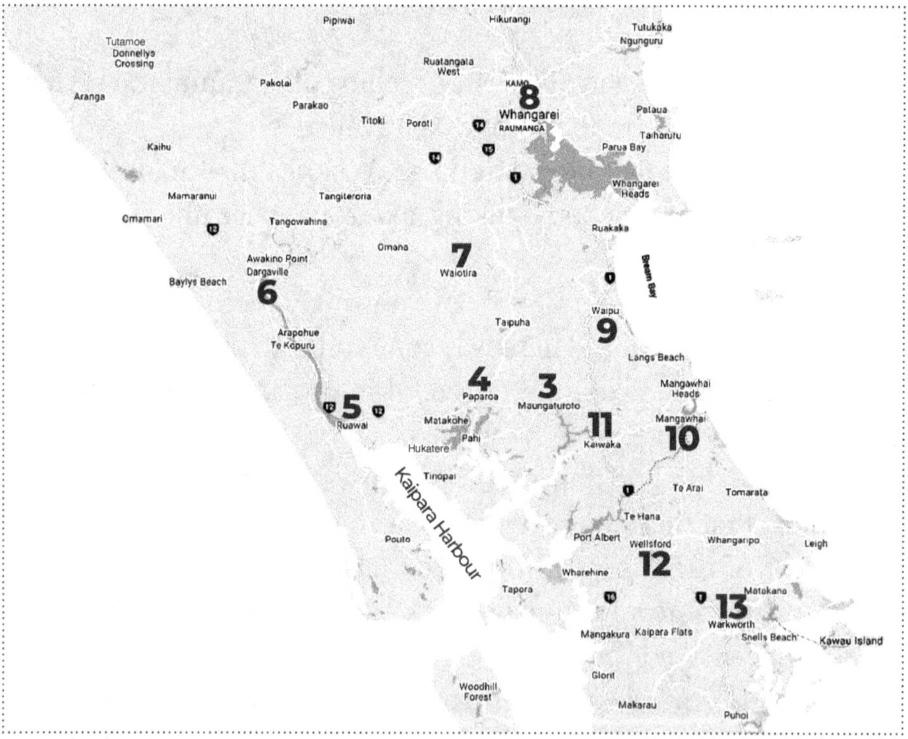

Contents

Photos and notes		8
Introduction		13
1	The beginning	17
2	First horses	31
3	Maungaturoto	49
4	Paparoa	83
5	Ruawai	101
6	Dargaville	119
7	Waiotira	129
8	Whangarei	153
9	Waipu	175
10	Mangawhai	195
11	Kaiwaka	219
12	Wellsford	249
13	Warkworth	257

These photo's were taken by Andre to illustrate the different positions of horse and farrier while shoeing. Laurel's horse, Shadow, takes it all in his stride. At the age of 11, he has done it all many times before.

1 This is where it all starts: lifting up the leg. My thumb is on this side of the leg, my fingers on the other side, gently squeezing the tendon. Putting on more pressure if nothing happens.

Release the pressure when the horse lifts his leg up. In Shadow's case, I hardly put any strain on, and in this photo we see that he is gently lifting his leg up. Lifting the back feet is exactly the same.

2 Shadow's leg is wedged in between my thighs, just above the knees, with his hoof sticking out from my apron so that I can work on it. It is oh so important where my feet are in relation to the horse. As a general rule: if the horse is happy, I must be standing in the right place, as they sure tell you if I am not.

3 Sarahlee did a good job of editing this photo. It is Shadow's hoof, seen by me from where I am in photo 2. The thickness of the wall is the same all way around which is good. The sole and frog are looking very healthy. The white line, yellow looking in the toe area, will transfer the weight, from the shoe on the wall, to the inner workings of the hoof.

4 The hoof well shod. The shoe, second time it has been put on, will give an enormous amount of protection to whatever ground-surface the horse is exercising on.

5 This position is needed to work on the outside of the wall, either rasping or folding over the nail ends to secure the shoe to the hoof. Any horse will tell you directly, if the tripod where his hoof is resting on, is in the right place. It is just a matter of finding the right spot.

1

2

TOE
white line
wall
sole
HEEL
frog
3

5

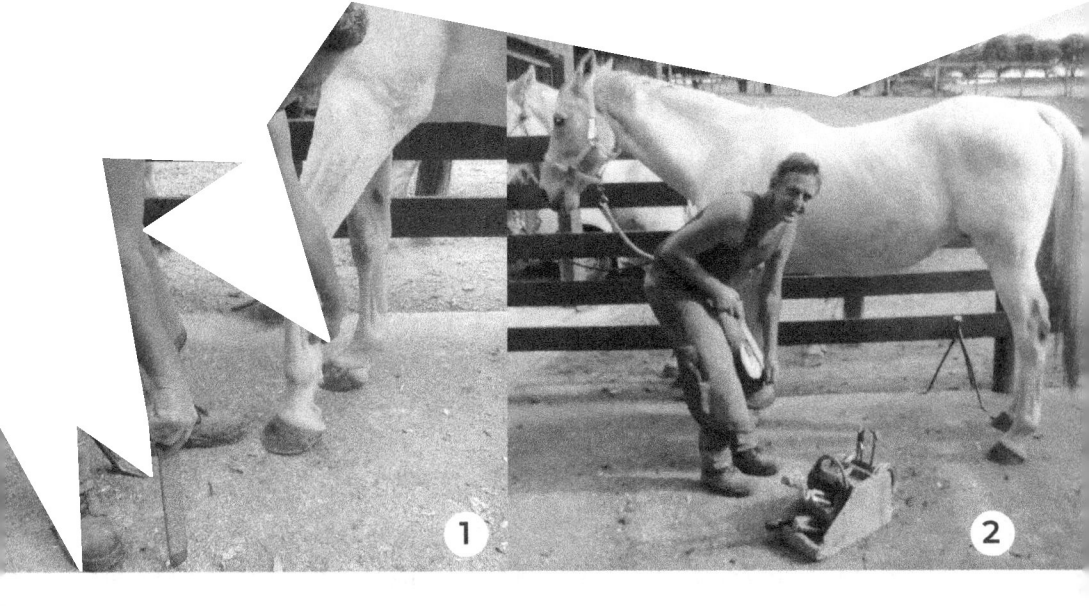

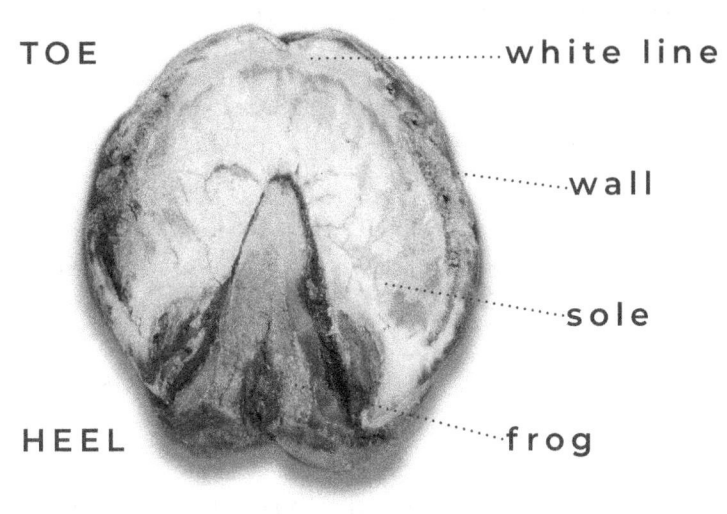

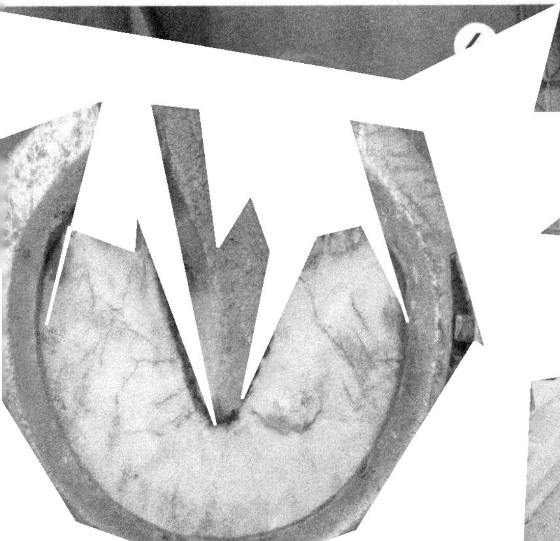

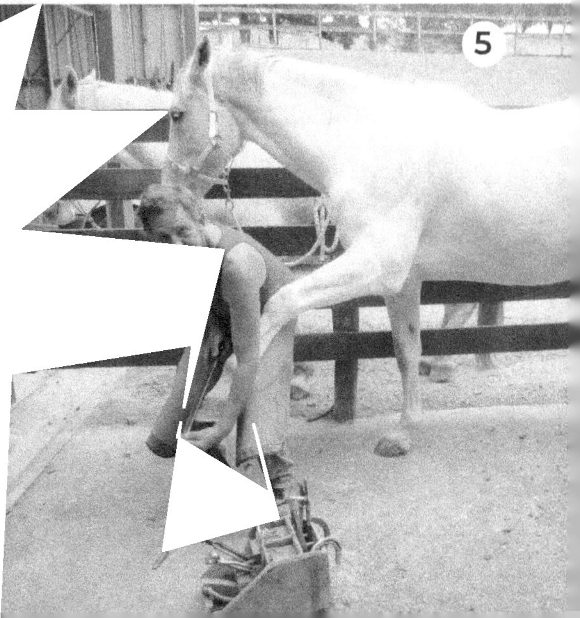

(6) ***Please note that Shadow's leg is not between my thighs but rests on my lap.*** If he would kick with that leg, he wouldn't do too much damage this way. Here I am securing the shoe to the hoof with some nails.

(7) When finished nailing the shoe on, I change position and touch his belly with my backside, his hoof on my left knee to fold over the nails and make it smooth with the rasp.

(8) Here I have changed position again and put my head almost underneath Shadow's belly so I can work on the inside of the hoof, which is resting on my right knee. Photo's 6, 7 and 8 are made without me putting the hoof on the ground. When changing position, I just take the leg with me, horses don't seem to mind.

(9) The tools of the trade. Permanently mounted on the back of my Ute at the bottom of the photo is the 40kg anvil to shape the horse shoe to the pattern of the hoof.

On top of the anvil on the right is the hoof knife; on its left is the old buffer. A buffer has two ends, one to clean the nail holes in the shoe, the other side is used as a chisel when placed on a folded over nail and being hit with a hammer to fold the nail back, so it will be easy to take the shoe off the hoof. This one has been hit a few thousand times compared to the new one on the left. Resting against this are a few different sized horse shoe nails.

On the left of the anvil is my reliable water bottle, I am not too worried if the water gets a bit warm in the sun. Above the bottle are two horse shoes, the left is a front shoe, the right is a hind shoe. Above these is my tripod, borrowed from one of my customers around fifteen years ago.

In the toolbox at the top from left to right: shoe-puller (good for anything steel), clencher (for folding over the nails), hammer (for driving the nails in) and the hoof-nipper, good for hoof only.

Between the top tools and the outstretched horseshoe handle are two little compartments which hold the nails. At the bottom of the box are two rasps, the new one is for hoof-work only, the old one is for nails and shoes. The wire brush is incredibly handy for cleaning the sole of the hoof and for cleaning the shoe as well. On the right of the toolbox are some aluminum horse shoes for race horses. The tool box is the fifth one I've made, changing the design a bit each time.

OF HORSES AND MEN

Introduction

This book is by no means a manual about how to shoe a horse. Instead, it is a collection of experiences gained while simply shoeing horses. On paper the job looks simple, and a farrier likes to treat all horses the same. While all horses like to be treated with some respect, they are so different to one another that a recipe approach has only a slim chance against a horse's own ideas and the personality and temperaments that nature has given them.

This book is not all about horses either as every horse needing my attention has its owner. The farrier would like to treat all owners the same, but they vary at least as much as horses do, apart from the fact that people like to be treated with some respect too.

Respect for the owner is simple because they are the ones who pay the bill, but while shoeing a horse, my respectful treatment of the horse takes on the form of a partnership, just like riding them. Trust is the word to describe this, and a two-way trust it is—horse trusts man, man trusts horse. There is just no way I can put the shoes on the hooves if the horse doesn't trust me.

Being blessed with an enormous amount of patience, I normally succeed in getting the job done.

The job is specifically the timeless tradition of putting new shoes on a horse. A set of four sturdily-fastened steel crescents, enable the horse to perform to the best of its ability, with maximum traction and protection from hard surfaces, much like an athlete with new running shoes. When the horse is happy, the owner is happy too, as they can now pursue their passion of riding their companion. When they are both happy, the farrier can be satisfied in a job well done. Aside from the horse and the owner, the weather is a critical factor in a farrier's trade. From cyclones that send torrential rain and gale-force winds, to nearly collapsing from heat exhaustion; from working deep in mud and slush that spread until all the tools and clothes are dirty, to sun scorched days when the sharpest tools seem blunt against bone-dry hooves, and two litres of water does not quell your thirst. A farrier says thanks to the weather gods when it is calm, not too hot, not too cold and above all dry. In the middle of a hot summer, battered by a relentless burning sun, a farrier looks forward to the winter. Yet when winter takes its toll, all of its unpleasantries make a farrier look forward to the summer again.

Through my career I would shoe a horse for a fifteen-year old girl one day, then suddenly she is all grown up and I find myself shoeing her daughter's little pony. There are a few horses I have been shoeing for twenty years now. But somehow time does not seem to fly because in every visit there is always something to talk with the clients about; the weather naturally, the horse, the family and whatever happened since our last visit.

There are over three hundred customer names stored in my mobile phone. Some customers I only see a couple of times a year, but others I see every four weeks. It is hard to remember their names along with their partners names as well. But remembering the horses' names is almost impossible, especially when an owner has a few of them.

Some horse names don't even indicate the sex so I get reprimanded regularly for saying "Good boy" to the horse when in fact the

INTRODUCTION

horse is a "Good girl". Nevertheless, a fair proportion of my clients and their horses are key figures in the stories in this book, and in order to protect their identities, I have changed their names.

For a long time I have been writing down these 'snippets', as I call them, of interesting things happening while out and about shoeing or trimming horses hooves. Human nature dictates that we do forget things, and some of these experiences are so funny or sad or unbelievable that it was important for me to write them down lest they be lost forever.

Aside from capturing the individual stories, another matter was finding a logical way to arrange them. In the end, I looked to my work routine for an answer. Every Sunday night after dinner I sit down for a few minutes with my mobile phone, diary and booking-book to make a plan for the coming week. In the booking-book I transfer the customers I should have seen last week to the coming week and write in all the new bookings. The customers are written down in groups based on their nearest town. I allocate five different towns and areas to each of the five working days. Once that is done, I start to text the customers in the Monday area, trying to stitch a nice little round trip on the map, and so on for the following four days. So, for example, one day I might go shoeing towards Northland's west coast in Dargaville and surrounding areas, while the next day could be spent in Kaiwaka and Mangawhai on the east coast. It all depends on the amount of bookings in a certain area. All my memories seem to come back to me when I return to the area in which they happened. I can drive past a customer's place and smile about a funny thing that happened there years ago. As it is the place, not the time, that memories come to me, so too is how the chapters of this book are arranged.

Two decades ago I would not have guessed that I would have a book worth of farrier stories. Having been a surveyor in the Netherlands, I came to New Zealand to pursue first a career in dairy farming, then cabinetmaking. Becoming a farrier, however, is by far the best, most interesting and rewarding job I have ever had. I give thanks to my wife Laurel, who is 'horse mad' as they call it, for introducing me to horses, pointing me in the right direction and supporting me all the way. After a lot of years of shoeing horses, I can honestly say that I still enjoy my job and that I will probably carry on in my retirement years, just hopefully not as many horses.

I would like to conclude my introduction with a fun fact: although I know my way around hammers, hooves and halters, actually riding horses never really appealed to me. Still I admire anyone who rides a horse. I don't know how they do it. They are so high up in the saddle that it seems a long way to fall if things go wrong. I feel much safer and happier with my two feet on the ground underneath a horse, shoeing or trimming their feet.

Frans Jansen

> Frans is a common Christian name in the Netherlands. It is derived from my official and baptised name of Franciscus. In English it would be Francis or maybe Frank. (Franz is German).
>
> Jansen directly translated in English is Johnson meaning son of John; Jansen means the son on Jan, which is a common male Christian name in the Netherlands. (Jensen is German or Danish).

1
The Beginning

The horse had enormous overgrown feet with a few big cracks. I did not know how to trim the hoof, but I once saw someone do it, so I knew what the end result should look like. With a hoof knife, a wood chisel, an old carpenter hammer and a rasp, I started. I was amazed at what the horse would let me do to his feet. How I picked them up and handled them did not seem to be any worry to him. Being pretty handy with a chisel and hammer, I managed to cut off most of the wall, the outside of the hoof, which was sticking out like our toenails, and with the rasp I took away the rough edges. Looking at the result, not overly pretty but rather compact, I was very proud of my handiwork.

Ribo was the horse's name and he was the first horse I ever touched at my age of twenty-six years. He was a thoroughbred and as a race-horse he won close to $30,000 in prize money, mainly when he had matured and went steeple chasing. They reckon he enjoyed that immensely.

When he retired from racing, someone took him out hunting — the old English fox hunting with hounds—only here in New Zealand they hunt hares as there are no foxes. He was pretty good at that too according to the master, the person who leads the hunt, who rode Ribo for a few seasons.

And now he belongs to Laurel, my wife to be, who hunted with

Ribo for a few years. When I met her, she was living in Matakohe, a little town world famous for its Kauri and Pioneer Museum which houses the world's biggest collection of Kauri gum, expelled from New Zealand's biggest tree. We did not stay long in Matakohe as I got a milking job in Ruawai, about twenty kilometres west. Ruawai translates to *Two Waters*—the place where the sea and rivers meet. The Ruawai flats are slightly below sea level, and it was only late in the nineteenth century that early settlers made a stop-bank around all the flat land to keep the water out, using shovel, spade, horse and cart. Now more than thirty years later, I still think of Ruawai as a small Holland, as that too is flat, below sea level and incredibly fertile from the sea and river silt.

We moved to Ruawai in the middle of winter into a nice house on the main road. We would call it our home for the next four years. Laurel and her daughters, Paula and Jolene, and I enjoyed it there, as did the cats, the dog and of course, Ribo. We married, and our sons, Andre and Lars, grew up there and we had a very good and happy time. That is except for Ribo. He was the hardest to look after as dairy farmers normally do not like horses. But there were a few side roads with enough grazing on the verges to keep him busy for a long time, provided we fenced him in and kept the wires hot.

Laurel had just returned from grocery shopping in Dargaville, a reasonable sized town twenty kilometres away, and checked on her beloved old Ribo, who was grazing on the side of a no-exit road near Raupo, just a bit north of Ruawai. Raupo was a very important place a long time ago as there was a ferry going to the Pouto Peninsula that cut the travelling time by car by more than an hour.

I met Laurel at the back door. I was still in my overalls and gumboots, having just finished the afternoon milking. "Stuck in the drain, up to his chest… poor Ribo is stuck in the bloody drain," she said, "What are we going to do?"

"We better have a look I suppose," I replied. "Might need the boss's tractor and some ropes maybe, but we better have a look first as it is still light. Maybe after you put away the frozen groceries, you can come over and we can take it from there?"

That was agreed upon, so I jumped onto my farm bike and went to have a look at Ribo.

He was stuck, all right. The drain was not very wide at all; he almost filled it all up with his body. If it were a stream, he would have stopped the water flow. I still did not know a lot about horses, but I could see he had given up trying. This is where he got stuck. Here he would make his last stand of accepting his fate, and here he would die, probably sometime the next day.

As I contemplated what to do, an old man appeared from nowhere on a pushbike. Even though the road was nice and flat, not many people rode push bikes around there. "Stuck ey?" he asked, but it sounded like a statement. "A fine horse indeed. I have admired him a few times on my travels. I live just down the road, and could see him from the main road.

The way you fenced off the roadside to graze your horse, I could not miss him, ey." He was silent for a while before proceeding, "Casey, Mr Peter Casey is my name, and I am delighted to meet another horse enthusiast. There are not many around here anymore. For you know I have a few of my own. You come and have a look one day, ey."

I managed to control a grin as his introduction sounded so much like James Bond's. After I told him my name, I explained that Ribo was my wife's horse and that she was horse-crazy, and that we had just started working on this dairy farm. I looked at the sky and noticed dusk was going to settle in.

Mr Casey looked old, of slight build, hunched shoulders and had a permanent limp. But maybe, he was just the man we were looking for to show us how to get this horse out of the drain.

I put a halter on Ribo and pulled the rope, hoping for a burst of energy to get him free. Nothing happened. He was going to die here instead of wasting futile energy in trying to get out. "Nothing happening, ey," Mr Casey remarked. He grabbed a spare lead rope and got right behind the horse.

"Now you, young fella," he said to me, "you will pull the rope again, but this time like you mean it—put some energy into it, ey. I will give him a severe belt on the back end so that something will happen. Ready? Go!"

I pulled with all my might while Ribo got a hiding. You could see him thinking very hard, but finally, after the second belt, his survival instinct took over and he leaped forward. His front feet moved up and forward but sank again deep in the mud. It would have been good progress if his back feet had followed, but they had not. We now had an outstretched horse stuck in the drain with the early spring night closing in.

My wife appeared, and after introducing Mr Casey we all wondered what to do next. "His back feet are stuck," Mr Casey said.

"Do we need a tractor?" my wife asked.

"If we do, how are we going to pull him out?" I asked.

"His back feet are stuck," Mr Casey said again. "We need another rope, ey." Luckily, we found some of reasonable thickness in the boot of the car.

Without much thought, Mr Casey hopped in the drain next to the horse to try to put a rope around the back leg of the horse, the lower the better. This scared both my wife and I. One little quirk from this big horse, and he would squash this little old man flat against the side of the drain. Suicide, we thought.

It must be said, Mr Casey had an incredible affinity with horses. Ribo totally accepted him crawling around his back end and putting a rope around his leg.

Mr Casey was finally satisfied with one side and crawled his way to the other side of the horse to do the same. The drain was about half full of water, and thank God it was not filled up to the edge. The problem was the stickiness and softness of the sheer black mud, as there did not appear to be a bottom to the drain, just mud. But Mr Casey kept ploughing on. He did get the second rope where he wanted it and climbed out of the drain, covered in mud.

"We'll probably only get one chance," he said, "So we better make it a good one, ey." Then instructing us separately he said,

"Mrs J, a lot will depend on you. You will have to be so strong in mind and voice to make the horse want to come out so that he won't give up after he starts. Pull hard, but when he tries and actually does go forward, loosen the rope a bit as he needs his head for balance. And if you can, try and steer him up the bank on the road side as there is a fence on the other side."

"And you Mr J, you pull with all your might and don't let go after the first step, he needs to have support so that he does not sink too deep in the mud again, ey. You take his right leg and I will take his left."

Glad that someone knew what needed to be done, my wife and I happily took our place and put some strain on our ropes. Mr Casey picked the left side with reason as his rope was long enough to make a whip out of the left-over bit.

"You both okay?" he asked. After confirmation he yelled, ***"Let's go!"*** and we all put our weight on the ropes while he lashed his spare rope once on the horse's backside, and again when nothing happened, my wife yelled encouraging words to the horse.

The poor horse, overcome by so much raw emotion, decided to play ball and again heaved his front feet up but when they went down again, he could not help but to lift both back legs as we basically pulled them out of the mud. When the back ones came down, they were in fresh mud so to speak and did not sink in too much as we still tried to pull them up. More yelling and pulling followed so as not to lose momentum. Ribo took another stride... first the front moved a little up the bank, surprising my wife who slipped and fell flat on her back.

Ribo used his front feet to pull himself up which was a little bit easier now. Before my wife could get up, she had to let go of the lead rope as Ribo took another stride, half up on the bank again as he did not want to jump on his boss, good horse as he was.

The next couple of strides he did by himself, and once firmly on dry ground he stood still, trying to regain his composure. After a couple of deep breaths, he started to shake to get rid of the mud, which did not work. He was one lucky horse. Mr Casey had landed back into the drain feet first again after the horse's second stride. He was literally covered in mud, his arms and legs completely coated in the stuff. There was mud on his face too, but unmistakably there was an enormous grin on the face of one happy man... happy to have saved this lucky horse.

My wife, unhurt as well, rushed to the horse and talked sweet little things to him, and as a surprise to all of us she took a couple of carrots out of the pocket of her jacket, saying, "Just been shopping you lucky horse, but don't you do this again."

Ribo sure loved those carrots. Mr Casey carefully undid the ropes from the horse's legs. My wife got a bucket and some towels out of the boot of the car, and I got the job of finding some clean water out of the drain to rinse most of the mud off Ribo's legs and belly. To make matters worse, he started shivering.

With the towels my wife dried his neck and back, then his belly and legs. She went back to the car and got a warm cover to put on the horse, and a big feed bowl full of horse feed. Within minutes the horse regained his normal composure and stopped shivering.

Now it was Mr Casey's turn to get the shivers. It was near dark now and a cool breeze came in from the coast. "We thank you very much for your help, Mr Casey. That was very much appreciated, so lucky we are that you just came by. We should be fine for now;

Ribo is getting nice and warm now thanks to you. Time for you to go home, hop in the bath and get clean and dry before you get a cold," I said.

"Oh well, that's what we do for a fine-looking horse like this, we do, ey. But yes, it is getting cold a bit. I might just hop on my bike and go home. Good to have met you. See you later," he said.

"Thank you, Mr Casey," my wife added when Mr Casey finally got on his bike. Those wet pants made it very hard for him to actually hop onto his bike.

Ribo had finished his dinner and was very happy to be in his little paddock on the side of the road wandering along doing what horses do best... eat grass.

Later at home, I commended my wife on being highly organised in getting all the useful gear ready. She explained that this was the third horse stuck in a drain that she had to deal with; she should have known by now. All I could think was that they were all very stupid to land up in the drain in the first place.

That winter Ribo aged a lot, since being exposed to the cold westerly wind was not good for an old horse. It was getting harder to graze him on the roadside, so we decided to find another home for him. We were very lucky that Jenny and Tony from Mamaranui, a settlement half an hour's drive north of Dargaville, were willing to take him in. They were very nice people and had 20 or maybe even 30 Welsh ponies running around the paddock below their house. They started with just a handful, but since someone dropped off a little stallion, the numbers exploded.

As the day came to an end, Jenny and Tony settled on the veranda with a cuppa, overlooking the valley waiting for the spectacle to begin. The ponies had been quietly grazing all day long, having a roll now and then or just standing sound asleep or admiring the beautiful scenery.

Now they started running, prancing, dancing, biting, rearing and kicking—it was play time! The ponies galloped towards the far side of the paddock, and just when you were sure they would crash through the fence, they would come to a sliding stop, the hind legs overtaking the front feet and touching the fence, the head and front feet miraculously turned away from the fence, all before stopping and scrambling away from it.

On a little knoll Ribo was standing to attention, watching them play.

The herd with the Welsh stallion in front made a nice loop around the little knoll, hoping to stir the old gelding up, but he knew how to play the game. A couple more loops later, the little stallion suddenly cut the circle a bit shorter and ended up right in front of Ribo, and slowed the pace enough to rear up and thrash around with his front feet close to Ribo's head. The stallion shrieked loud and clearly as if to show Ribo how strong he was, "This is my herd, these are my mares, their off-spring is mine too, and I am their boss. Don't you forget it!"

This then was the start of some lovely animal play of chasing and play-fighting. Ribo would cut some young fillies from the herd but when the stallion noticed what was happening, he would gallop past Ribo to take his fillies back to the rest of the herd. By the time he thought he had them all together again, Ribo managed to get some youngsters from the back again to follow him instead. And so, it went back and forth till everyone slowed down about half an hour later. As if someone blew on a whistle to end the game, all the horses suddenly lost interest in playing around and just stood there looking very happy with themselves indeed. "Time to watch the news," Tony said to Jenny, "but I know already that watching these horses play is much more interesting."

Only a couple of years later Ribo passed away in what Tony described as a beautiful way. Ribo, at the end of the day, after chasing these young fillies out of reach of the Welsh stallion, suffered a heart attack and was gone very quickly, doing what he loved doing.

After Ribo died, Laurel took a liking to Appaloosas, the spotted coloured horses the American Indians used to ride, and she joined the Western Riding Club where she met Nick and Vivienne who had Appaloosas. 'Western' refers to the style of riding developed in the Western United States, which looks rather relaxed compared to the stricter English riding. Nick became interested in shoeing his own horse, not necessarily to save money, but for sheer convenience: you can shoe your own horse in your own time at your own pace and at your own place. At the time, he was working on a Landcorp Farm north of Dargaville big enough to support a manager and two or three shepherds. A shepherd had to have a set number of working dogs and, if possible, a horse as there was a lot of rough country unsuitable for a bike.

It was an ideal job for anyone interested in the outdoors. Aubrey, the manager, was shoeing his own horses, plus a few more for other people for years; and did not mind, in fact, would enjoy teaching Nick and me some things about shoeing horses.

One Saturday morning the three of us got together with a few horses: it was my first lesson in shoeing. Not in my wildest dreams would I have thought that many lessons would follow, and that I still would be learning when I retired.

Aubrey knew a lot about shoeing horses, having had to shoe his own horses on some far away stations (really big beef and sheep farms), and he had been around horses his whole life.

I learned how to handle the horse while shoeing, what to do, and, more importantly, what not to do. For certain, don't get angry while underneath a horse. Aubrey had a soft way of handling the horses, so they were a pleasure to shoe; you just touch their legs and they will lift their legs up by themselves. I trimmed one hoof, under close supervision, until it was ready to take the shoe. I even managed to nearly shape one shoe on an anvil made from a piece of railway iron. Aubrey finished shaping it and nailed it on. If I wanted to nail a shoe on for the first time, I had better use my own horse, he told me, which I suppose was fair enough.

After that, nothing much happened for a few years. My wife and I started share-milking on the other side of Ruawai as well as rearing our family. After a couple of years, we left for Maungaturoto, share-milking on a farm behind the dairy factory. We walked the cows from Ruawai to Maungaturoto, guided from horseback. There was a car in front for the job of putting some bailing twine across the gateways, and three horses at the back to keep the cows moving.

We were lucky that on the farm in Maungaturoto we were allowed a couple of horses. Horses and dairy cows don't get on very well together. It was here that Billy Irvine came to shoe our horses. Billy taught me a lot. If a horse ever became lame, for whatever reason, Billy would instantly take the blame, saying that he must have pricked it or something. By doing so, he instantly diffused any arguments which might have arisen, so we could look at the real issue straight away.

Billy never married, and he lived at home looking after his mum. After she died, other family members wanted a piece of the house and things like that. It was in the days where we had just gotten the hang of the answer phone.

Billy's invite to leave a message was interesting and rather unusual:

"Hello, this is Billy here. If you are a lawyer, piss off. If you are a member of the family, you know where to go. If you are a customer, please leave your name and number. Thanks."

Billy got a bit sick of me. I could feel it. He just got sick of all the questions I kept asking, "Why this, why that? What happens if you do this, what happens if you do that?" And all the while I watched every move he made and how he did the things he did, there was always the question 'Why?' I suppose I behaved a bit like a two-year-old with all the why's.

Then one day, just after he arrived, he put his hand in his pocket, retrieved a scrap of paper and gave it to me. "Here," he said, "Manukau Polytechnic are organising a farrier course in Pukekohe. You better go there to learn a bit more."

And so, a few weeks later, Nick and I were on a two-hour drive to Pukekohe, just south of Auckland. To make it more interesting, we brought along my oldest daughter's horse in the horse float and arranged the night before to stay with my brother in Pukekohe. We were looking forward to this one-day course in shoeing your own horse. Big was our disappointment when the course was cancelled early in the morning. It was time to go home again.

They did run the course a couple of months later. Nick could not make it, but I did. It was held at the Pukekohe racecourse, at the Forge of Earle Adlington.

Earle had appeared in a few articles in the Horse and Pony and probably other horse magazines and appeared on TV on Country Calendar.

He was a master farrier with a wealth of experience.

There must have been 12 people at Earle's shoeing area, very often called 'The Forge', at the Pukekohe racetrack. We all wanted to learn and we were all keen to shoe our own horse or at least be able to trim it's hooves. How you can teach all that in one day, or maybe better still, how you can learn all that in one day, is probably impossible. To become a farrier is a four-year apprenticeship. That's probably why they called it an introductory course. It was hard to put all his years of knowledge and experience into a day-long programme.

But we managed just fine. This time I did not bring a horse, but a few other people did. With so many years of experience, Earle made everything look easy. He trimmed one hoof and put on a shoe without any strain on his body while the horse remained very relaxed with this professional approach. And then it was our turn.

Before too long, a learner was putting on a shoe under Earle's close supervision. And then so did the next person, grateful to further their skills on someone else's horse. We all kept on trimming and putting on shoes, and when we were only watching, we took note of anything that Earle said.

At morning tea time, Earle showed us a piece of hoof he had cut off from a neglected horse. It was rather long, around 100mm. Time had made it contract some, as all the moisture had disappeared, I told Earle that it looked like part of the antlers from a deer. "No," he explained, "the feet of this pony were so incredibly long that I had to cut them off with a hand saw. Not cut the feet off, just to trim the hooves, like we have been doing this morning. I only cut off what was sticking out, and this was part of what was sticking out. The hoof nippers were too small to cut it off, so I had to use the hand saw."

The piece of hoof looked horrible, especially once we understood what it was, where it came from and how it managed to get that long.

Not in my wildest dreams did I ever think that years later I would possess a similar piece of overgrown hoof, sawn off with a hand saw because it was so long, stored in the back of my Ute, for educational purposes, as I call it.

"Hold it right there," Earle said with a lot of urgency in his voice to the guy who had just picked up a horse's left front foot to start rasping the wall. "Put the foot down please. Not in my workshop, no way!" The poor guy did not know what was happening, but now he was the centre of attention, with everyone curious to find out what Earle did not like. "We talked a lot about safety this morning; we talked a lot about common sense, about what to do in certain circumstances and what not to do." It was very quiet in the workshop. We all felt there was something important coming, something that all of us seemed to have missed.

"Many years ago," Earle continued, "there was this guy, like John here today, who started rasping the horse's foot. As I have told you a hundred times this morning already, horses are unpredictable. Don't you ever forget it. We get a feeling for it when things are likely to happen, but they can happen much quicker than we can ever understand.

"For some reason the horse this guy was shoeing got a fright. The guy had his rasp close to his stomach, like this." Earle picked up the rasp from John and held it lightly with the tang, the point where a handle could be fitted, to his stomach.

All became instantly clear.

"The poor guy spent weeks in hospital, the tang had perforated a few organs, and he was lucky to be alive. So that is why I say, not in my workshop, not when I am around. All it takes is a handle, and they are not that expensive. Here, take this one please John," and Earle handed John a rasp with a handle. All was well again, and John resumed his work after taking a deep breath.

Earle made everything look so easy. Where we were struggling at home with a piece of railway iron, Earl had this massive anvil probably weighing over 100kg. Everything is easier, especially when you put the horse shoe in the coal forge and make it red hot, so it's very easy to bend and shape. Of course, it is not easy at all as I found out much later. You have to know on which point to hit the shoe to make the bend or straighten the steel, combining this with the amount of force to hit it and the angle to put your hammer on, it is still rather difficult.

The day came to an end when Earle's friend and colleague dropped by. Earl put a bit more coal on his forge and threw in an old rasp. When it was hot enough, he picked it up with his tongs and put it on the anvil. He held a cutter on top of the rasp and his mate started hitting it with a small sledge hammer. When the cutter almost cut through the steel, the blows became a bit gentler as not to blunt the cutting tool when it would cut through the rasp and onto the cold hard steel of the anvil. After the cutting, a third from each end, there was bending, twisting, tapering and a lot of other things I did know about. And every time when the old rasp became too cold to work on, it was put back in the forge to heat up.

Sometimes Earle directed his mate to hit it here or there, pointing with a steel rod to show exactly where; other times he did everything himself. It was a beautiful exhibition of good old fashioned tradesmanship and it took a while before we could visualise what he was making. It turned out to become an absolutely stunning looking boot-puller.

"Wow, what a nice hobby this would be," I was thinking, just as if I needed another hobby. The boot puller was given to a young lady who had shown an incredible amount of perseverance in trimming a couple of feet on her frisky young horse.

We all went home with a feeling we were much richer in understanding the horse, knowing more about their feet and feeling very comfortable in trimming and in some cases, putting on a shoe.

Coming home on a high, I told my darling wife that I could shoe a horse now, and if she could please let me just do it. I needed a few more tools, but they were not too hard to get hold of.

2
First Horses

Peacock Smart Fellow looked at me after I tied him up on a rail in the cowshed yard. He knew something strange was going to happen.

"It is the wrong time of the day to go anywhere. My rider is nowhere to be seen, so it can't be a pleasure ride around the farm. It can't be the vet either because there is nothing wrong with me. The dentist has been, not too long ago, so it can mean only one thing—the farrier is coming. Oh no, not that again. I enjoy it when my shoes are on, as it is much easier riding over the farm races, but it is such a nuisance holding my leg up all the time, backwards, forwards and sideways. It is not an enjoyable time really."

I looked at the horse with renewed interest. He was a beautiful chestnut with a white blanket on his backside. At sixteen hands high, the old height measurement for horses, surprisingly still in use, he was very tall for an Appaloosa: the result of breeding with a thoroughbred, the galloping race horse. One hand is four inches which is approximately a hundred millimetres. Sixteen hands convert to 1.6 metres, measured from the ground to it's withers, a horizontal ridge line between the horse's neck and back.

Today was the day I would try and put four shoes on his hooves. I learned enough to give it a go, I thought, and had the permission of his owner, so here we go.

Peacock Smart Fellow, his registered name, or 'Fella' for short, kept on looking at me. He wondered where Billy was. My gear was a little bit 'Mickey Mouse' as they call it. The apron was of a flimsy sort of leather and did not even reach the knees. The hoof nippers were the cheapest ones we could buy, the knife old and blunt, the rasp also blunt, the hammer was again the cheapest. But we managed to find some shoes and *on they must go.*

It all looked so easy when other people did it. It really did. So, I must be able to do it as well, I thought.

Dressing the hoof, that is trimming the hoof accurately so that it is ready for a shoe to be put on, was not too bad. It was the shaping of the shoe on the anvil which proved to be the biggest hurdle. The anvil was a piece of H construction steel, but it looked like a big I. Figuring how to hold the shoe in or on the slot cut in the top of my so-called anvil, which sat on a big stump, was the hardest. Then the matter of working out how hard and on which angle to hit it proved to be very important as well.

It took time, a lot of time. I relayed back and forward between the horse and the anvil: lifting the foot up, holding the shoe in place, and seeing what needed to be done: where to bend, turn, flatten and widen it; then at the anvil, trying to bend, turn, flatten and widen it; then fitting the shoe back on the horse and wondering what happened. Why did the plan not work? Didn't I hit the shoe hard enough with my hammer?

As I kept on thinking, fitting and shaping, I came to the conclusion that there were too many variables. Determined to work it out, and to finally put my first shoe on a horse, I kept on going backwards and forwards. Fella, who had shoes put on his hooves on a regular basis, was wondering what the hell was going on.

"What is happening to this guy who normally only feeds me, shifts me to a new paddock and sometimes catches me? He is not trying to put some shoes on me, is he? I certainly hope not. Oh my,

this is going to take ages, and I haven't eaten enough grass yet this morning. I better start misbehaving a bit, and then maybe he will let me go."

So, when I thought I already had some difficulties, everything suddenly got much worse with the horse's misbehaviour. But I did get closer in shaping the shoe, and suddenly, as if by magic, the shoe fitted like a glove. Now it was only a matter of nailing the shoe on. I had seen that done a few times by then and it did not seem too hard.

I had the feeling as if I needed another hand, as two did not seem enough: one for holding the shoe in place, one for holding the nail and one for operating the hammer. So in reality the one holding the shoe has got to hold the nail as well. Easy… then there is the angle at which to hold the nail and hit it with the hammer. I managed, but it was a struggle. The horse did not like the nailing, and I was very worried that the nail would go the wrong way and hurt the horse. I was very scared indeed that the horse would pull back his foot with a nail still sticking out that could end up in my hand or leg. But I did get there. I did. If it were not such an agony, I would have been proud of myself, but the nails had to be folded over before I was finished, and it proved to be very painful to rest the hoof with shoe on my knees. With the rasp, I had to make the nail ends the same length and fold them over with the hammer, then make it all look nice and tidy by running the rasp over it lightly. Easy, really… but I was exhausted from all this work I was not used to. I might have been reasonably fit, but of all the muscles I used that day, there must have been some I never knew existed, let alone needed to work for me.

It was time to straighten up, yes, but not a time to celebrate. There were still three more feet to do. Shaping the other front shoe seemed to be less of a problem as I got a bit used to working this so-called anvil. But poor old Fella had had enough of it. Billy could put four new shoes on within an hour, whereas I managed to put on one. I did succeed at putting the other front one on, but by then I could hardly walk. The pain grabbed not just my back, but all the muscles at the top and back of my legs. Looking at the feet, I was proud I actually put the front shoes on; though I was not very happy at all with the way it looked. Nevertheless, it was time to put Fella in his paddock, have a cup of coffee and go and get the cows to be milked. There would be another day tomorrow.

Two days later, I felt recovered enough to attempt to put shoes on Fella's back feet. The day before would have been totally impossible as my back and my legs were way too sore. The actual fitting and nailing of back shoes is exactly the same as it is for the front. The big difference is in the handling of the legs as they are different: you don't put the back hoof in between your own legs as you do with the fronts. There is an enormous amount of potential energy bundled up in those hind legs, and when that power gets unleashed, it will send you flying.

The shape of the hooves is different too: the front ones seem rounder in shape than the back ones which are more pointed.

The outside of the hoof is called the 'wall' and can be compared to our toe nails. The difficulty I encountered while nailing on the hind shoes was the fact that the wall seemed to have a much steeper angle than the front feet. The thickness of the wall seemed to be thinner than the front as well. It is real scary stuff putting back shoes on for the first time. To be on the safe side, it will be better to nail them a bit low: the nail will come out of the wall very quickly, but it will not have much holding power. Just let's hope for the best and at least not lame the horse. By the time the back shoes were on, I was determined never to shoe a horse again, not even one shoe. Not even a nail. My body was sore all over, especially the lower back and the back of my legs. I did not know how farriers did it and my appreciation of them was enormous.

There was no way I would think it possible that I ever could make a good living out of shoeing horses.

Two days after shoeing Fella, the first shoe came off. A hind one, of course. Most people call them 'back feet', some, mainly professionals, call them 'hind'. As I was a little busy and Laurel was not riding anyway, I left it for another day, still trying to get over all these sore muscles I didn't know I had. By the weekend, he had lost another one, this time a front one. It was time to take some action. To try and try again is what I learned from Aubrey, Billy and Earle. So, off I went, putting the horse in the yard, tying him up and starting again. It was plainly obvious why the nails came out of the wall too quick: there was not enough hoof underneath to secure them. A bit of sticky mud would have been enough to suck the shoe off the hoof.

But it takes courage and a lot of experience to put the nails a bit higher as there is the chance to seriously lame the horse when the nails go the wrong way. The nail can go into the sensitive part of the sole causing almost immediate lameness. The sensitive part of the sole is on the inside of the white line, which is the part in between the sole and the wall. If a nail is hammered into the middle of the white line, with the angle of the nail too much inwards, the chance of lameness is very high as it puts a lot of pressure on the sensitive areas. This is called a 'nail bind'. It is dangerous business really due to too many variables. No wonder that to become a master farrier is a four-year apprenticeship. And here I was trying to master it in a few days.

While catching Fella, I managed to stumble across one of his shoes. The other was found by one of our children; it was a very unusual thing to find both shoes. After taking the old nails out and cleaning the shoes, I could see and feel that there was something wrong. I remembered Earle saying at the course that the front feet and the back feet have a different shape: the front ones have a round shape, almost looking like a part of a circle. The back feet have a pointed hoof and a more oval shape overall. The manufacturers of horse shoes, in this case the New Zealand Horse Shoe Company know this, so they make front and hind shoes in a lot of sizes, thicknesses and widths of mild steel. It has to be mild steel; otherwise there is no easy way of shaping them.

These facts are all clear and obvious now, but that still does not explain why I put a hind shoe on Fella's front hoof in the first place. It does however explain why I had such a hard time in shaping the shoe. What a way to learn! Indeed, once I realised where I went wrong, shaping the shoe suddenly became much easier.

The next problem, of course, was the nailing. Now there were suddenly six old nail holes in every hoof, and ideally, I had to dodge them all. One hoof was worn a lot on the inside, leaving a very thin wall to put the nails in. Fella wanted to be good, as he had realised a long time ago the benefits of having shoes on. But he had got me sorted out a little while ago. He knew that I was not a farrier, he knew I didn't really have the 'know how' or the experience.

He reluctantly let me carry on my clumsy way of putting the shoes back on. There were only the lost two to replace. They were done in record time, too, I realised when I was finished—it only took an hour.

Looking at Fella's feet, I knew it did not look good at all. The nails were still way too low, the shape of the feet left much to be desired, and judging by the shape of the shoes it would be half a miracle if Fella would even walk properly, let alone enjoy a farm ride. As long as I could see what was wrong and how and where I could improve, there was hope. In the meantime, I hoped Billy was not coming by too soon, otherwise I would be in big trouble.

Billy came by six weeks later, which was two days after I had shod Fella for the second time not counting the two lost shoes. I was reasonably pleased with my effort and the time it took, only two and a half hours, which I thought was not too bad. Billy was not sure if he should laugh or cry.

"Well", he said, "you did manage to put some shoes on your horse's feet. That will have to be an accomplishment, I suppose. If the horse is not lame, you succeeded in the horseshoeing philosophy that the shoes should give the horse's hooves protection so that the horse will be able to go the extra mile. I will have a quick look."

Billy took his time explaining what he was looking for, while lifting every foot and looking at the angles, levels and any gaps between the shoe and the hoof, especially near the heels.

"Right", he said finally. "The shoeing will not cause any lameness. But as you can see, it will be a miracle if the shoes stay on the feet longer than a couple of weeks. You are on the right track, as the basics are reasonably good. Just don't take the horse to any show or something like that until there is a big improvement in the way it looks."

And with that I had to be satisfied, thankful really, that at least the basics were right. Maybe in a few more shoeings I might not have to be ashamed to take the horse out somewhere.

Things were going not too bad at all. I shod Fella a few more times, and slowly the shoeing started to look a bit better, yet still short of looking professional. Billy came by a few more times, pointing out what I could do better here and there, but then he suddenly retired and shifted to the Hokianga, another beautiful harbour up north.

There was a girl living down the road who would occasionally come and ride over the farm where we were share-milking. She heard that I had started shoeing horses and asked if I could please put some front shoes on her pony as he was getting a bit tender walking on the gravel. "I will try," I said, as I almost felt it an honour to help somebody.

"But he doesn't tie up," she said.

"You will have to hold him then," I said.

And with this pony, standing not even 14 hands high, the second major test of my horse shoeing career was about to start. The test was one of patience and the lack of knowledge of how to deal with a strong-willed pony.

The pony did not want to lift his foot up. When I finally managed to pick it up, he would snatch it back out of my hands. There was not even a possibility of putting his leg in between my thighs. Sometimes when I managed to pick up a front foot, he just walked forward, causing me to just follow him. This was getting ridiculous.

This pony was a spoilt pony, or a very strong unhandled one who might not be used to any discipline. Certainly, the girl did not show any inclination to try to make the pony behave. What to do, oh, what to do? The girl was sweet and kind to her horse, and it would take a long time to tell her how to handle the pony when he misbehaved, especially as I was not sure myself what to do.

"I am going to hang on to his front leg for as long as I can. When the pony goes forward, I hope you can stop him from doing so. Let's try," I said.

The girl replied with a soft "Ok."

I managed to pick up a front leg and off we went. The pony went forward, but so did I. The pony kept going, probably even enjoying it. But instead of stopping, the girl more or less kept steering the pony in a safe route around the tanker loop, a rough road used by milk tankers with their trailers to pick up the milk from the cowshed.

As the pony's leg was not too big, I was able to keep my grip tight enough just above the hoof. But the pony was too short for comfort: I had to bend my back to try to make things work for when the pony would take off again. He would stop sometimes, but when I changed position, he took it as a signal to go again. It seemed impossible, but my old nail box with all my tools came into sight again, and I realised we had travelled the whole length of the tanker loop.

Still, I was not prepared to let go. Sure enough, the pony took off again, and after a while it stopped on the other side of the tanker loop. I could sense a change in attitude and patted the pony's shoulder. Then I patted her leg all over, brought the leg forward and backwards, and slapped the bottom of the hoof with my hand. There was no reaction. I let the leg go to finally straighten my back.

We walked to the toolbox and I managed to again pick up the foot we had struggled with, cleaned it and even trimmed it without as much as a flicker. While the going was good, I thought I might as well try to put a shoe on. Luckily for me the shoe did not need much shaping, and now I was hoping the pony would not mind the nailing. The pony did mind the nailing, so there was a lot of snatching back of the foot and trying to move away again. But we managed and after a while the shoe was on nicely, leaving only the other front one. The hind ones looked alright and I didn't think they needed trimming.

Just when we thought that the pony would be okay from that point on, the pony decided to revert back to his old ways. Around the tanker loop we went, on three legs—the fourth being held by me, my arm getting a bit longer each time the pony took a surge forward. At exactly the place where the toolbox was, the pony stopped and said that he would behave if I did not take too long. And indeed, it did not take too long, and the pony did not misbehave. This pony taught me that with patience and sheer determination it is possible to put a couple of shoes on a horse who definitely does not want to be there.

The girl became a very good vet south of Auckland. I managed to shoe and trim the pony for a few more years with different owners, but it was a pity that there was not the slightest change in attitude: the pony would never be easy for me to handle. The children, however, could not wish for a better riding pony.

Horse number three was Deirdre's, a nice and quiet quarter horse. Quarter horses originated in the United States, being the ideal stock horse working the bulls, cows and calves and sheep. Apart from that they excelled at sprinting, with their favourite being the quarter mile, or around four hundred metres, so that's where the name comes from.

People used to race quarter horses in the States, but nowadays they are sought after as stock horses and easily-managed pleasure horses. Deirdre was living over the hill from us and she and Laurel used to ride together all over the farm.

This horse made me understand that the quieter the horse is, the better the job we can do. Simple really. She came over riding her horse, tied it up on a rail in the cowshed, and went to have a cup of tea with Laurel. By the time they finished their cuppa and a yarn, the horse was shod.

Then of course, Paula's and Jolene's ponies had to be shod as well, and like Deirdre's horse, they were nice and quiet.

FIRST HORSES

One day an anvil arrived. For what seemed a long time, I had been looking for an anvil. There was no TradeMe in those days. Word of mouth was the best way to go. Putting an advertisement in the newspaper was and is still common, but not something to go out of your way for. Whenever I met horse-people, farmers or engineers, I would ask them if they had an anvil lying around somewhere. This practice had served me well in the past, and did so this time as well.

A girl from our local pony club had asked me a while before if I could shoe her horse, but I declined, saying it was too hard without an anvil. So here she was. She had helped her grandfather reorganise the garage and the workshop, and this is what they found. A nice 20kg anvil, a real beauty, light enough to be mobile, but heavy enough to be more than a toy.

I found an old stool to put it on, just the right height, and I felt as rich as a king.

An old engineer's hammer given to me, complimented the anvil, and this was the start of something good, I could feel it. Years later I would buy a 100kg anvil (the one on the back cover of this book) and I would tell anyone that I was happier with that anvil than with a new car. It only shows that we are all different and that we have all got our own hobbies, or maybe obsessions.

With the arrival of the anvil, my mobile farrier services started. I kept on saying to myself, "Have anvil, have car, will travel."

First stop was a pony in Ruawai needing to be shod belonging to Carmen who became my longest serving customer. If first impressions count, I do not know why she ever asked me back, as one of the shoes came off within three minutes, a record which still stands today.

I had just finished shoeing her horse and put all my tools away, including the anvil and its stool, when her loud yell caught me from halfway across the paddock.

After the yell came, "Lost a shoe!" still in a very loud voice. She was standing in the middle of the paddock on the other side of one of those very small drains only a foot deep and wide.

I waved to indicate that she had better come back so we could put it back on. After she arrived, I asked her what the hell happened.

"I led my horse through the paddock to put her in the next paddock along," she explained, "but there is this little drain right in the middle. The silly tart jumped it, and the back foot slammed on the back of the front foot, ripping the shoe right off. I could not believe it. Here it is."

She showed me the shoe with all the nails still in but with an enormous bend. It is amazing with how much force a shoe can be ripped off. I took the nails out of the shoe, flattened it, and put it back on. It was all good.

One happy customer led to another, and I started to enjoy this going out and about while at the same time making sure not to neglect the milking of the cows and the associated work. Share milking in the late eighties was not easy at all. There were a few very dry summers and a lot of wet winters. The interest rates were the highest they had ever been at 24%, and the outlook for the milk price was not good at all—there was one season where they even cut the pay-out in half. Who, in any job or business, can survive that? We did, only just, but we decided to sell our cows to try something new.

As it turned out, we sold our cows a year too late as the prices had more than halved from a year before. There was just enough money left for a deposit to buy a lifestyle block seven kilometres out from Maungaturoto towards Whakapirau.

I found myself a job as a cabinetmaker in Maungaturoto to pay the mortgage and managed to shoe a few horses each Saturday morning.

Word of mouth is probably still the best advertisement there is. A man by the name of Liam rang me to see if I could shoe some horses for him. He had heard about me from a lady down the road where I had been a couple of weeks before. Liam and his wife Emma were running a very successful trekking business a few minutes outside Waipu.

"I will come and have a look and see how we go," I said. This was my standard reply. I never say that I *will* shoe the horses, as it is possible that for some odd reason, I might not be able to.

I was there the following Saturday at eight in the morning. I parked my little red mini and walked around the shed to the old cowshed. There were horses tied up just about everywhere, and after a few counts I settled on twenty. My instinct told me that if I had any brains, I would turn around now. Maybe this job was just way too big for me.

Liam came over, we introduced ourselves to each other, and I commented on the fact that he had a swag of horses present—standardbreds, a couple of thoroughbreds, and ponies of all different colours and sizes.

In about an hour's time he and a helper would be taking a dozen people on a two-hour trek in and around the river, through the bush and up in the hills. Then I said we better get to work then if he was so busy.

Liam untied a horse and led it through the others to the shoeing bay. Here he tied the horse up with a rope on either side of the halter, so that the horse was facing the yard.

I could see by the way Liam handled the horse in that short period of time that he was a horseman, so he and I would get along just fine. If the horses would behave as well, life would be a breeze.

"This is Shadow, and he would like four shoes on please, then the three horses tied up over there on that little raceway. All of them four shoes please, but I will probably be back before you finish. They all have been done a few times before so I do not suspect you will have any problems. If you could do that for us, that will be really great. Next week is going to be nice and busy," Liam said.

"I will just try and see how we are getting on, thanks. You'd better get cracking, too, if you want to get away on time," I replied.

I got all my gear out of the mini and started work. Shadow was nice and easy, willing to cooperate. Life would be good. I knew it.

I loved going to Liam and Emma's place. The horses were good and there was always something happening. There were people coming and going, and each one of them left with a huge smile on their face. Apart from the horses, the customers also loved the scenery—whether in and by the river, through the native bush, or upon climbing some hills, all resulted in some awesome views.

Although there were a lot of horses, I will always remember four of them. I had just lifted the front foot of Gizmo, a black horse, big, strong and bold, and put it in between my thighs when the back foot on the same side came forward in such a hurry, I thought it would smash my face. By a miracle it stopped just short of my nose, giving me a hell of a fright and causing me to lose my balance. I let go of the front leg, and ended up on my backside in front of the horse. That was way too close for comfort.

Then there was a little grey pony called Blue, of course, and it had developed Laminitis: an inflammation of the laminae surrounding the coffin bone, the last bone in the horse's leg in the middle of the hoof. Though I did my best to make the horse comfortable and fit for riding by putting shoes on, the result never looked nice, since there was always a big gap in the toe area. But apart from the odd day after a shoeing when the pony would be a bit tender, he stayed sound for many years until he finally earned his retirement.

Peanut was a classic. Many times I have referred to his personality when people were talking about hard-to-shoe horses. To put shoes on Peanut was sheer hard work. It was not that he was young, because he was a mature horse, but his mentality did not change over the years. Sometimes he was almost impossible to handle, so I called on the expert. Liam would untie him and make him do a few circles, first one way, then the other. He tied him up again and Peanut would behave for the duration of the shoeing. It was pure magic. But I suppose you have just got to know what you are doing. Liam proved himself over the years to become one of the best natural horsemen around, even though he did not like the direction that natural horsemanship philosophy was turning, as a whole. In later years, he ran very popular clinics in Europe that combined horses and human-ship.

It was just after I had shod Peanut for the second time, needing all my wits and strength, when we had a cup of coffee. I told Liam, "You know I started to shoe horses late in life. Even so, I've handled a lot of them by now, and over the years I've learned a lot. Well, I am still learning, but I have got this gut feeling that tells me that if a horse continues to be bad while being shod, the horse is no good for anybody. In short, I cannot see Peanut being any good for your trekking business."

"That certainly is a bold statement and I can see where you are coming from," Liam replied. "I learned a lot too over the years, and I can tell you that Peanut is the best horse we have for giving lead rein rides to real-young children. I haven't got a horse that could come close to the safeness and character of Peanut. He stops if the child even looks like it is losing its balance or if the child is not sitting properly—he just feels it. At times he is my best-earning horse."

"At that rate I better just keep up with him, keep my mouth shut and keep on fine-tuning these theories I have about horses," I said, and we both had a laugh about it.

And then there was Aussie and his mate, who could have been identical twins. They were standardbreds and did not make the grade, probably for being not fast enough. Like thoroughbreds, they have a brand, but the standardbred one is a bit harder to decipher.

Liam would probably know who was who, but he was not there. According to the list, I had to put shoes on Aussie and do nothing with the other one.

Emma appeared from just around the corner, so I asked her which of the two Aussie was. "We only got them a couple of days ago," she admitted, "and I have not worked out yet who he is. After a while you get used to them and know exactly the differences, but for now I do not know. But I will find out. I think it is this one. Just give me a couple of minutes, and I will tell you for sure."

How she would find out, I did not know. She did not look for her cell phone to ring Liam, as he would probably be out of reception anyway on the back of the farm, but instead she started stroking the belly of the one she thought was Aussie while slowly whistling.

Yes, that will certainly tell us what his name is, I thought. Now and then she would look underneath as if suddenly a name card or passport would appear. As she seemed very determined, I just kept quiet and looked on. Then the horse's penis started to appear, and finally it made sense. The whistling is a trained habit for racehorses in case they have to give a urine sample to check for any illegal substances. It takes a while but they can be trained to urinate on request.

But it still did not explain why Emma was doing all this, and it looked rather weird, really. When his penis was almost full size, she called me over to her side.

"Look," she said, pointing to a black spot on the pale coloured skin, "that black spot looks exactly like the map of Australia; there is even a dot in the place where Tasmania is. This is Aussie all right."

That was the strangest way of finding a horse's name I ever

would come across, and I was sure that this story would come up over and over again when horsey people start talking about how their horses got their names.

I said, "Thank you, Emma for going to extreme measures to determine the name of the horse. I will take it from here and will put some shoes on him, thanks."

"I am sure I will be able to recognise him next time by just looking at him." Emma said with a smile on her face.

3

Maungaturoto

I had more and more customers, so after four years working in the furniture factory, I tried my luck at shoeing horses full time. The summers were good since riding horses is essentially a summer sport. The winters were bad as most people turned their horses out, but I was fortunate enough to find a job here or there giving builders a hand or working in one of the many local furniture factories. Those first few years were very hard.

Financially I would have been better off with my regular job in the factory. The little red mini died, but we luckily found a cheap replacement—a blue mini. I don't think the bank manager would have lent me any money if I showed him my balance sheet. But we got by, we always did. I just needed more customers, the closer the better, of course. There was a farrier covering the Warkworth area, sixty kilometres south of Maungaturoto, who had just left for Singapore to shoe race horses there. I picked up a lot of his customers there as well as in neighbouring Puhoi. One customer in Puhoi had a driveway so steep that the poor old mini could not get up the hill. After a couple of failed attempts, I had to give up. I took the anvil out of the back and put it on the floor in front of the passenger seat. This gave the front wheels that extra bit of weight needed to pull us up the hill.

Apart from Liam and Emma, it seemed that all the new customers I got only had one horse, sometimes two, and only a few had three or more horses. You don't have to be an economist to work out that the more horses there are in one place, the better the financial returns will be. I needed a few big customers to make everything worthwhile. That is why I was over the moon when Barry rang to ask if I could shoe a horse for him, hopefully that very week, just down the road from our place on one of his farms. I admit that I was a little apprehensive since the horses he had were big show jumpers and hunters. I had to do a very good job as Barry would be a very good customer to have. As it turned out, there was nothing to worry about. Bonnie the horse was of mature age, had shoes on a hundred times before on her beautiful strong black hooves. I did the best I could, and when finished, I was very happy with the way the hooves with shoes looked. Barry was happy too, as he remarked that they looked nice.

I sure must have done a good job because Barry rang me the week after to shoe a couple more. He had more work for me the next week. The weeks turned into years.

Barry knew a lot of horse people around the country and managed to sell a lot of horses over the phone, and people got to know about the good name he had made for himself and that the horses were exactly as he described them. If Barry said that the horse could jump one meter and ten centimetres, it would mean just that. If he said the horse was very quiet, you could take his word for it. By the same token, if the horse was a handful, he would tell you so.

With all the work handling the horses, the breaking in and riding on, Barry needed help so he employed two girls who were very keen to ride them and learn a bit more about turning almost wild horses into friendly show jumpers.

One Monday morning, the two girls managed to quietly guide four youngsters into the yard. They were big and bold, since apart from a regular drench in the race of the enormously high and solid stockyards, they'd had no handling whatsoever.

The gate to the drenching race was open, and quietly Barry herded the horses into the race, the first one being the hardest one to get in of course.

"So far so good," he said to his two helpers. "Now all we have to do is put the halters on. Simple really, but seeing this is your first day at the job, I think I better show you how to do it safely as there are a lot of things that can go wrong. Always think safe."

The drenching race had a nice and solid walkway built onto it, of such a height that you felt as if you were towering over these horses, which were all sixteen hands high, which would make it much easier to put on a halter than from the ground.

"Whatever you do," Barry continued, "watch your hands so that the horse's head doesn't knock them against the rails." After that he just put the halter on the first one without too much of a struggle and asked the girls to do one as well. These were real horse girls and they managed, leaving number four for Barry.

Then he picked up a very strong but soft rope and put it through the halter of the first horse, around the neck, and then made a bowline, making sure that it was not too tight or too loose. One of the girls opened the gate at the front, having instructions to only let the first one go. Barry was already on the other end of the rope. He was not serious about teaching the horse to lead, as he was concerned about getting out of harm's way and coaching the horse to any one of the four sides of the yard. Each side had a big sheet of ply nailed to the rails with a hole in the middle, in front of a big post to tie the horse to. As if by luck, the horse just parked himself in the right spot in front of the post, appearing overwhelmed really, so Barry managed to tie him up without any further excitement.

One-by-one, the rest followed in just the same way. The result was four big Stationbreds, three and four years old, tied up for the first time in their entire lives on their own side of a square pen, itself part of a big stockyard. The sheet of reasonable thickness ply in front of the horse prevented the front feet from going through the rails if the horses played or thrashed around.

One of the girls was a bit nervous and worried about what might happen when the horses were going to test the rope. She had been taught that you had to first be able to lead the horse before you tie the horse up. She asked Barry about that a bit later, feeling a little worried about the way he might react. Barry, at all times, was the perfect gentleman. If there was time to explain things, he would. If there was no time, he would say so, but would always come back to it later. He did not get angry at nor ridicule even the most stupid question.

"Today I caught the horses by surprise. It is all new to them," Barry explained. "The first time in the yard, the first time tied up. I used to lead them for a while in their own yard to try and teach them some halter manners. It was incredibly dangerous and time consuming. The day after, when I would do it again, it was still questionable if they even learned something the day before.

"So now I do it this way. They will be tied up here till four o'clock, when I will undo them, leave their halter on to make them easy to catch in the morning. They will throw a wobbly now and then—one will start the other off. The odd one throws himself on the ground, but not many as their self-conservation is still paramount.

"Let us say it this way—I have done a lot of them, and apart from the odd scratch they all came through just fine." Barry wondered if he had made some sense to his new helper, so he added, "You can just about do anything to, or with a horse, as long as you don't do it in anger. That is my cut off point: don't get angry.

"These horses in the yard have got a rope to deal with, preventing them from going where they want to go. But the rope does not get angry or short tempered, and never raises its voice. The horse has a choice how to deal with the rope, and in my experience they all accept it as part of their new lives."

From the expression on her face, Barry could see that she accepted his reasoning but still had her doubts.

Exactly a week later it was my turn with these four horses for their first set of shoes. It is amazing how some horses can change in a week. There were two horses tied up in the covered yard as well as one of Barry's hunters to assure them all was well. The other two were on the other side of the rails, and through the railings of the next pen one could see next week's horses already tied up, contemplating their fate.

These four had been put through their paces. Just before Barry let them go that very first day, he made sure they would move away from him when he approached them, a very useful habit. They came in every day after that: they had their legs lifted up, got used to the saddle, the bridle and the bit, and they had all been ridden in the round pen for a few days by that point. The next day they would go riding all over the farm, so they needed some shoes on.

The shoeing of these horses was very good once I understood that it was up to me to reassure them that everything was fine. The quieter and more easy-going I was, the easier they behaved.

If they did play up, I tried to hang on for as long as I could, and by the first sign of the horse relaxing, I relaxed myself with all my might.

Of course, we had some scary moments now and then, but apart from some cuts and bruises there was nothing major. It was a pleasure being there, and I learned a lot.

All went well until one day we had a very strong horse. Barry and his helpers had trouble getting on top of this one. He was hard to handle, and everything they tried to teach him took twice as long as any of the others. If he had not shown so much potential as a show jumper, he would have been gone a long time ago.

Wary, alert and quick would be a reasonable description. Together with being big and strong, this horse was a challenge, to put it mildly. To approach the horse and try to make him stand still was a major exercise, as if he thought I was out to kill him or something, so I spent a lot of time just petting him and telling him all would be fine. It made only the slightest bit of difference.

We just had to try our best and lift a front foot to try and dress it the best we could. Even though it took four or five attempts, I succeeded. As for the back one, that took more doing. One second he would be submissive, the next he was gone and way out of my reach. It took a lot of doing but I did manage to dress all the four feet. But there was no way I ever could put the shoes on.

I felt it and I knew it. He had way too much power for me to handle. There is just no way I could hang on to any of the legs to keep it still enough to put the nails through the shoe into the hoof.

"Maybe I will just rope him up for you." Barry said, as he must have understood my predicament.

A little while later the horse looked at me with frustration in his eyes, as one of his front legs was securely but safely strapped up. Shaping the shoe to the hoof was easy, so I was soon up to nailing it on. The poor horse really did take a dislike to all this stuff happening to him and tried his utmost to get away from it all, to no avail, as I kept on coming back, again and again.

We managed, but I did not look forward to even attempting to do a back shoe. Still, Barry put the straps on the back one, and the horse accepted all that, as he had done it a few times before, more than any other horse.

It was up to me once more. Once again, the shaping of the shoe was easy, but this time the nailing failed in a big way.

After the first couple of taps on the first nail, all hell seemed to break loose. The horse just wanted to get away from me and my hammer but he forgot he only had three legs to stand on. He completely missed a beat and his back end came to rest on the concrete floor soon followed by the front which got pulled down as well. He was lying flat on the ground, realising one of his back legs was strapped up making it extremely difficult to get up again. Instantly, Barry seized the opportunity and sat on the horse's neck, making sure the lead rope was long enough.

"Quick," he said, "put the shoes on while he is lying down, will you, it will save us a lot of hassle."

I could not believe it—putting shoes on a horse that was lying down on the concrete floor. How long would it take, and how long would the horse allow us? Would it be even more dangerous with the back legs? Even though one is strapped up, he could kill me with the other one.

"I will try and see what happens. I just hope that he doesn't kick me." I said to Barry.

It felt safe enough, but the angles at which to hammer the nails seemed all wrong. There was a lot of guesswork to be done. But the horse took it all in its stride, well, only because Barry was sitting on his neck. I felt that the pressure was on, but there are not many shortcuts you can make in putting on a shoe. With some difficulty I put in the remaining nails of the strapped up hoof and folded the nails over. I shaped the second hind shoe the same as the first one, hoping that it would fit as well. It did fit not too badly, so I decided to put it on the hoof of the free leg which was underneath the horse. This presented even more problems, especially in folding over the nails. But hey, let's first see if we can get it on, without getting kicked, shall we?

I don't know if it was luck or good management and handling skills, but the horse did not do one thing wrong even though I had to pull the hoof a good foot off the ground to be able to get underneath it.

Still, I did not want to jump up and down to celebrate as there was still one more hoof to go. According to Barry we might just be able to make it so I got busy again. The horse, I could feel, was up to something, and it would not have surprised me if he would have chucked Barry off his neck, got off the ground and then kicked the stuffing out of us.

It must have been my lucky day. Just as I finished, Barry could not hold the horse down anymore, and he and I got out of harm's way pretty smartly as the horse pulled himself up. Soon he was standing on his three legs again and realised there were some pieces of steel nailed to his hooves which made a stupid sound on the concrete. He had a few shakes, tried the lead rope, as you never know something might have changed, pranced up and down a bit and then slowly settled down. It was now time to take the leg strap off, and a quarter of an hour later he just stood there thinking about what exactly had happened a little while ago. Somehow, I think he could not work it out, but hopefully he realised that this was all part of his new life as a riding horse.

Barry was very grateful we managed to put the shoes on without injuries to the horse or human, and while it must have looked rather dramatic, the horse seemed to be unfazed by the ordeal.

When I asked about the horse's name to put on the invoice, Barry replied that the horse did not yet have a name. I wrote on my invoice "No Name", and he went on to become a good to handle, well-placed, likable show jumper.

On my next visit Barry gave me a few photos of No Name lying on the ground with Barry sitting on his neck and me in the most stupid positions putting on the shoes. I never noticed there was a photographer.

MAUNGATUROTO

Maungaturoto became very popular after the Kaipara District Council allowed farms to be split up into four-hectare (ten acres) blocks, enabling the farmer to retire and townies (Aucklanders) to buy their slice of heaven: a lifestyle block. One could build a dream home or set down a relocated home, buy a horse or two, a horse float and a four-wheel drive and live the life.

On the north side of Maungaturoto was a nice lifestyle block where the sheep were sharing their block with some donkeys.

"This one is a movie star," the young lady owner told me. "In a few weeks' time he will be on TV starring in an advertisement for Mitre 10. It was supposed to be his mate, the one over there in the corner, New Zealand's smallest donkey, but he had an off day when they were filming.

He was not necessarily naughty, but nothing went nice and easy. So, we tried Kong and he really excelled, just as if he really enjoyed all the attention. We had a busy few days filming but I must say it was fun. I never knew there was so much involved in making a little ad of maybe a minute; I don't really know how long it is. He is famous now." The lady was obviously incredibly happy with this accomplishment.

"I must say that it is an honour for me to give this movie star a pedicure," I responded. "I never knew I would go this far up the ladder. And now I better get on with the job, otherwise it will never get done," I said as I started trimming the hooves of the "World Famous in Maungaturoto" donkey named Kong.

Kong and his mates did not wish for anything; they were well looked after. They had a sand pit to play in, a rocky area to trim their hooves naturally and to dry them out and, of course, a new little paddock regularly, complete with shelter from the rain and sun.

There was an old shed from which a lean-to with a concrete floor was built. It was a good place to groom them and trim their feet. It was just a little bit low for me as I regularly knocked my head on one of the beams. And every time, I had to think of this Old Dutch saying, "A donkey never hits the same stone twice."

The donkey lady regularly took one or two donkeys to the park, to the beach, to visit donkey friends, to go to A&P shows or go to the rest home, where their company was really appreciated. Now that Kong was a movie star it was a joy to take him to the Mitre 10 store in Whangarei or Warkworth. Kong proved to be a top attraction—children instantly knew the name of the donkey and wanted to pet him, and everyone was amazed at how small he really was, as the advertisement didn't really do justice to his size: 32 inches tall.

In the advertisement, Kong's owner has a hell of a job to keep Kong confined to his enclosure. Kong proves to be a Houdini artist in escaping and ending up in the most unusual places. The man keeps on modifying the yard to no prevail as Kong escapes again, sometimes in the most atrocious weather.

Finally, the man's young daughter takes him to Mitre 10 where they get advice, study some plans, buy tools and materials and go home to start their "do it yourself" project. The end result is a replica donkey made from timber and what have you, a mate for poor old lonely donkey Kong. With his soul mate nearby, there was no need for Kong to escape anymore.

After trimming the feet of Kong and his donkey family, it was time to shoe the last horse of the day. As I knew I would be home just after four o'clock in the afternoon, I had asked my son Lars to put his horse Jack in the yard the minute he came home from school. I put on my apron and picked up my toolbox and walked over to Jack, who was almost asleep, tied up in the yard. Jack looked at me and sniffed me, and that was the end of it. It was as if my smell caused an instant dislike. This normally very quiet and well-behaved Thoroughbred horse suddenly acted as if a bee had stung him. I could not even touch him. He wanted to get as far away as possible from me. When I followed him to the end of the lead rope where he had to stand still, he simply tried to bowl me over to get away from me. I am not a person who gives up easily, so I tried a little while longer. But Jack had made his mind up. There was no way he would let me near him, let alone shoe him.

While I put my tools away, I started to think that the smell of the donkeys I had trimmed just before might have upset him. It was a far-fetched theory as I had never had any problems like this before, despite routinely going from donkey to horse and vice-versa the whole day long. The next day was a Pony Club Rally day, so I decided to shoe Jack before the event if he would let me. I let him sniff me, and all was well; he was a completely different horse than the day before.

To get to the bottom of the problem, I made sure Jack was in the yard a few days later when my last job of the day was indeed another donkey. Jack took a look at me, had a sniff, and that was the end of it. Again, there was no way I could get near him. Good old Jack, the only horse in my books who takes such a dislike to the smell of donkeys that everything else goes by the wayside.

On the southwest of Maungaturoto, a big six-hundred-and-fifty-acre beef farm was converted into sixty-five lifestyle blocks. It was here that Mighty spent his retirement years, and his owner was sure that, for a while, Mighty was the oldest horse in New Zealand. From the previous two owners she had established that he was forty, but because she could not prove it, she did not make a fuss about it. Ponies can even live a bit longer than that, but for a reasonably big horse he had done extremely well.

Or maybe I should say that the owner had done very well in

providing him with everything he needed in life. In his later days he knew he was pretty special as he got three bowls of hard feed a day—he had no reason to complain about anything. He lived on this new subdivision jutting out onto the Kaipara Harbour. When the tide is in, it is absolutely beautiful. At low tide a lot of mud flats appear, and the water is reduced to a stream in the middle, but is still nice to look at. Mighty had to share his ten acres with two other horses. There were a few trees in every paddock to provide a bit of shade in the summer and shelter in the winter. It was the ideal life for a horse.

It was somewhere in the middle of April, just after twelve o'clock. Mighty stopped doing what he was good at (eating grass) and straightened his neck out as far as it could go and listened with his ears pricked forward, his eyes fixed on the other side of the water. Something obviously took his fancy.

Once you looked carefully in the direction the horse was looking, you could faintly see some little dots crisscrossing the side of the hill on the other side of the inlet. A little bit behind the dots, a few people on horseback appeared, one of them was wearing an unmistakably red coat, springing out in the green of the immaculate-looking sheep farm. Hunting! Better described as hunting with hounds. One of the past-time passions that came over from England, where the noble men found it pleasurable to hunt foxes with hounds and follow them on horseback. Riders, dressed up to the nines in proper hunting attire, on horses groomed as if they were ready to go to a Royal Gala day, they would set off after the traditional Stirrup Cup (an alcoholic beverage of some sort) to go cross country through the fields (as they call them there), galloping after the swift canines.

The hounds, derived from beagles and cared for by the hunts man, had a few centuries of breeding behind them. They were bred for their ability to pick up scent and their good stamina. These hounds on the other side of the water were still zigzagging along the hill side, trying to pick up the scent of a hare, as there are no foxes in New Zealand.

A pair of binoculars would have been handy as things were fast changing: a couple of hounds found the scent of a hare, and they let the others know by baying—they would be stronger with thirty of them than acting on their own. Rather than the long howling of a lone wolf, this baying was short and repeated quickly three or four times in a row.

Mighty was listening and watching it all with the keenest of interest. Now here was some excitement. He used to do this. He loved it—it was his passion; it used to be his reason for living.

The hounds were very alert now, all following the leaders, like a ribbon moving over the hill side, now coming better into view. The horses on the other side were beside themselves, too. In a mad gallop their riders took them to watch a spectacle unfold.

"What am I doing here?" Mighty pondered, *"I am wasting my time here. I am wasting my life here. Over there, on the other side of the water, that's where the action is. I love it. I love hunting, galloping over those hills, trying to outdo my mates over there."*

It was the sound of the hounds, like a war cry, which made him very edgy, on the top of his nerves. He could not help it; he could not stand still anymore. His head was going up and down, left to right. He took his front feet off the ground and when they made contact with the ground again, he let fly with his back legs, never mind the horse-cover. Up came the front legs again, but this time they came down much further. It was the quickest way to start a canter, which was followed by a gallop, to his target on the other side of the water.

Most good hunting horses can jump a seven-wire fence. This is a traditional boundary and sheep fence, consisting of 120-centimetre high posts with seven wires strung on them, onto which timber battens are nailed so stock can't worm their way through.

Mighty must have jumped many of them in his day with someone sitting on his back steering and coaching him in the right direction just as if he could not do it by himself. Of course, he could do it by himself now, even better, as he was fully in control of his own head.

So there he was, forty years young, galloping down the hill towards a near new seven wire fence. He checked his strides himself as he approached, and slowed down just that little bit to allow him to plant his back legs firmly in the right spot so his whole body could use the spring created by the back legs to jump as high as he could over the fence. He jumped plenty high enough, and it was very graceful and beautiful to watch.

Mighty was a horse again, feeling young and strong, so he went a bit further, but not too far, as there was another fence. Mighty slowed down a bit since he knew this place well, and knew what was on the other side: mud, a whole lot of mud. It was low tide and the mud would be sticky like, well, Kaipara Harbour mud.

By the time he reached the fence, all the speed was gone and he stood suddenly very still, breathing very heavily for a while. His eyes focused on the other side again, his ears pricked to pick up any sound. The hounds were on the far side now, almost out of sight, their noise barely registering through the wind that had picked up a little. There were a good twenty riders out there, close on the heels of the hounds. Mighty enjoyed every second of this performance.

"Better watching this than watching television," he thought. As the last horse disappeared around the hill, he let out a deep sigh and said, *"I think I might just go and eat some grass now."*

Amigo was a beautiful Appaloosa mare, mainly white with black spots and dark legs. She was living on State Highway 12, not far from Maungaturoto. The owner did not know a lot about horses in general and even less about this one, except for the fact that she was well bred. Apart from being well bred, she was also very well fed, not handled a lot, and above all she was full of beans.

Someone must have trimmed her feet at least once, but the last time must have been a very long time ago. Facing this, a farrier just has to take a lot of time, be quiet, be patient and make all movements' slow. We managed the job, and survived it too. Despite a few scary moments when the horse started panicking, when she didn't not know what was expected of her.

The second time I trimmed her feet, Amigo was her usual self, full of energy, and had not had a lot of handling since last time. This time she even reared up a few times when I was busy with the front feet. Oh, would it not be lovely if someone tried to make a nice horse out of this monster!

Third time lucky? Not this time. The horse was lame. The vet was coming at four p.m. and I was asked if I could please be there as well. I could not, as that evening was my birthday dinner in Whangarei with most of the family, but I could come earlier if that was suitable.

The owner could not be there till four so I had a look on my own. The horse could not even walk to the gate, as lame as she was. On the sides of steep hills, any livestock will make tracks to secure a stable footing while grazing. It was with this hill as well, and it was on one of these ruts the horse was standing, feeling very sorry for herself.

Indeed the horse was very reluctant to move forward or backward. I tried very hard once I put on the halter and lead rope. There was no way short of hitting her with a stick, to make her move. It was one of the back feet that the horse refused to put any weight on, and it was very awkward screwing my body into a position it did not want to be in, lifting the horse's leg in a position she did not like either. I managed to clean the hoof, pinpointed the sore area and started digging. I dug a reasonable hole with my freshly sharpened hoof knife, but the closer I got, the more tender it seemed to be getting. Amigo did not like it when my knife came near the sore spot and pulled her leg back in a big hurry. After four or five times, it became obvious that she would not let me anywhere near her sore foot. All the while it was a literal balancing act on the side of the hill on this narrow track, so I made the decision to call it quits.

I had to ring the owner and tell him what was going on.

"Can you please ask the vet to sedate the horse and dig the hole I dug a little bit deeper to release the puss which has built up in there from an infection called a stone bruise? I am sorry I have to go to attend my birthday dinner," leaving the owner none the happier. "And you have to get the horse to the gate or at least to a flat and level place. The vet won't be able to do anything where the horse is now. I know its hard, but you'll have to. Good luck with that."

I felt sorry for the man who was not a horse man by any standards. I really hoped that he would be able to get the horse to some flat ground, and that a vet would come who knew a thing or two about horses.

A few weeks later I was at Sarah's place in Kaiwaka. And here was the beautiful Appaloosa with the name of Amigo. The owner had gone overseas, Sarah told me, and needed someone to look after the horse. She remarked that the horse did not seem to know much.

"Last time I was there, the horse was lame as could possibly be," I told her. "It was on my birthday, so that's a few weeks ago now."

"Not lame anymore," Sarah said. "But the owner told me that she was so lame that she did not want to put any weight on it at all.

He said you had been and could not quite get it clean, and that he better shift the horse to some flat ground. It took him two hours to get Amigo a little bit up the hill, but he managed.

"The vet insisted on taking an x-ray. Amigo did not like that at all and kicked the whole x-ray set-up far away. The owner did not mention the vet fixing the lameness. The vet probably gave the horse some painkillers and the like. After suffering some broken x-ray equipment, I don't think the vet was looking to get some broken bones herself. But hey, that's all water under the bridge now. She is definitely not lame anymore."

Katie had two horses already, but soon after Cain moved in, they were looking for another horse, so they borrowed Amigo for a while to see if she was any good for them. If she was, they would buy her. The first time they looked at her, they put a saddle on and both of them rode her. I told them they were very brave and lucky to be alive.

"No, no, she is really cruisy so far," she reassured me, "not fazed by many things. Bit strange really that the owner did not know much about her except that she was well bred. She is not very young either but we treat her that way as she does not seem to have much riding experience. But so far, she is not doing anything wrong. So, can we have some shoes on her please?"

"I will try," I said, and knew that I would at least be able to trim her feet as I had done before. It is always amazing how the temperament of a horse can change with a little work. When it was time to try to put the shoes on, the left front one was as good as could be, like a 'normal' horse. The left back one was good to shoe as well, and going around the tail to the other back, this one did not strike any trouble either. Now on the home run, our spirits always lift a bit. The shoe was easily shaped, and in a couple of minutes the nails would be all in.

The simple noise of my driving hammer hitting the shoe while it was on her hoof was, in her mind, the most terrifying experience she'd had in her entire life. She snatched her leg back, and it went up in the air as the other front one came up as well. Balancing on the hind legs with her front hooves high in the air she was thinking, *"Should I hit Katie who is still holding onto the lead rope? Or is it better to try to get that nasty man who wants to put a shoe on my hoof?"*

She came down in orderly fashion, Katie having walked a bit backwards while I escaped sideways. Well, let's try again, shall we? It is exactly like they say, if you keep doing the same thing, you will get the same result. It was not entirely true as the second time she did not rear up as high in the air. I just could not get the first nail in. I had not even hit the nail yet, just the shoe.

Cain found us an old stirrup leather. I had to pick up the foot, tie the stirrup leather above the hoof just under the fetlock, then bend the leg, and loop the leather strap above the knee and back to the buckle. When done properly, there is no way a horse can pull its foot out, and at the same time, it is almost impossible for the horse to get injuries from the stirrup leather.

Amigo did not like this contraption on her leg. Not one little bit. It took away her freedom, her power to take off and the power to strike. But if we would think that because of this she would settle down, oh no, *"This little stirrup holding up my leg will not at any stage immobilise me. I am too strong for that. I am clever—I can walk on three legs and I still can rear up and snatch my leg back. You just watch me!"* she said.

We were watching and taking note. While the stirrup itself might have been safe, there was a real danger that the horse would throw itself on the ground which can cause various injuries. She was tied up to a tree on the side of the driveway with heaps of gravel around.

The most sensible thing to do was to move her onto the lawn.

Do not think of this lawn as the kind you find in some residential areas manicured to perfection to resemble the best golf course ever. This lawn looked more like an extension of the paddock. The whole summer long you can do anything on it, but in the winter, it gets transformed into a bog.

The lawn was dry enough, so here we go I told myself. It was amazing how well she could move on three legs. I saw trouble coming. Every time I came close to Amigo, she just moved away. It took a while before I could touch her, get hold of her leg and tap it gently, which was to her a signal to be off like a rocket. This was going to take ages as she was not overly upset at all—she just wanted to, and could, get away from me. Basically, if you keep on trying without losing your cool, you will eventually get there.

We did it, but it took a very long time. Somewhere along the line the horse gave up. Or the horse gave in. Or the horse surrendered. It does not really matter what you call it but you have to recognise it happening, otherwise you will lose the plot yourself. That precise moment is hard to see, and it is harder to describe what actually happens. Maybe the handler can see something in their eyes or behaviour. Yet, as per normal, I only sensed the physical contact with the horse, mainly the legs. But I felt it and immediately relaxed, so that the horse would relax even more. Then I asked for Cain to pass me my tools, and within a minute I had the shoe on. In another half a minute the clinches were folded over. It did not look very nice, but we were not going to a fashion parade anyway.

That shoe came off after just a week, and when I got there a week later, the other one was off as well. The left front was easy to put back on. I shaped the right front one and tried a couple of times to put a nail in, but really had no luck. I needed a considerable amount of time to put it back on.

Cain must have sensed that I was in a hurry, or you know, very busy and running late. He said, "Leave it up to me. Just give me the shoe and a few nails. I have got the rest of the gear. I will do it quietly later on today. I seem to be able to do almost anything with her, so I don't mind giving it a go."

I did not need much convincing because I knew Cain used to shoe his own horses for a long time. "Make my day," I said, "because it will take some time. She is not a dirty horse, maybe she just does not like me, but with some quiet handling and a lot of time, I am sure you will get there. Thank you." And with that I was free to see some other customers.

Cain did manage to put the shoe on, and it lasted pretty well. But inevitably it had to be done again in time. This time I decided to use my brain and made a plan. She liked standing this way, tied up on the tree in front of her, with her backside almost touching the other tree with a little fence in between the trees a metre away. It was her happy place. I would try to not disturb that. Then I would go as quietly as possible, make all my movements slow but steady, and keep my voice to a sweet steady soft monologue.

The plan worked and I also decided to put the shoe on the right front first. She did not like the hammering, but with nice soft hits with the hammer and a lot of talk to put her at ease, we managed brilliantly. Katie informed me that she had spent a lot of time just hammering that foot. I told her that it had paid off very well indeed.

With this foot out of the way, the other three would be a piece of cake, after which I could shoe their other horses too. This was just another day in the office.

"Ninety-two," she said.

This took me a bit by surprise, so I asked her, "What do you mean by that?"

MAUNGATUROTO

It was the second time we met, sitting in one of the big lounges of one of the biggest cruise ships of the time in the middle of the Mediterranean.

We had met the previous morning in the breakfast cafe when my wife and I joined her and her friend at their table. We talked about the food, the cruise and what to do that day. We talked about what we did for a living, and I was happy to tell them that thanks to the sterling efforts of my wife working in real estate, we could afford to see my family in Holland, as well as go on this splendid cruise.

In return, my wife said of me, "And he puts shoes on horses and works on our little farm in his spare time, so now there is absolutely nothing he can do here but eat, sleep and rest."

"I love horses," one lady replied, her eyes looking somewhere in the far distance. "Is it hard to put the shoes on?"

"Just before we left," I began, "I met a new customer who was determined to learn how to shoe a horse. She asked me the same thing, and I told her it was very hard work. She said 'In that case, I don't want to learn anymore,'" which made the three ladies at the table giggle.

My wife told them about her horses, and the ladies were very interested. Before you know it, breakfast was over, and it was time to go ashore to see a new town and enjoy new experiences, people, language, food, customs and money—the joys of traveling. We said our farewells and hoped to see each other again.

The next day was a rest day for us. To get ashore you had to go in a rescue boat, which they called a 'tender' so as not to scare us I suppose, and be ferried to shore where a bus would take you to town on a two-hour journey in the sweltering heat. It was nicer to stay 'home', enjoying the air conditioning. My wife bumped into an old close friend from her school days, a chance of one in a million, and they decided to have a morning to themselves for coffee and talk about those good old days.

It was when I was stretching my legs, trying to walk a few kilometres to keep up a little of my fitness, when I spotted the two ladies from the day before in the lounge room, who seemed to have a day off as well. I said hello, they invited me to sit down and we introduced ourselves. They were Mary and Sonja from the United States. They both looked to be in their thirties, Mary with her bright red hair would stand out in a crowd, and Sonja, the one who liked horses, had long dark blond hair and still had that distinctive distant look in her eyes. It was when I sat down that I noticed the white stick with red bands on it leaning against her chair.

"You are blind?" I asked her, immediately regretting the bluntness of my question, so I added quickly, "Sorry, I did not mean to be rude, I just did not know. I did not notice before."

"No apology necessary. If you did not notice yesterday, I must be pretty normal then," said Sonja.

"Oh, she is normal all right," Mary added, "as her best friend I am supposed to help her, but most of the time she is just fine and not slow in coming forward."

"I would love to hear some of your horse stories," Sonja said.

"See, I told you," Mary said.

"My wife is having a coffee and probably lunch with an old class mate she met yesterday. They have not seen each other for twenty years or more, so I suppose I could bore you with some of my wisdom. Did you ever see a horse?" I asked.

"Blind since birth," Sonja said, "but I have met them a long time ago and petted some of them. They seem so cuddly."

"They can be cuddly alright," I said. "Do you have any idea what their feet look like?"

"I did go to school, you know, and I learned that a horse belongs to the equine family: horses, donkeys and zebras. They all have one toe, a hoof, at the end of each leg."

"Well done," I said. "Now that we have arrived at the horse's hoof, would you like me to shoe a horse for you? It will be a challenge for me to explain it in a way that you can see it. Did that sound alright?"

She smiled and said it would be wonderful if I could.

I took a deep breath and decided I might as well start at the beginning.

"The horse is tied to a post, or someone is holding the animal. You approach a horse from the side, the horse's right side in this example, and you aim towards the shoulder, for if you aim for the back, the horse will go forward, and if you aim for the front, the horse will go backwards. You touch the shoulder with the back of your hand. That is movement number one. Then, for most horses, movement number two: you let them sniff the back of your hand so they know who you are and that they have nothing to fear from you. Some really want to smell you while others don't care. Now I have to try to explain where you stand, or your position in relation to the horse. If you don't get it, you tell me, ok?"

"Ok," they said in unison while I was hoping I would not make a fool of myself.

"You stand beside the right side of the horse with your legs slightly apart and your feet are in line with the two front feet of the horse, which are a foot apart, so that their feet point forward and yours point backwards. With your right hand you can touch the horse's shoulder and you basically look at the back leg and the hip of the horse. Sometimes, the horse's head turns around and starts nibbling your shirt. Overall, it really looks like the horse and you are going in different directions.

"Movement number three: with the back of your right hand you touch the shoulder, and in one gentle motion, keeping contact with the horse, you slide your hand downwards past their knee, which is the same as our wrist, and stop just above and at the back of the fetlock joint, which is like the first one of our knuckles. While doing this you cannot help but bend your back.

"The fourth movement is to gently squeeze the tendon between your thumb and fingers of your right hand, just above the fetlock joint. The horse will react by lifting his foot up, which you will grab with your right hand. You move your right leg a bit more to the right and slightly bend it some more. Your right hand will move backwards around your right knee and then push the hoof forwards between your thighs where your left hand will pick the hoof up and pull it forwards to just above your knees. Automatically you will bring your knees together and the horse's bottom leg is caught. Now you have to try to be comfortable and at the same time make sure the horse is comfortable too.

"At the sixth handling you can finally do something with the hoof which is nicely rested just above your knees and you start with cleaning. A hoof pick or the back of the hoof knife will be fine, and you try to clean all the soil and dirt out of the bottom of the hoof. If needed, you use a wire brush to make it really clean, as any remaining fine gravel will make all my tools blunt. Now it is time to have a look at the hoof.

"It looks a bit like a saucer. Clydesdales have feet like dinner plates, and donkeys' are even smaller than a tea cup. The outside of the hoof is called the wall and is exactly the same as our toenails, consisting of a million and one hairs just like those growing on our heads. It is the part of the hoof that carries the weight and transmits it through a complex but marvellous system to the last bone in the hoof, the coffin bone, which is the same bone as the one that sits underneath your toe nail or fingernail."

I saw the ladies touching one of their finger nails, so I had to add, "The middle one, as evolution has it; the others disappeared over time. The horse's legs have the same number of bones as we have and probably a few more animals, but I am not really sure about that."

Her interest rising, Sonja said, "The specific feet, legs, body and the whole shape of an animal is perfected for their living circumstances. I remember that from school. Anyway, would you like a cup of coffee or tea maybe?"

"You are the same as most of my customers," I mused, "they always ask me that. I would love to, but maybe after we put the shoe on? I have got to concentrate for this one, same as in real life."

"Okay, you are the boss," she said.

A few more things about the anatomy of the hoof—it sort of looks round like a saucer from the bottom, but it gets a bit elongated towards the heel. Again, the outside of the hoof, the wall, is like our toe nails. To stop the wall from splitting at the heel, where enormous pressure occurs when galloping, a rubber-like triangle called the 'frog' is located at the rear of the foot. The hoof can now expand and contract like a proper shock absorber. When the horse puts pressure on the hoof, the frog takes pressure as well, and it has the ability to pump the blood back up to the heart. This amazing invention enables the horse to sleep standing up, making it one of the best flight animals—they can go from being asleep to galloping in two seconds.

"Between the frog and the wall, you can see the sole and the white line. The sole, which takes up a large area of the foot, keeps on growing and then flakes away. This is called exfoliation. Between the sole and the wall is the white line, designed to let the wall grow down and to assist in the weight distribution towards the coffin bone.

"The details of all these things are complicated, but we fellas take it all in very quickly, especially when we decide that the foot we are working on is a 'standard foot'.

"You see that the wall is pretty long so you will cut it off with your nippers, which are in truth oversized end-cutters. That done, you will have to have a look to see what you have done and pick the hoof back up in your right hand and let it loosely balance to have a look at the angle and the level. The hoof goes back in between your thighs.

"With the rasp you will take off what is necessary. Experience is a good thing, but you just can't see the level and angle from this position. So, you put the hoof back in your right hand and have another look. If you are lucky, you only have to rasp a little bit off a couple of high spots, and then you use the hoof knife to cut a bit of the sole away, as the shoe will have to rest on the wall. The shoe should be regarded as an extension of the wall.

"You take the hoof from between your legs and have another look. Indeed, it looks good. While holding on to the hoof, you will change your position in a slow manner to not upset the horse. Still holding the hoof in your right hand, you shuffle backwards and then around so that you are standing in front of the horse, underneath his neck. It is then that you will bring his whole leg forward to put the hoof on the hoof stand, a steel tripod around fifty centimetres high with a ball on the top like a tow ball, taking care that the horse is comfortable. All the while you have not straightened your back, and you are now looking at the outside of the hoof. The first thing you notice is that the toe is long and the heel is short. You may have not measured them for a while, but you know that if the toe is four inches long, the heel will be around one inch.

"From the coronet band, where the hoof starts, to the bottom of the hoof, has to be a straight line. Straight is strong, bent like a banana is not. All you have to do is rasp off the splaying-out bits, being careful not to take off too much, concentrating only on the outside of the hoof. You change 'camp' again, as I call it, by simply walking around the hoof stand, your back away from the horse, your head underneath his neck, and rasp the inside of the hoof, only the part which is sticking out from the straight line.

"When this part is finished, the hoof is 'dressed', and ready to take a shoe," I declared. "That is a lot of work", Mary said. "And all the time you are bending over?"

"Indeed, as there are only two requirements for this job—a strong back and not too many brains," I joked.

"I just want to tell you how interesting this is. And now you are going to put the shoe on for us?" Sonja asked.

"I sure will," I replied, "I always like to shoe a couple of horses before I have a cup of coffee. By now you have worked six or seven minutes, and in another six you will have the first shoe on.

When you go to a shoe shop, you sort of know which size you take. But sometimes they are a little bit too big or too small. It is the same with horses. If you think it is a size three, or maybe a four, you will take both and put them on the sole of the hoof to see which one the horse will like. Once you find the right size, you will have to shape the shoe to fit the hoof nicely. This is pure panel beating, really. A lot of farriers make a shoe or heat up a factory-made shoe before they shape and fit it.

"I refer to myself as one of the best cold horse shoers around. We can talk about that later if you like, but let me show you my way first," I said.

The ladies nodded silently. If they only knew that I felt myself treading in very deep waters. It is almost impossible to show someone how to shoe a horse without tools, let alone a horse, even before the fact that your listener is blind. But somehow I had their attention, so there was no going back.

"Most horse shoes are made in China or Malaysia and are made of mild steel, which is relatively easy to bend and shape. When I put the shoe on the hoof, I break things down to 'left and right' and 'in or out'. I say to myself: the left side of the shoe has got to go a bit out until almost the heel and then come in again, or the right side has got to come in a bit before going a little bit out.

"I take the horseshoe to the anvil, which is permanently mounted on the back of my Ute, get my shaping hammer and basically hit the shoe in various places until the shoe fits like I want it to fit. This may take two or three runs, sometimes even more," I explained. "You fit the shoe by trying it on and shaping it on the anvil until its perfect.

"To put things into perspective, a good dressing of the hoof is still more important than a badly shaped shoe. More cases of lameness are caused by having the wrong angle and level than a wrongly shaped shoe. Of course, we ideally want both to be right.

"When you are happy with the way the shoe fits on the hoof, you only have to secure it with a few nails. You put the hoof in between your legs again and place the shoe on the hoof, holding it with your left hand. You grab a nail and hold it in between the index finger and thumb of your left hand while holding the shoe in the proper place. You grip your shoeing hammer in your right hand, hold the nail on a good angle and give it a couple of taps with the hammer to see if the nail goes the right way. If you are happy with it, you keep on hammering. If not, you will take it out and do it again, and hammer until the head of the nail is firmly embedded in the crease of the shoe. There is a little bit of nail sticking out from the wall, which can do damage to your leg if the horse pulls back. On the other side of the hammer is a little slot which you slide over the protruding part of the nail and give it a twist to breaks it off.

"After the first nail you can still shift the shoe if necessary. When all fits well, you put the second nail in." I paused, "By now you will be wondering if it hurts the horse and if the nail is in the right place."

"We sure do," Mary confirmed.

"The wall of the hoof is normally wide enough to take a nail. And like our toenails, it is not sensitive. The placing, however, is crucial. It has got to be on the outside of the white line and the nail has got to come out of the wall; it must to be visible. To help us, the manufacturers of horse shoe nails put a bevel on the point of the nail so that it will travel away from the bevel. To make it easier for us they put a stamp on the head of the nail on the same side as the bevel.

"After you put six or seven nails in the hoof, you then put a bit of steel underneath one of the nail ends, which as you recall, is already much shorter after having being broken off. A couple of hammer hits on the nail head will result in the nail end being bent perpendicular to the wall of the hoof.

"You repeat this for every nail. Then you will change camp again and bring the hoof forward, resting it on the hoof stand. With an old rasp you rasp over the sticking-out pieces of the nail to make them all the same length, about three or four millimetres, and rasp a little bit of the hoof away underneath every nail. Then you get your clencher, a tool that looks a bit like a pair of water pump pliers: a pair of adjustable pliers where the inside of the mouth have serrations. Because of these, children call them 'alligator pliers', referring to the serrations. With the clencher you fold the nails over one by one, before making the whole side of the hoof smooth by running the rasp over it very lightly.

"You change camp and do the same on the inside of the hoof. Then you put the hoof on the ground and stand back and look at it. If all went well, you should be very happy with a well shod hoof."

"That must have been hard work," Sonja said, "you must be ready for a cuppa by now."

"Almost," I said. "While we have got this far, I feel I have to show you how to do the back feet. It won't take long—the shoeing is the same, but the positions are different.

"Having finished the front foot, the back of your right hand touches the horse's shoulder, and while keeping contact with the horse's side you walk towards the back until your feet are in the same line as the horse's back feet. Your hand goes over the backside, down along the leg, over the knee until just above the fetlock. If the horse has not lifted his foot up yet, you will gently squeeze the tendon, harder and harder until he does raise his foot.

"You grab the hoof in your right hand, just like before, but now you lift his leg up on your lap and take a couple of little steps forward to make it more comfortable for the horse and yourself. As well as your back, your legs are a bit bent as well. You are standing probably two feet behind the other back leg and you would like to feel assured that you are in control of the horse. From this position you dress the hoof like the front one, and when finished you walk back and plant your backside under the horse's belly and lift the hoof up onto your bent knees.

"From here you will dress the outside of the hoof. You keep hold of the hoof and turn half a circle so that your head is almost under the horse's belly to dress the inside of the hoof. I must say that it is this position that you feel the most vulnerable. Yet soon the hoof is dressed and you can let it go. Now you only have to put the shoe on, but that is exactly the same as the front one."

Done. I did it. I was suddenly finished, and I hoped it made some sense to the ladies. "That was hard work," I said. "Once that shoe is on, you are only half way. But the rest is all the same as these first two."

"Ninety-two," Sonja said as Mary got the attention of a waitress.

After we had ordered our coffee, I asked Sonja, "Ninety-two, what do you mean by that?"

"Ninety-two different stages or positions to shoe a horse," she elaborated. "You started counting and I just carried on from there. Twenty-three different movements per hoof, and I suppose some are more if the shoe is hard to fit or something. Then I just multiplied it by the four legs. Simple."

"That is a few movements I must say," I remarked. "I always

start counting, but I have actually never got to the end. That is amazing really. Ninety-two, I will have to remember that. Thanks for that."

"I really thank you very much for taking the time for us, it was really enjoyable," Sonja said. "You are welcome; I just hope you can visualise it all. It is a very physical job, but when you have a good quiet horse, it really is enjoyable," I said.

"Dangerous too, I bet. Many accidents?" Mary asked.

"Had a few nasty kicks from donkeys on my face; one horse kicked me in the head which resulted in being unconscious and a broken nose; a lot of cuts, bruises, sprains; and a sore back once in a while. All in all, I think I am very lucky," I replied with a grin on my face, as I did not think that they would agree with the last bit.

"Sure you were lucky?" enquired Sonja with a smile on her face. "All in the name of doing your job was it?"

"Indeed," I said. "Apart for some freak accidents like the horse kicking me in the face, a lot of injuries can be prevented by listening to the horse or donkey and to stay out of harm's way. If you get kicked, you were definitely in the wrong place."

The coffee arrived and we were busy putting the sugar in and stirring it. I enjoyed the taste of the coffee just as much as if I had really shod a horse. Some things don't change.

Sonja asked, "What I don't really understand is why the horses have to have shoes on. They seem to get by alright in the wild, don't they?"

I said, "Not all horses need shoes, luckily for me. It is just that when you ride them a lot, the hoof wears out more than they naturally grow, so the feet will become very tender. In that case it is a very good idea to put some shoes on. If they are jumping or racing, they normally perform much better with shoes on. I would not want to go without my boots or shoes for one minute; I just could not get around. The Kenyan marathon runners all used to go barefoot in the good old days, but now they all wear the best running shoes they can get their hands on. The key word is protection, while we also have to take into account that the horse is very domesticated. The modern horse normally only lives in one paddock, but in the wild they had thousands of acres to roam around on. It does change the hoof a bit. And, of course, there is the fact that there is someone on their back, so a horse will welcome a bit of extra support for their hooves."

"It sounds as if you really enjoy your job," Mary said.

"This is the best job I have ever had," I said truthfully. "I travel our beautiful countryside, stop here and there to shoe one or more horses, have a cup of coffee from my thermos flask in some amazing places, trim a few donkeys, do a bit of socialising, have some lunch on top of a lookout hill somewhere, have a yarn with some other customers while I shoe their horses, and finally go home again, knowing that I have done enough physical exercise for the day that I don't have to go to the gym."

That made the girls giggle a bit, so I went a little bit further. "I can't go to the gym anyway," I said. It goes against my philosophy." I could see I had their full attention again, so I continued, "If I work up a sweat, I want to get paid for it. It goes against my grain to pay the gym owner so I can work up a sweat. It just does not feel right."

They had a laugh about that. "Good on you," Mary said.

With the coffee all gone and the horse well shod, it was time to catch up with my wife again. To Mary and Sonja, I said, "Thank you for the opportunity to talk to you about my passion—shoeing horses. I really enjoyed this."

"The perfect job isn't it," said Sonja. "Thank you very much again, and I must say we thoroughly enjoyed it. Thanks for your time to make horseshoeing visible for me. And you never know, we might see each other again." Mary thanked me as well.

As I walked away, I thought the chance of meeting again would be very slim since there were three thousand people on the ship, not counting the crew. But the odds of my wife meeting an old class mate from Whangarei on the other side of the world were very slim as well.

We did see them again at the finals of the karaoke contest. The auditorium was packed full on the last night of the cruise. Mary helped Sonja onto the stage and directed her to stand right in the middle, and then it became eerily quiet before the music started. After a couple of beats Sonja started with a voice so clear and warm that it did not take long for the crowd to get right behind her. It was a sterling performance with a powerful finish resulting in a standing ovation just as powerful.

I considered myself well paid for showing her how to shoe a horse.

4

Paparoa

Bob Kenny, like most people moving into our area, came from Auckland, but his accent would tell you he was a Scotsman. He relocated to our region because some of his friends from Auckland moved north, and after visiting them a few times, he came across a lifestyle block in the middle of Paparoa and bought it. Now he was the proud owner of some desirable grazing land and was busy putting up his American style barn with living quarters upstairs, shed and stables downstairs.

When I came to Bob's place for the very first time, there seemed to be no one home. But after a couple of minutes, Bob came down the circular staircase with a cup of coffee in one hand and a saucer with a couple of chocolate biscuits in the other. I thanked him very much and found a box to sit on to enjoy my cuppa. Never be too lazy to make yourself comfortable.

After he lit up his cigarette, he told me, "That's what I do for the farrier, that's the least I can do. I did it in Scotland, I did it in Auckland, and now I do it in Paparoa."

In all the years to come, whenever I came to look after his horse's feet, in summer or winter, there would always be a cup of coffee with biscuits.

He swapped his slippers for gumboots, but as they had holes in them, he first had to put his feet in plastic supermarket bags. He also wore heavy black glasses, broken in the middle of the bridge over the nose, but fixed with an abundance of sticky-tape. It is a good cuppa, I reflected; let's hope the horse is good, too.

The horse turned out to be an Anglo Arab, the offspring of a Thoroughbred and an Arabian horse, the two most noble horse breeds. Astraban was his name and he was probably three or four years old, well fed and under worked. He looked absolutely beautiful. There is no way you could keep a horse like this on its own, and Bob was lucky he had found a nice old Thoroughbred to keep him company. It did not take long before another two horses arrived, and with that Bob was set. He was happy, the horses were happy, and he could enjoy the later stages of his life.

It must have been the fourth time I had come to trim all these feet again when I finished another nice cup of coffee with a biscuit and wondered where to start. Bob had made himself a bit of a court yard between the stables and the race to the paddock. Although unfinished, I could see it would be really nice one day. The horses enjoyed it in here, and the horse standing next to me was quiet, so why not make a start with this one? Bob would be back soon from putting the coffee cups away.

I lifted the right front foot up and put it in between my thighs and started cleaning the hoof. Astraban was standing a couple of meters away, watching what was happening.

I could hear a horse approaching, and when I looked up, I saw Astraban coming for me with his mouth wide open. There was nowhere to go, so I leaned my head and right shoulder against the side of the horse whose leg I was still holding in between mine.

Astraban advanced a couple more steps and very, very quickly got hold of my left shoulder; my whole shoulder disappeared into his mouth. He lifted me off the ground and suddenly dropped me.

By the time I realised what had just happened, I knew I had to do something. Somehow I had to smack him, growl at him or even throw something at him to make him realise that this kind of behaviour was totally unacceptable. But I did not have the chance. After Astraban let me go, he turned on his back legs and took off, faster than many a horse out of the starting gates at the races. He knew he had done something wrong.

By now Bob was back again, a bit out of breath rushing to see what all the noise was about, and now was the time to survey the damage. My shirt was torn to pieces. My singlet was not much better. At the front of my chest there was a hot red bruise forming where the teeth had luckily stopped. It was the same on my back, right up to my shoulder blade, and I was probably lucky that I could not see it then. In days to come it would become a kaleidoscope of distinctive colours—red, blue, purple and black. And it would be very sore and stiff for a week or so.

"Oh well, another experience," I told Bob, who was very sorry and almost embarrassed about what his "pride and joy" had done to me.

"Shall we trim the other three and come back next week for Astraban?" I offered. Bob thought this was a good idea and soon he had put a halter on the first one and we were in business again. The pain was not too bad yet, so I thought I might as well carry on.

I did not go back the following week. I hardly did anything that week, suffering from a very sore and stiff shoulder. As with a lot of injuries and accidents, we feel very sorry for ourselves, but at the same time we feel very lucky indeed as it could have been so much worse.

If Astraban had been more serious about it, there would not have been much left of my shoulder and if he had got hold of my head instead of my shoulder, I would not be here anymore to talk about it at all. I do think I was bloody lucky.

It was three weeks after the incident (incident sounds so much better than an accident) until I felt emotionally strong enough to try to trim Astraban's feet. There was something going on with his behaviour that I could not work out yet, something that could not just be explained by the fact that he was an Anglo Arab, the most 'hot-blooded' horse there is on the temperament scale, followed closely by the Thoroughbred and the Arabian breeds. Less temperamental are the warm-bloods such as the Hanoverian, and after a whole lot more breeds of horses, the scale ends with the cold-blooded Draught horses, such as Clydesdales. Just being hot blooded, however, is not a reason to try to rip someone's shoulder off his body.

Most horse owners, at some point, like to give their horse a little treat. It is something to say thank you, I like you, or you have been very well behaved today. One of my customers had the habit whenever he walked past the horses, of giving them a bit of a carrot. One day he did not have a carrot so the horse bit his finger as he walked past. Did the horse think his finger was a carrot, or did the horse say, "Where the hell is my carrot?"

Regularity fosters expectations. Bob did not routinely give his horses carrots. He might have done now and then, but carrots were not the problem. He gave his horses, well, at least Astraban, sugar cubes.

What is the danger in a little sugar cube, we always wonder. Horses absolutely love it. How much energy can there be in a teaspoon of sugar? There is not a lot of energy in it when you compare it to the horse's weight. The problem is purely in the habit of getting a sugar fix, and if you do it every day at the same time, the horses will get nicely addicted to it. With this habit comes the association that links the owner to the horse's happiness. The owner equals a supply of instant satisfaction. When the owner suddenly runs out of sugar cubes, watch out for the consequences.

When the owner is not there, but the farrier is, and the horse has not had his sugar fix yet, he might just take to the farrier, as there is no one else around. And who wants to argue or fight with an Anglo Arab in the prime of his life with an enormous amount of energy to burn?

Bob had been around horses all his life and he realised what was happening. So, immediately after the last episode, he stopped giving Astraban sugar cubes. If he ever needed a treat, he would resort to carrots. Bob had a hell of a job to wean him off his addiction. Astraban did not take no for an answer and threw a few wobblies. But after a couple of weeks he was manageable again. Whenever I came to attend to Astraban's feet from then on, Bob also made sure he had a firm hold on him.

There was something happening at the Showgrounds at Paparoa. It could have been a ribbon day of the Ararua Pony Club or some other horse event, but regardless it was well organised with a lot of advertising so there were a lot of people. The highlight of the day, at lunch time, was an exhibition of a top dressage rider who was either going to something prestigious like the World Cup, or had just come back from it. She and her horse gave a beautiful performance to music for a large enthusiastic crowd ranging from young pony clubbers to elderly folk, who specially came to witness this event.

She just started her routine when Bob came along as he only lived a few hundred metres away. And why not bring his trusted Astraban along so he could see and learn what would be expected of him in a few years' time. As Bob came a bit closer, I could see that at least he had left his leaky gumboots at home. He was wearing the shiniest riding boots I had ever seen, well-fitting jodhpurs, a white shirt with matching stock and a beautiful patterned riding jacket with shiny buttons. On his nose rested what looked like brand-new glasses, on his head was a new-looking riding hat, in his free hand was a beautiful dressage whip and in the other a well-polished leather lead rope fixed to a leather show halter. Astroban had been in the bath too, and looked like a million dollars. His four white socks were bright like snow, and his four white feet were nicely oiled. His dark chestnut coat was showing a beautiful sheen. Bob must have started very early that morning, probably having washed the horse the day prior and kept him in the stables overnight.

Bob led Astraban along the drive. On his left was the big hedge of the old Bowling Green, on his right, a big double row of spectators. There was nowhere to go but straight ahead, and that was the plan. But Astraban stopped and looked around. He was not very happy. He obviously did not like it here. There were too many people, so many colours, all this excitement, the music, and nobody was looking at him, for they were facing something happening on the rugby field. And then he spotted a horse and rider in the middle of the field almost halfway through their dressage test to music.

"And what is that horse doing over there in the middle of the rugby field? I want to say hello. Do I know that horse? Look, there is someone sitting on his back. Come on Bob, let's go, I want to say hello to my mate over there. Come on, let's go and introduce ourselves, shall we? Might be an old mate of mine; Oh, come on; don't be boring, we did not come all this way to look at the backs of all these people, did we? Besides, don't they know who I am? Generations of selective breeding made me what I am: One of the finest, most noble and pedigree horses around. Can I show them Bob? Can I show them what I am made of, how incredibly good looking I am with the most refined motions? I bet you I can outperform that black horse on the field out there any time. Why don't you just let me go to check that horse out? Oh, don't be such an old fart, let me go, will you?" Astraban said.

Bob had the intention of showing off his pride and joy and just wanted a quiet time with a yarn to some people here and there, but he found it was getting increasingly harder to control the horse. By now Astraban was really prancing left and right, and the lead rope was not long enough. The front feet came off the ground and he started neighing, pawing the ground with his front foot and generally fidgeting around.

By then the people close by had turned around to have a look at what was happening. Unhurried, they still moved out of the way of this very unhappy horse, keeping one eye on the very nice dressage exercise and a wary eye on the horse at their backs working himself up. More and more people moved away as Astraban made a loud shrieking noise as he reared up. A few minutes before, the horse was facing a wall of people, but now they had parted to the left and right, leaving a nice pathway to the dressage arena. All it took was another rear up, with a change in direction when he came down again, putting so much strain on the lead rope that poor Bob had to let go. Now freed of his boss, he galloped a few strides towards the dressage arena. The arena was fenced off with a rope about a foot high of the ground, and strangely enough Astraban saw it and jumped it gracefully. After a few more high-speed strides he slowed down, as if his mission was almost accomplished.

"This is where I belong, in the middle of the arena, in the middle of the limelight. I can relax now. And look at all these people looking at me—I am loving this," he thought.

According to the music, the dressage test was almost finished. Unfortunately, the rider could not finish as there was this horse suddenly standing in the wrong spot. If he had stood anywhere else, she could have gone around him, but not there. In the end she just slowed down her paces and stopped when she was facing the judges and bowed her head, to finish. It was not quite the finish she hoped for, but it was nothing to get upset about either.

In fact she thought it very comical, this being the first time that another horse stopped her performance. There was a lot of clapping of hands and other sounds of appreciation. Horse and rider had just made an incredible impression on all the people present, especially the pony club riders as this is what some of them were hoping to achieve in a few years' time. At a walk, the rider wandered over to Astraban, said hello and picked up his lead rein. The horses seemed to like each other at first sight. Bob came over to meet them, feeling oh so embarrassed while the lady thought it was rather funny.

"Did you see how your horse behaved when all the clapping was going on?" she remarked. "Your horse thought it was for him, for being so special. I am sure he even bowed his head a bit."

After Bob apologised profusely, he really appreciated that Astraban had settled down from the moment he entered the arena, very much in love with this fine-looking dressage horse. They talked a bit more about their horses before Bob lead Astraban home a little later, both of them on cloud nine.

I continued trimming Bob's horses for quite a few more years. Every time, there was a cuppa coffee waiting and a little bit more progress to be seen on his piece of paradise. Every time, Bob looked a bit older, moved a bit slower and always seemed to be out of breath. After the mishap at the Paparoa Showgrounds, Astraban had not gone out anymore. As Bob was getting older, he knew that his show days were over, while Astraban had not even started yet. He really should have been going somewhere where he could be ridden and shown here and there, to find his potential, to see what he would be good at.

Bob's health took a dive, but luckily he had some distant relatives, or maybe good friends, in Auckland, where he would spend the remainder of his life. His place was as good as sold, so that was a big worry off his shoulders. The same people who were going to look after Bob were going to look after Astraban and his mate as well.

A local lady would take care of the pony since her daughter took a liking to her and they had done very well so far on the lead rein. That only left one old horse, which I picked up for him and took home as I said I would if Bob ever got stuck.

The only thing left to do was to say goodbye. Bob thanked me for my services over the years, and I told him the pleasure was all mine and wished him well.

Finally, the fourth date for our appointment was okay. The first time I texted her it was too muddy. The next available day it was supposed to be raining. The third time it was too windy, but finally, this time she would be there as the weather forecast was good. I would be there at eight in the morning even though she preferred nine for some reason. I got there on time, noting that it was the furthest I had travelled down this no exit road. I was almost at the end of a peninsula jutting out in the Kaipara Harbour out from Matakohe on the way to Tinopai. A beautiful place it was, and so was the nice weather to top it off. But there was no horse or owner. This certainly was a really good start to my working day.

After a little while, a mature lady appeared from the house, and sure enough she proved to be the owner. After I introduced myself, I commented on her nice place amongst this ideal farm scenery on the edge of the harbour. This led to the inevitable talk about the beautiful early morning sunny weather, while I was really wondering where the horse was.

"I asked you to come at nine, because at nine he always comes over to the house. Would you like a cup of tea maybe?" She asked.

I had the feeling she was playing for time, waiting till it is nine o'clock when the horse would ceremoniously appear from who knows where. I tried to look for the horse in this open, clean farmland, but I could not spot it anywhere. "I just had my breakfast and a cup of tea, thank you. We will be fine for a while," I replied. "Whereabouts is the horse anyway?" I could not help asking.

"Over there, under those trees over there," she said, pointing to a long, long way away where a little clump of trees stood. Indeed, just then, because I knew where to look, I could just make out the silhouette of a horse.

"I don't think he will come over in a hurry. Would you like me to catch him for you?" she asked.

I felt like saying, "Now that will be a splendid idea!" but I had the feeling that might be overdoing it a bit. So I said, "Yes please, that will be nice thanks."

She put on her leggings, gumboots and coat, and off she went. I was watching the horse as the lady moved closer and closer to him, but he did not move one step. The lady put the halter on and walked all the way back, trying to look for the driest spots and dodging the biggest pug holes. When she finally arrived, I could see that this horse was a magnificent animal, probably in his prime. He was a Chestnut with four even white socks and a not too big a white blaze, a stripe of various width and length running from between the eyes to the nose. Closer to seventeen than sixteen hands high, I had the feeling the horse would have too much power for the owner. But she said that he was good to ride, and when I asked her how the hell could she even mount him, as she was not very tall at all, she pointed to an aluminium stepladder, and not the kitchen one with two or three steps, no, but the builders one with seven steps, thank you. I came quickly to the conclusion that these two must have had a wonderful working relationship in accepting each other.

"So, now you have arrived, we better have a look at your feet and give them a trim, shall we?" I began. Hardly ever does the horse reply, but it never hurts to have a yarn with them when you first meet. He was good to trim, but when underneath the back legs, I could feel how strong this horse was.

This first time was the start of a long customer relationship. It was the only time I saw the owner catching the horse. All other times, the horse would be ready and waiting with nice clean feet. In later years the owner worked different shifts, so I would often catch the horse myself. That became easier again when they put in a farm race all the way to the clump of trees and a bit further to the water's edge.

It was nearing the end of summer when I was called again to put some shoes on the horse as the owner was doing more and more riding. Stopping at the gate, I could see no horse, and like the very first time, he was standing under the clump of trees. This time I decided to drive the Ute all the way there and tie the horse to the Ute when I got there. It was going to be a piece of cake—I had done it all before.

I caught the horse and began taking the shoes off, trimming the hooves and putting shoes back on. It was simple really, and went well until there was just one shoe to go—a front one. There were just seven nails to put in, and the job would be done. Life was good. I was making plans of what to do next, such as having my lunch right there, such a beautiful serene spot it was.

But it was to be a long time later that I would be able to eat my sandwiches, as swarms of flying ants drifted in, disturbing the peace in a big hurry. They had come out of nowhere. The horse did not like it one little bit. He was up and down, shaking his head vigorously. The bottle of 'Buzz Off' insect repellent was quickly put to good use, but the spray could not come quick enough. I protected first my own face and hair as the bugs seemed to congregate around my head.

Only then did I realise that these little flying ants, or whatever they were, in their hundreds, were just the scouts for vast flying colonies still incoming. The horse was gone, all its hundreds of years of domestication wiped aside instantly, the basic instinct of flight taking over. The flight was a direct result of an enormous fright from of a cloud of flying ants buzzing around his head trying to get into his nose, eyes and ears. The piece of bailing twine tied on the Ute, on which the lead rope was tied, was no match for the brute force of a horse trying to get away from this horrible danger.

With the horse gone I only had to worry about myself. In this situation, you keep your mouth closed, fair enough. You don't want to eat these little buggers. You keep your nose closed as well. Now that's a bit harder. You close your eyes, block off your ears, swish with your arms, wipe your face clean with your hands, and spray more 'Buzz Off' around your face. Still, they keep on coming. They make a noise too, not as loud as a bee swarm, but similar. Running around helps, that is for sure, but the moment you stop, they are back. They are like a bad dream; you just can't escape them. I see the horse resting relatively happily in the shade with a few cows as company. Why didn't the swarm follow him? Do they like me better? The funny thing is, they don't even bite. But they were awfully annoying, trying to get in your airways, ears and eyes.

Amidst the chaos, there was a brief spell when they descended like mad onto the bonnet of the Ute. I sprayed all over them.

A towel over my head seemed to work a bit. If you keep them out of your ears, you have won one little battle. When you drape it over your nose and mouth, it's only the eyes to worry about now. Keep on walking, keep on walking.

Then suddenly they took off. It was as if an in-built alarm went off. They probably had an appointment somewhere else. I saw not one flying ant anywhere, only handfuls of dead ones on the bonnet. Unbelievable! I stood there thinking that if I ever described this to anyone, they would never believe me. The mobile phone I had at that time did not have a camera in it. Oh well, that's life. Now that it was all-clear, it was time to get the horse again.

As if nothing ever happened, the horse let himself be caught. We were making the little walk back towards the Ute when we were ambushed. There is no other way of describing it. There were none to be seen, but next second there was a swarm so big it covered the horse and me together.

Suddenly, the horse was off—well, trying, as he was a strong horse. When he threw his weight at the lead rope, I knew all about it. I did not want to let go as it would be the second time he got away, and I might not be able to get him a third time. As I tried to hold on to the horse and swipe at the insects around my face, the horse was throwing his head from left to right and up and down, and these silly flying ants, for some reason, were thinking they were in heaven.

The horse had had enough and did not hesitate to tell me, "Let me go, let me go!" So off we went, the horse going around and around me like an over the top lunging session.

Luckily the lead rope was one of the long ones, but I had to hang on as we covered some ground away from the Ute as well. And all the time this cloud of flying ants kept on buzzing around us. It would have gone viral if anyone was to film this and put it on YouTube, but that was far from my mind. Away, away, is what the horse was thinking, as fast as we can. It was a recipe for disaster. Further and further we spun away from the Ute. We could not outsmart them; we could not run away from them. I decided to go back to the gate of the paddock, now only 400 metres away, we covered 100 already. At first I thought I was imagining it, but the dark cloud of ants became a bit thinner. We were very close to the gate but there were still too many for comfort. By the time we reached the gate they were almost gone. You should have heard the sigh of relief from both of us.

Standing still at the gate, where there was a sort of yard, proved to be a big mistake. They were back, in vengeance. You should have heard the sigh of desperation from both of us. This was about our last straw; we could not handle any more punishment.

As if the good gods had mercy on us, the swarm suddenly disappeared. They seemed to have just vanished in thin air, with not a cloud of them to be seen anywhere. I could not see a single one.

Immediately, the horse settled down again and checked the food bowl to see if maybe someone had put some food in it for him. I, for one, would have liked to give him a good feed, as he had been very good. "Okay boy, let's tie you up, I have to go back to get the Ute. You just stay here and be good, and you better pray that our nightmare won't decide to come back."

By the time I came back in the Ute, the horse still had not got any unwanted visitors, so that was good. Only a few minutes later the seven nails were in, and the hoof finished. I gave the horse a mighty pat; this was some experience for both of us. Finally, it was time to have my sandwiches. Just another day at the office.

It was a horrible day, even though it was dry. The forecast told of heaps of wind with a few showers. It was the rain which always worried me. All the tools get wet, muddy and slippery; the horses are wet and muddy; and I get soaked as well. As I only had one body, I better look after it and not get wet, cold, or sore in the muscles, especially not my back. I made money over my back, so I had better look after it.

Ellen, at any time, had three or four horses in work for herself, her friend Danny or her customers. She broke them in, rode them, took them to events, sold them and all the other things you do with horses.

She loved her eventing and found herself competing in Rotorua or Taupo for the weekend now and then. The more professional the people are, the better organised they normally are. Ellen only had a few acres, probably around six, so the horses had to be stabled or penned up most of the time, especially in the winter.

It was blowing a gale by the time I got there. Next to the stables, two horses were tied up waiting to be shod. On either side of the float was another horse tied up ready for Ellen to ride. The horses to be shod were tied up with a strong chain from the halter to a steel pipe fastened to two big posts. The drive and the yard were flat with muddy limestone, but underneath the horses to be shod were a couple of long rubber mats. At least the horse's feet were out of the mud.

The horses, being in work, were well handled and did not mind the wind at all.

Most of the time horses don't mind wind, and I sometimes think that it is a human thing to say that horses get spooked because of the wind. Everything around the horse moves. With their 180-degree vision they take in every movement from every tree, shrub or patch of grass. I do not think that the horse's nervous system can be on full alert, ready to jump out of their skin, every second of a twenty-four-hour day. Certainly they will settle down and accept the moving things as normal.

I talked about this one day to my friend and customer Liam who was running a horse-trekking business just out of Waipu. He took groups of people horse riding through river and bush, climbing a few slopes, and finishing on top of a steep ridge overlooking bush-clad hills.

"Horses don't mind wind at all," he said. "They accept things as they are. Better than us humans who worry too much about these things."

Indeed, the horses were all at ease, going about in the normal manner as they should have been, which was standing still until called upon to either be ridden or shod.

Routine and work combined with a lot of tying up makes for a quiet horse, so there were no problems. Everything was fine, and the gale blowing was just a bit of a change in case we got bored.

The first horse was shod without any problems, so it was time to change them over, as I like the horse which is being shod to stand nice and close to the anvil at the back of my Ute. It is neither economic nor safe to walk around one horse's back feet all the time to get to the second horse.

I had finished taking the shoes off the second horse, cleaned and dressed all of its feet and was busy nailing the first shoe back on with the right front leg held in between my thighs when it happened. I did not see what it was at first, but I noticed the horses get an immense fright. A gust of wind had gotten hold of a corner of the rubber mat and pulled it a little off the ground, which was an unusual enough movement to upset the horses. The next gust of wind was even stronger and ripped the rubber mat from the ground, scooping it up to the horse's legs, which the horse did not like one little bit. He was trying to flee from it while I still had his leg in between mine, but not for long. There were legs everywhere, all trying to get away from this mat still flapping against the horse's legs.

With all the horse's might, he pulled on the chain to try to get away. There was no give in the chain, but the posts did bend over a lot until finally the halter broke and the horse was gone.

The other horse was off as well only a second later, also breaking its halter. Nothing could stop them. The other two horses at the float saw that something was happening, that two of their mates had broken loose, and this rubber mat was still flapping and flying in the wind, with only me holding it down after having been ceremoniously dumped on the ground. One of the pair broke loose as well, and the other one was not very happy at all being the only one tied up.

Ellen, who had just come out of the tack room, had heard the noise and wondered what the hell was going on. Three horses were on the run, trying to get as far away from the mat as possible. The mat came to rest a few metres away, the wind picked it up after I finally got up.

After I explained what happened, I said I would take a few minutes off and have a cup of coffee out of my thermos flask, which I often refer to as my life saver.

That was one of the biggest frights I got in my life and it would take a few minutes to settle my nerves down again.

The coffee was good and because of the time needed to enjoy it, things settled down again to normal. The mat was put back into place, making sure that the wind could not catch it again. Ellen caught the horses, and when they realised that the mat was not going to jump up anymore, they were happy to take their place on it again. Half an hour later the job was finished and I was off to the next customer.

5
Ruawai

I had just finishing shoeing the bay horse on the driveway next to the kumara paddock. The horse belonged to Ivy, and unlike her sister Carmen, she was not competitive at all—just wanting to do a bit of trekking and a lot of farm riding. She was just going to walk the horse home, put the saddle on and go for a big ride around the neighbourhood. She lived on the other side of the paddock, and as it was hoe'd up to plant the kumaras, there was no way she could not walk him right across the paddock.

She was not even half way when we heard an enormous yell. I stopped working on Carmen's horse to see what was going on. Ivy was holding a front hoof up, indicating there was something wrong.

"There is a nail in her hoof," she yelled.

Well of course, there were seven to be precise to keep the shoe on.

"A roofing nail," she yelled across the distance.

That sounded serious. But a roofing nail? In a kumara paddock? I thought I better go and have a look, so I took some tools and my Iodine spray bottle.

I should not have doubted Ivy when she said it was a roofing nail, as rural girls just know a lot about practical things. It was indeed a roofing nail I saw sticking out of the middle of the frog while Ivy was still holding the leg up. A roofing nail differs from an ordinary nail because it has a tight-fitting washer at the top so it has a bigger surface to hold the roofing iron down and stop the water going in. To prevent the nail from being pulled out by prolonged wind trying to lift the iron of the roof, the shaft of the nail is square but twisted like a corkscrew so it won't come out easily. Mostly they are sixty or seventy millimetres long, and the head of this nail was still sticking out by around ten millimetres or so.

"A roofing nail," I said, "in a kumara paddock. At least fifty metres from the nearest house. Incredible! That nail has to come out."

There was no way the poor horse was even thinking about putting his foot on the ground. The pain of the nail in the hoof would be considerable; to put it on the ground would be excruciating.

I sprayed the entire sole and frog liberally with Iodine. For all I knew, the blood could come rushing out when I pulled the nail out. The nail was right in the middle of the frog, almost square to the level of the sole.

"Right, let's do this," I said to myself. I picked up my shoe puller, put it in position and pulled the nail out as straight as possible. The horse let out a sigh of relief as the immense pain subsided. Immediately I put on a bit more Iodine on the tiny hole, but no blood came rushing out. I didn't even know if that was a good sign or not. If some blood did come out, it might take along any bugs as well, which was our biggest worry. We all know what stepping on a rusty old nail can do to a human foot.

"Look Ivy, the nail is out. There is a big chance of infection with the bugs on the nail going in that deep. The vet is just across the road—I would get some drugs into the horse to fight an upcoming infection, just to make sure. That's about all I know and all I can do, sorry."

This injury happened in the days that mobile phones were only for the rich. Ivy would walk back to Carissa's place to make a phone call. At first, the horse was very apprehensive of putting any weight on the sore foot, but after a few steps, realising that the nail was gone, the horse dutifully followed Ivy, slightly favouring the injured foot. Ivy came back and said, "I have to be there in half an hour at the clinic, so that's good. She will be just fine."

She was not fine, however, despite the vet pumping the horse full with all the horse might ever need to fight infection and inflammation in the hoof. It was not enough, or the cocktail did not have the right ingredients, or something inside the hoof was damaged.

The poor horse went really lame for a long time. Not quite bad enough to be put down, she came close a few times when emotions ran high, or low, depending how people looked at the problem. A lot of people would have called it quits if they were in Ivy's shoes. But she carried on caring for her horse, making sure that she had enough to eat and drink as she could barely walk, change a bandage here and there, and trying Stockholm tar for a while to draw out the infection. The foot was soaked in Epsom Salts to soften it up. When the hoof was getting too soft, removing the bandages and sunbathing was the word.

Almost a year passed before I met up with Ivy while shoeing Carmen's horse again.

"I went for a ride the other day for the first time since that stupid nail," she said, "and all went well. She is an old lady now, so I don't think she will be needing shoes anymore. We just hack her around now and then and we both are happy."

"That's good to hear," I said. "You have done very well with her. I hope she did not cause you too much financial strife."

"We do know that owning any animal is going to cost you money at some stage. The first visit was the worst, but we managed. After that, the vet came by now and then and gave some advice here and there, so as not to break the bank. And here we are, isn't she looking great?"

"She looks wonderful," I said as she was in good condition, had a shiny coat and looked incredibly happy.

Carmen's horse had a crack in his front right hoof, almost in the middle, from top to bottom. It had been there a long time and never seemed to be any more than a shallow sand-crack. But during the last few shoeings, we noticed the crack getting bigger, especially at the bottom end, where, underneath, a biggish hole was forming.

Carmen showed me a video she found online about how to fix a crack like this, which appealed to her because of its simplicity. She showed it to me on her mobile phone. I watched it again that night at home on a big screen. It involved screwing on an aluminium plate over the crack. So far, all I had ever used was some builders bog, and while many times were very successful, a couple of times were disappointing.

I ordered the necessary materials the very next day and they arrived a couple of days later. I dressed the hoof and put the shoe on as normal, but I did change the front shoes from ones that had clips on the toes to side-clipped ones for a little bit of extra support. I screwed on an aluminium plate with heaps of holes in it.

I got given six different sizes of screws with different thicknesses, but above all, they had different lengths. We do not want the screw to enter the sensitive laminae on the inside of the hoof wall, do we? But how do we know the thickness of the wall anyway? Adding the thickness of the wall to the thickness of the plate will give us the size of the screws. Simple really. I had a really good look at the thickness of the wall, as it shows underneath, and took a nice-looking screw that would not poke through the inside off the wall.

Now we just had to work out how high we are going to screw the plate. I decided to screw it on right in the middle, and attached it there with five or six screws on each side of the crack. Now that looked nice and solid. All we had left to do was fill in the entire cavity with the new bog we bought. It comes in a little tube and you need a special dispensing gun for it. It releases the right amount of the two components; they just need a little bit more mixing with a wooden spatula, the ones they use for making ice blocks.

Using the spatula to spread the mixture, I not only filled in the hole, but also put a layer of bog on the plate, covering it all the way to the shoe. Done like that, it was never going to look nice, but with a little Glad Wrap, it might help. So I wrapped it around the hoof a few times, not too tight, not too loose. When that was done, it was time to wait five minutes for the bog to harden, but fifteen was better, according to the instructions. Luckily the horse had a few more feet to keep us busy. After taking off the Glad Wrap there seemed nothing more to do but run the rasp over it a couple of times to make it look nice.

The second time, five weeks later, it still looked so good that I decided to leave most of the bog alone, including the plate. I took the shoe off, did a minimal hoof dressing and put the shoe back on.

On the third time the horse had lost a shoe: the one with the plate and the bog, of course. When I trimmed the hoof, the bog and plate almost fell off by itself. The bog was solidly attached to the plate. The toe had grown rather long now, so there was a lot to trim off. But the whole hoof looked so firm and the crack had become so small that I did not put on another plate or apply any more bog.

The fourth time I attended to the horse, he had gone lame— very, very lame. It was the problem foot, of course. I cut heaps away, and that tiny split was now an enormous V-shape. I dug with my knife as deep as I dared. I was sure there would be an infection in there somewhere and hopefully I could open it up to relieve the pressure. All I got was one spec of puss. That's all. I put the shoe back on and filled the hole with Stockholm tar and cotton wool. We just hoped for the best.

I texted Carmen a week later as I was so curious how the horse was getting on. She replied that the horse was galloping around the day after I had a look at him. Eight months later we could not even see that there had been a crack in the hoof at all.

It was still in my early days of becoming a well-established farrier when there was a little white hand-written envelope in the mail. In immaculate, old fashioned and precise handwriting, with the curls and whirls all the same size and angle, the writer asked very politely and very formally if Mr Jansen would be available in the not too distant future to be kind enough to shoe a pony in Ruawai as there was a lot of riding to be done.

Signed sincerely; by no one else but Mr Casey.

It must have been a few years since I last saw him and thought he was old. He was very old now. His head seemed to be fused to his body—when he went to turn his head, he had to turn his whole upper body. His lazy eye got even lazier and stayed shut a lot of the time. But the biggest change was his limp. That really slowed him down. The sore leg had to make an arc to get to a new place. He had broken his leg in a horse-related accident and had to spend some time in hospital. From the neighbour, I heard that they nearly lost him. The nurse in charge had decided that Mr Casey could do with a good wash, which would also be good for her student nurses to experience. After the initial shock of actually seeing someone so incredibly dirty, the nurses went to work with soap and brushes and were busy for a long time. Whether his body reacted badly now this protective layer of dirt was gone, or was it an allergic reaction to the kind of soap they used, they could not establish. He was lucky in a way, because since it happened there, they managed to save him.

His polite manner and his general dislike of all things modern had, however, not changed a bit. Tied up on the rails of the stockyard, the pony was fat and dirty. First impressions always seem to be short and to the point. The front feet showed obvious signs of laminitis—the heels were very high, the toes were pushed to the front and upwards, and the s-ridges on the outside of the hoof were clearly defined.

"And how exactly are you getting on your horse with that leg of yours?" I wanted to know, because if he could not hop on, I did not have to shoe the pony, really.

"Don't you worry about that," he said. "We are well used to these things, ey. I can climb on any fence with rails or a wooden gate and tell the pony to come real close, and then I gently hop on. Been doing that for a while now."

So here we go. At least this pony was used to all this, having had it done a lot of times before. "These people borrowed my shoeing gear and never brought it back. I just can't remember who they were. That is so bad. That's what's wrong with people nowadays, ey. No conscience, ey," Mr. Casey said, not losing any of his old ways. "I got hold of that friend of yours, Mr. Eastman, he trimmed a few horses for me, ey. But he reckons he has got a sore elbow now or something. Then I got Mr. Baker, now he is a good professional, ey. Too busy he is now with harness horses you know, a lot around Kumeu way I believe, ey.

Then I got talking to this hairdresser lady in town who has got a horse grazing on the stop-bank and she told me you were shoeing her horses. I found your address in the phone book and wrote a letter and here you are, ey."

I always got a lot of work done when the owner was having a monologue, especially when they talked as slow as Mr Casey.

"And next time we better trim some of these old horses, they haven't been done for a while. And Marcus of course, over at the back, needs doing as well. Old Johnny died a while ago—just lucky I got Marcus from him out of the old Clyde mare. Just as if I knew that old Johnny would die, ey. And you heard of course I have got a partner, ey?" he asked.

"Well no, I have not heard about that one," I said.

"A *business* partner," he replied, putting a lot of emphasis on the word 'business'. "Mrs Brown she is, and she runs a few horses up at her place in Dargaville, and in fact she has got a couple of nice-looking Clydesdale cross-breeds in the next paddock over here. Good lady she is, ey."

I wished Mr Casey well with his partnership and wondered if something would change around here. It did not take long to shoe the old pony, and Mr Casey was very happy indeed now he could do some serious riding again. He said he would give me a ring in six weeks' time.

It was nearly three months later, when he rang, but all the shoes were all still on.

After inquiring how Mr Jansen was today, he told me, "If you could shoe the pony first, then we will do Marcus's feet, I have got a big Standardbred in the yard you can do after that while I will get the big mares in, ey. People always think I am stupid or something, but I can organise my day just fine, thanks. And yours too come to think of it, ey. Not bad for an old fellow, really." As polite as he always was, he was just a bit shy of people.

The pony was quickly done. But even though it was all flat in Ruawai, I could not see Marcus because of the rows of Macrocarpas here and there obstructing the view. Some of these trees were so old they might have been planted when past residents drained the whole of the Ruawai flats by constructing a stop bank to keep the floodwaters of the Kaipara Harbour at bay. These imported trees made beautiful shelter belts but took up a lot of room. If one tree was lucky to get some nice straight trunks, it could be cut into very good and nice-looking timber. After it was discovered that the fruit of the tree caused cows to abort their calves, farmers slowly got rid of them all, noting it sure makes excellent firewood.

How to get to the old stallion was the problem, solved by Mr Casey himself.

"We could drive over in the Ute if you like? It is as dry as it will ever be."

He threw the halter and a big rope on the back of the Ute, and off we went, out of the house section into the first paddock. We veered to the right, where there was a gate. I stopped in front of the gate, waited for Mr Casey to ready all his muscles and balance his weight in the right place before he climbed out of the Ute. I quickly opened all the windows as the smell was, to put it very politely, not very nice.

He had a problem opening the gate as both strainers were leaning over dramatically, the top dog was gone where the top hinge was supposed to swing from, and it had been replaced by a bit of bailing twine. The gate had been left sitting on the ground so Mr Casey had to lift and drag the gate out of the way little by little.

He climbed back into the Ute, which really was a big exercise, and started talking about these stupid big dairy farmers in Ruawai who pumped so much water out of the ground that the water tables, the groundwater levels and everything else was out of balance, and that's why all the strainers on his farm were on a lean. And that's why the gates did not work anymore. It was a shame really.

Driving through the next paddock was a bit of a challenge. There was heaps of what looked like ancient dried up riverbeds. They could well have been, but they were a bit hard to navigate with the grass being two feet high and ruts in the dirt from years of heavy animals pugging the ground.

The next gate proved to be a nightmare. The gate was in the middle of a very old and unkempt row of Macrocarpas. There were dead branches on the ground to be avoided, but the worst were the overhanging ones, some of them almost a foot thick and I involuntarily ducked my head as I drove under the last one. This gate was almost falling to pieces. To save a lot of time, I hopped out, and with careful manoeuvring I managed to drag the gate to lean it against a tree.

After one more gate, we finally arrived in Marcus's paddock, the furthest away from the house, far enough away from any mares for him to get excited about.

Marcus sensed trouble—probably never in his life's memory did a Ute enter his field of vision. He became as frisky as only an obese old stallion could, pranced the perimeter of his world in slow motion. His boundary consisted of electric fence tape and standards, but the tape was not hot and not very tight, and here and there it touched the grass.

Mr Casey got out of the Ute, retrieved his halter and rope and went over to catch Marcus. He might have been caught a thousand times before, but today Marcus said, "No." He was not a horse of many words. "No," he said again when Mr Casey got a bit closer. "What is it you don't understand about the word No?"

As overweight as he was, he was still much quicker than Mr Casey would ever be. With his head between his shoulders, Mr Casey would limp his way over to where Marcus was, but with three paces to go Marcus would wander off about ten metres to wait for his boss to come close before wandering off again.

Still sitting in the Ute, I thought what a marvellous thing it would be if there was a way I could film this somehow and let others enjoy watching this unique interaction between horse and man. This wish did come true a few years later with the advent of sophisticated cell phones and something called YouTube.

It was not cruel to watch, nor mismatched or sad. This was nature, the ultimate in natural horsemanship, a show of the nature of horse and handler, a coming together of man and beast. Every time Mr Casey came too close Marcus would wander off, mostly only ten metres, but a couple of times he trotted around the paddock. For a horse so out of condition, carrying way too much weight, I must say he put in a stunning performance, with his head high up in the air and a trot so slow it looked elegant, while noisily expelling air from his nostrils.

I did see the moment that Marcus gave up—he stopped and said, *"You can catch me now."* Mr Casey saw it too, of course, and came close enough to touch Marcus on the shoulder and then let him sniff his hand. Marcus approved and said that his boss could carry on.

When Mr Casey almost stood up straight, right in front of the horse's chest, Marcus's head was a couple of feet above his handler's head. How he ever was going to put a halter on, I could not even visualise.

It must have taken a while for both parties to catch their breath, but then I saw Mr Casey uncoiling his rope. It was thick and strong enough to tow a truck, but after a while he managed to swing one end over the horse's neck and rein it in a bit.

Okay, but now what?

Mr Casey fumbled a bit with the rope, but after a while it became obvious that he had made a decent knot in it and slowly started to pull it a bit, making sure it was positioned high up on the neck.

As if Marcus was a highly trained dressage horse, he slowly lowered his head. But that was still way too high, so he lowered it a bit more, with his eyes level with Mr Caseys. Handicapped by his inability to move his upper body or barely straighten up, Mr Casey had a hell of a job to put the halter on. His face was facing the ground, both his hands slowly going upwards with the halter open to take the nose of the horse, who gently obliged and put his nose in the halter. After a couple of tries, Mr Casey managed to flick the halter strap over Marcus's head, and by touch he managed to find it on the other side. By sheer feel, he guided it through the clasp and tightened it.

I was impressed and wanted to give them both a medal.

The rope was around three metres long and Mr Casey proceeded to guide the rope through the bottom eye of the halter, after which it would finally be my turn to do some work.

As I have an incredible natural respect for stallions young or old, a respect I would carry with me for the rest of my shoeing career, I approached this stallion with all of my senses primed to their maximum ability. Let us face it; the odds were heavily against us. The ground, covered in heaps of long grass and full of pug holes, was not good for balance or a good footing if you wanted to get away in a hurry. The handler, although a real horseman, was obviously not going to rescue me if things went wrong. The stallion, although quiet by nature and slow by virtue of being obese, was probably twelve times stronger than me.

With utmost caution I proceeded to do my job, while Mr Casey, somewhere underneath the horse's neck, softly spoke to the horse, changing to a very low growling tone if Marcus moved a bit. Marcus had only to nudge him and he would fall over—if he lifted his head up in a hurry, Mr Casey would be dangling in the air.

Not thinking about what could happen, it was important to focus and make this a pleasant experience for Marcus. The feet were only slightly smaller than a pure-bred Clydesdale but the wall was incredibly long so there was an enormous amount of hoof to trim. As the nippers can only cut off around twenty millimetres at a time, I had to make two or three cuts in the dry and hard hoof.

This was simply very hard work, and after the first front foot it would get worse doing a back one. It could have been a couple of years since the feet had last been trimmed and the horse had been handled, so the back legs were the ones to look out for.

We did have our moments, and most of them had to do with balance because of the enormous pug holes. When I was comfortable in a particular spot, Marcus did not seem to be comfortable. Where he was happy, I just could not get my feet on an even level. And all the while Mr Casey was growling in the heaviest voice he could master.

It seemed like the longest it had ever taken to trim a horse, but we got there, and I must say that Marcus was indeed a true gentleman. I counted all my blessings that everything turned out fine.

The day was not yet done, as there was the Standardbred to do in the yards. As we did not have to close the gates, Mr Casey planning to do that maybe the next day, we got to the yards in reasonable time despite driving at walking pace through the paddocks.

All my experiences with Standardbreds had been good so far. Because they are normally well handled, they are very good with their feet, especially if they have raced or came close to it, because of all the straps and hobbles needed around their legs.

But this horse exceeded all my expectations. He was simply enormous—the biggest Standardbred I have ever seen—tall and, not unexpectedly, very overweight. But somehow someone had put a firecracker up his backside. Well, how else to describe his behaviour, as he could not stand still for more than two seconds in a row. I did not fancy my chances in trimming his feet, but one has to try. There was the remote possibility that the horse would settle down with some human contact.

I entered the yard with all my senses sharpened up, put a lead rope on the halter, which looked as if it had been on there for a long time, and waited until I could pet him. I needed just to touch him, anywhere would be good.

I did not get a chance. Up in the air he went, feet going way higher than my head, the scary thing being that you don't know where the feet will land, but luckily I stayed out of harms way. Sometimes it is only a one-off thing and the horse settles down after that. Not this time. I got the feeling he could do this for the rest of the day so I unclipped the lead rope and let him into the outer yard just as Mr Casey was bringing in the two mares from the other side. They were even more solid than the Standardbred, with bigger feet as well, but with a really placid nature.

By the time their feet were done, so was the day. All that was left was to get paid for my services, so I followed Mr Casey into his little barrack.

As the few windows were quite small and dirty, it was pretty dark inside on this hot summer's day. When my eyes got used to the dark, the first thing that got me were the flies. There were a million and one of them. On the far side was a bunk of sorts with a few blankets on it, a sink bench on the side covered with dirty dishes and a kerosene burner. Next to where I entered was a toilet room, but I was probably lucky the door was half closed. In the middle of the small room stood a kitchen table with two chairs, one of which was occupied by Mr Casey writing out a cheque in his most beautiful handwriting. Above the table hung an old kerosene lamp from the rafter, the only light in the place.

The flies were just terrible, but Mr Casey did not seem worried by them or the filth and dirt he was living in. He was actually very happy with the way things went today and sincerely thanked me for a job well done.

Only a couple of years later, for the first time ever, Mr Casey was not there. He was normally either inside, in the yard or around the house looking for chicken eggs. The dog was lying in his normal place, having given up on the idea of being a guard dog a few years ago, and the chickens went about their business. But it was rather quiet. I silently prayed that he was not dead, lying inside on his bunk covered with flies.

Walking around the yard, I looked over the farm in case he might have been bringing in some horses maybe and there in the distance I spotted him. Something funny was going on here, I thought, before I went to look for a place in the shade to have a better look. On the race that ran from the yard to the back of the farm, were three old ponies with Mr Casey following behind, herding them into the yard. The ponies were already very old ten years ago, but they still seemed to enjoy life. One by one they walked three or four metres and then stopped. Maybe that's what they do when they get old. When it was the last one's turn to take a few steps, I managed to get a good view of Mr Casey.

In his left hand he carried a makeshift walking stick. He was in the 'at ease' time, his feet placed close together near the fence. His right hand would go as far forward as it could along the top wire of the fence. Once there, he grabbed the wire, shifted his weight onto his bung left leg and the stick and pulled with his right hand to bring his right leg as far forward as he could, which was as far forward as his right hand was. Then, with all the weight on his right leg, he would shift the stick, making sure not to put it in a hole, and heave his left leg forward, making a very straight, stiff arc while doing so. Once that foot found a bit of level dirt, it was 'at ease' time again.

And then, he would start all over again. At this rate it would be a long time before he reached the yards. I wandered over to meet him to make sure he was alright. He was in good spirits and did not see anything being the problem apart from maybe going a bit slow.

"But what is time anyway young man, ey? It's only time," he said, and prepared himself for another step.

"I will take these three ponies and give their feet a trim," I said, and as he nodded, I tried to get a little bit of speed out of these old ponies. They did not understand why anyone would be in a hurry either. They were sure they would get there in good time, like their boss. In the yard, I put the halters on and started to trim their feet. Occasionally I would take a look at Mr Casey's progress which was steady but oh so slow.

By the time he came to the yard, I was just finished. It had taken him three quarters of an hour to walk fifty metres. But like he said, what was time again? Don't the hare and the snail celebrate Christmas on the same day? He got to the yard safe and well.

I opened the gate to the yard after asking if he had left the gate to the paddock open, which he had done.

The ponies were not in a hurry, and after all the excitement they decided to hang around a bit longer before walking all the way back. They might have even gone back the following day.

As usual, I followed Mr Casey inside where he would write out my cheque. There were more flies around this time, which seemed almost impossible. Mr Casey looked exhausted, so I asked him if he was alright.

He reassured me he was fine, "It's just me bung leg, ey. Just slows me down a wee bit. I will just have a little afternoon nap and then I will lock these ponies away."

"The ponies are just fine, Mr Casey, they can walk to the paddock by themselves. Would you like me to ask the neighbour to call in a bit later to see if you are okay?" I asked.

"Don't be a fool, young man. I told you I was alright, didn't I? Thanks for trimming my ponies again, and I will ring you next time to do old Marcus again, ey."

I wished him well and said goodbye.

Four days later I was at Ralph's place. He used to borrow one of Mr Casey's horses many moons ago to pull a sledge with hay to feed the cows in the winter. Ralph's wife Natalie asked how things were, and out of the blue I replied that Mr Casey was still alive.

"No, he isn't," she said, "his death notice was in the paper a couple of days ago. The funeral is tomorrow, but we can't go—another hospital appointment."

We talked a bit more about what had happened in the world before I went to shoe Ralph's horses. All the while I wondered when Mr Casey died. It did not occur to me to ask Natalie when, as I thought I would find the notice in the newspaper at home. But somehow, I never found it, probably just the day when the paper did not arrive in the mailbox.

Much later, I heard that the neighbour found him the day after I trimmed his ponies' feet. The neighbour had been quietly keeping an eye on him, ringing him most days. As there was no reply, he went to have a look and found Mr Casey fully clothed on his bunk, covered by a million flies.

He had gone for his little afternoon nap just after I trimmed the ponies, and never got up again.

It was not a big funeral, but at least there were a few neighbours, friends and fellow church members. Unfortunately, I could not make it, with my lame excuse of being too busy and not enough notice. How old he was, I still don't know. His place was sold very quickly, and his business partner made quite a few dollars in doing so.

One of the neighbours, who was a horse person, got called upon to do something with the horses.

The three old ponies were beyond re-homing. They had probably never ever left the place so they went to the hounds. Strangely enough, they enjoyed the ride once they were in the truck, it being probably their first ride ever. Old Marcus was old, like the ponies, but it would not have been fair for him to make the trip with the ponies—his legs probably could not stand up to such a shock. The vet and the drain digger came at the same time to help him out of his misery. The white electric fence tape was still there, barely visible amid the overgrown grass, but there was no way he would ever step over it.

The new owners must have had a hell of a job cleaning the barrack, and the farm, for that matter. The overgrown Macrocarpas did supply a huge amount of firewood though. After two years of tidying up and fencing, it looked a nice block of land again.

6

Dargaville

A little past the racecourse in Dargaville was another horsey place. In a round pen, there were two horses with halters on, waiting to be reshod. When it was dry, like a midsummers day, I could drive in. All I had to do is first tie the horses up, then open the gate and drive the Ute in. It is so nice to have the Ute close by when shoeing. All the gear I need is right there including the, oh so important, anvil. I enjoy walking, but we all know how time consuming that can be.

I finished shoeing the number one horse, the biggest one, when I noticed black clouds on the horizon. The forecast had said something about it—some heavy showers in the afternoon, coming from the west.

I had better hurry up. The number two horse was a bit smaller, and the hooves were a bit smaller too, which made it a little bit quicker to shoe. A couple of raindrops fell, but hey, a couple of drops didn't mean much, yet. The sky above Dargaville was black. Seldom have I seen clouds that black, and thick. It was amazing really, as if all the clouds in a five-hundred-kilometre radius had gotten together for a meeting above Dargaville. Hurry, hurry now, I reacted, with two more shoes to be put on. A few more drops were falling. It was still nice and warm, but who likes getting drenched? There was one shoe to go, but then I could call it drizzle. With a bright yellow raincoat over my singlet, I put the last shoe on—done, hooray!

There was still something going on in Dargaville, the looming black clouds even blacker and thicker than before.

I had to get out of the round pen, leave the horses tied up, open the gate, drive out, and only then let the horses go, yet it is amazing how often this simple logistic challenge gets stuffed up.

So the horses were safe and well in the big round pen while I was safe and dry in the Ute at the end of the little raceway leading to the round pen. It sure must have been time for afternoon tea—a freshly made cup of coffee with hot water from the thermos. In my cup I put two teaspoons of sugar, one teaspoon of coffee, add hot water, stir it and enjoy. I did enjoy this one while I watched more clouds hurrying over to join the others. I considered myself lucky in this prime spot, watching the clouds go to war. It was getting a little dark, and it was only close to three o'clock.

Ellen arrived shortly after three, according to plan. Surprisingly, it was still dry. I told her to look at the sky, and suggested that since it was going to rain soon, we had better wait for a little while.

"In that case I better get these two three-year olds in and do some long reining while it is still dry," she said, and off she went. She turned around straight away and said, "I can't, there are horses in the round pen."

I got out of the Ute and said, "Let's put them in the little race on the other side of the drive. But we better be quick, it is going to rain, you know."

With one horse each, we led them across the drive and put them in the race. We put some tapes up so they would stay there.

While Ellen went her merry way, I dived back into the Ute as it was starting to rain. Just soft, warm rain to start with. But the thunder and lightning above Dargaville was a real spectacle, and I heard later that the whole Dargaville area was without power for a couple of hours. We were not that far away really, and the soft rain was soon replaced by real rain with some of the biggest drops I have ever seen. The wind picked up very quick and made being outside suddenly very unpleasant.

Out of nowhere, Ellen appeared with two horses in tow. She did not stop until they were in the round pen. Then she made a dash for her car. Hopefully she had a set of dry clothes with her as she was soaking wet. The wind and rain were lashing the Ute, and big puddles were forming all over the driveway, for as far as we could see. The traffic on State Highway 14 slowed down to a crawl, and some just stopped and waited for the rain to ease. Everyone had their lights on as it was very dark now.

As often happens, the rain looked as if it was never going to stop. For a little while it even got heavier, with more thunder and lightning not too far away.

"When are you in Dargaville next?" Ellen texted—we were too far away to talk through an open window, especially with this downpour.

"Next week is fine, but I am prepared to wait till 4 p.m," I replied.

"Horse trials at Barge Park in Whangarei this weekend where the two you are shoeing are going," texted Ellen.

After a while it was time to clean the windows as they were totally fogged up. Was it my imagination or was it getting lighter? Was the rain slowing down a bit?

As my vision through the windows was slowly restored, I could see a break in the dark grey clouds. Those in the far distance seemed a little lighter. It was a quarter to four. Five minutes later, it stopped raining. Unbelievable!

Ellen and I got out of our vehicles. If we had been on an army exercise, we would have been making a plan of attack. But that is exactly what we did. I had two horses to shoe, she had to ride them as well as long-reining the two young ones.

Ellen was off to get the two horses that needed shoeing. She was back quickly and we tied them up in the little race behind the Ute, out from the round pen. As I got started, Ellen tied the other two there as well, so we were both busy. If I could please open the gate to the round pen for her and her horse number one, and close it after her, she would be fine. It was the second time she was long-reining these three-year olds. After going through her routine and the horse doing what was expected of her, it was time to open the gate for her again. She would tie the horse up and take all the gear off, to put it on her horse number two. By the time she finished long reining horse number two, I had finished my horse number one. We were doing well.

When I started my number two horse, she put her two back in the paddock and then saddled up my horse number one. I asked her again if she was all right, as she still was soaked to the skin. She looked very, very cold and pale. She did not have a raincoat in her car and no dry clothes either. She said she was alright, and with that she was off on her horse, putting on the finishing touches to prepare the horse for the trials. By the time I finished my horse number two, Ellen came back very happy. "I am warm again," she beamed. "There is nothing like a good workout."

While I packed my gear away, she put the saddle on the last horse.

"Looks like we made it after all," I said. "Look, I won't be surprised if the sun will come out in a minute."

"That certainly was a lot of rain. Thank you so much again; I will see you next time. Thanks." Ellen said.

"Thank you, see you next time," I replied.

It was amazing what could be done in an hour and a half when we both were organised. All in a day's work. I was even on time for dinner after an hour's drive home.

DARGAVILLE

A cyclone was supposed to hit us, but at first light at 6.30 in the morning it looked like a promising day. It appeared very quiet, so why stay home? Quickly, I made one phone call, sent a few texts and assured myself of a busy day around Dargaville.

In the afternoon, the wind started to pick up. By the time I got to Lurlene's place it was really blowing. I had to get her off the couch as she forgot I was coming, but it did not take her long to catch the young stallion and put him in the implement shed.

There was a big gap between the floor and the bottom of the sheets of corrugated iron that made the wall, and the wind was howling through it. In the corner of the shed were some left over sheets of the same corrugated iron, and they were flapping as wildly as they could while being held down by a couple of strainers, those really big posts used at the start of a fence. To top it all off, the whole building creaked, and there must have been one or two loose sheets of corrugated iron flapping somewhere to add to the noise. It was not a beautiful setting to shoe the young stallion for the third time in his whole life. He was not the easiest to shoe, but his immediate surroundings did not seem to have any effect on him, so I thought I had better just get on with the job.

The gusts of wind battering the shed gave me more frights than the stallion. I had just gained hope that we would be able to manage without a disaster when it suddenly struck. The stallion gave an almighty squeal and jumped in the air, and I was so lucky to get out of his way by the time he came down again. Lurlene was having a hell of a job trying to handle him, the stallion managing to drag her fully outside the shed. By then it became obvious what had happened. The three other horses, which were happily grazing in the paddock on the other side of the race, suddenly came into view. That was all it took to disturb the stallion. He thought he had never in his whole life seen them before, and you never know, there might be a mare in season amongst them.

It took Lurlene a while to settle the horse down again. We were fortunate that the other horses decided to go back to where they came from, and that they were not the slightest bit interested in him. The stallion went into the shed again, and I managed to put on the last shoe in orderly fashion. All done, all good. Lurlene had another horse to shoe, but that one would have to wait for another day as it was not really a nice horsey day anymore.

It was in the middle of nowhere, too far to travel to really, but there were four horses to trim, which made it almost worth my while. It was around three hundred metres above sea level, on the side of Tutamoe. It was not too far from Waipoua Forest, the home of Tane Mahuta, the king of the forest, the biggest Kauri tree in New Zealand. There were not too many big trees where I stood, all having been felled in years gone by to make way for some beautiful farmland. Early every new year, there were some pony and horse races at a nearby beach and the owners thought it wise to trim their ponies' feet before they went.

The two ponies were good to trim, but the owners had just acquired two Clydesdale cross-breeds and I would have to go and trim them in the paddock, as they had not been out of their paddock yet. Dark clouds had been moving in for some time now, and we were all hoping that we might be able to finish the job before it started to rain. Dad and daughter caught the horses easily enough, but the problem was finding somewhere level enough to trim them. By the sound of it, it was to be the second time that they had ever been trimmed, and by having a quick look at their hooves, I saw that they certainly needed doing. In the corner of the paddock, there was a reasonably flat little area. As they had stood there a lot, there was no grass, just a bit of grey topsoil. It was getting really dark now even though it was the middle of the day. As a precaution I took along my raincoat, and as the first drops began to fall, I put it on. There was really no alternative—waiting for the showers to finish could take a while as the forecast indicated solid rain for some time. Coming back another day was no option either, as the place was far outside my normal boundary.

So, let's just get stuck into it, I concluded. The wind picked up as I lifted the first foot. Yes indeed, Clyde feet—big, with heaps to cut off. After the cutting, which was still pretty hard to get through, there was also heaps of rasping to do. It was hard work at the best of times, but the incoming rain made me go as quickly as I could. The flat area was just big enough to keep the two horses, and beyond the flat, the land sloped down quick and steep, and it looked slippery, too.

The second hoof of the first horse, a back one, looked very big as well. The way to lift it up without spooking the horse is the secret. The covers were still on, which made the job a bit hard for the two youngsters, one about only two years old, the other three years old. The wind was picking up, the covers were flapping, more rain drops were falling, big enough that you could feel each impact and I was stuck working in between the two horses, each weighing probably seven hundred kilos. Where to stand was a big issue: was getting squashed between two horses better than getting squashed between a horse and a seven-wire fence? Looking on the bright side, I was happy that there was no electric outrigger on the fence with seven thousand volts going through it. By the time I was going to start the number three hoof, the horse somehow resigned to the fact that this was what was expected for the immediate future.

We were so lucky that they belonged to the quietest horse breed, one defined in the temperament scale as 'cold-blooded'.

It became obvious that we were not getting out of there dry, despite all three of us people being well dressed for rain. By the time I started the last hoof of the first horse, it was raining, and not just a little bit. It was raining 'cats and dogs' as I learned in high school in Holland at the age of twelve. The things you think of when you should have all your eyes and ears open, all your senses primed on what is going on around you with the horses and the handlers. The rain was so bad that I had to put the hood of my rain coat over my head which resulted in making my world very small—narrow vision and worse hearing. I prayed that everything would work out fine. At least the first horse was done. On the other hand, to get the number two horse in position, more or less where the first one was, proved to be very difficult indeed. Our little flat solid area had turned into an inch of slush, which made it very slippery, and the horse began sliding down the hill when it put a couple of feet on the slope. But they took it in their stride, so to speak, and after some more manoeuvring, the horses were finally swapped around. I was happy to start number two horse.

Everyone was pretty wet by then. The rain seemed to get even worse and it was dark as if the sun had set. The feet of this horse were even bigger than those of the first one. It took a lot to clean the feet as all the grit underneath was caked on, now iced with a new layer of fresh mud to keep us on our toes. My hands were covered in mud, as were my tools. I could not even find my rasp for a time covered in the fresh mud as it was, like everything all around us. But we made progress, a little bit at a time, making sure to keep that contact with the horse, and hoping their concentration span was pretty big. They were very forgiving, to be fair. We all know they like standing still when it's raining, but do they really enjoy it when someone tries to trim their feet in the pouring rain? Suddenly, well not really, the end was in sight—last hoof, mud everywhere. The mud on my hands worked its way up into the sleeves of my raincoat up to my elbows. My legs were wet and muddy; my leather working boots were full of water and totally covered in mud.

Oh, what a relief it was to tell the owners that the horse's feet were finally all done. I gave the horses a pat as they have been exceptionally well behaved. Next, I was off to a shed lean to, by my Ute, where I could finally dry myself a bit with a towel given by the owners. Luckily, I had a full set of dry clothes with me, so all was well. That was except for the socks and boots, which would dry over time as long as the rest was dry and warm.

It must have been almost two years later that we met again. They had sold their place in Tutamoe and found themselves a nice lifestyle block in Hukatere, which is on the way to Tinopai, on the outskirts of the Kaipara Harbour. The daughter presented me with a one-year old Palomino whose feet she could lift. If she could, probably so could I, and sure enough, it was no problem trimming this one's feet. The next one was only eight months old and had only ever lifted the front feet up once. With its head in a feed bowl, this horse was very good, even with its back feet. His feet had a little bit of separation here and there, but that was soon filled with cotton wool and Iodine spray. The dad told me to have a little break while they would take these two horses away and bring the next ones in.

They came back with a four-year old Clyde cross, steel grey with four even white socks. It was the very same one I had done last time. The feet were the longest I had seen for a long time. I asked the owners if they had a handsaw handy, and I was presented with what I call an heirloom—a rather big, old and probably handmade saw with a beautifully carved handle on a shiny blade of old-fashioned long length. It was a real beauty with a sharpness to do its owner proud. The hoof was so long, that to cut it with my hoof nippers would have taken three or four cuts, which would have been hard work as summer weather makes hooves like rock. I put the first foot on my tripod, and after making my mind up where exactly to cut, I started sawing. I thought the horse might take a dislike to this, but nothing happened. The cut was completed.

And after that, I finished it off with the rasp. It was then that the dad described the encounter they'd had the year before when they could not get hold of me. They found another farrier to trim the horse's feet, who they were sure was very capable, but they could not understand why none of the horses seemed to like the man. The animals all seemed to play up, which only resulted in the farrier losing his patience, and from then on it seemed to be a nightmare to try to make the horses behave and stand still. It was especially true with this horse I was trimming right then. I could not believe it, as this one was as quiet as a lamb, and I had just managed to put the back hoof on the tripod, which normally takes a bit of balancing.

The big horse behaved as if he wanted to please me, so I started sawing on its raised back hoof. It was rather amazing to see the end results compared with the two feet that still needed doing. After the four feet were done, the horse looked rather smart, whereas before the trimming he looked rather neglected, like the ones we see on TV now and then in programs like 'Animal Rescue'.

It was ten o'clock on a summer's day, and my singlet was soaking wet from the sweat. We did a couple more trims, including another Clyde cross, when the dad's dad came by for a look. He was on crutches but got by well enough. When we were finished, the dad's wife came by, also on crutches, with a leg in plaster. I could not resist remarking that I hoped there was nothing contagious going on here with all these crutches. We all had a bit of a laugh, and then it was time again to go to the next customer.

7

Waiotira

"Can you shoe two of my horses tomorrow at 8 a.m, please?" Harry asked.

That was a bit short-notice. I guess some people don't understand how busy life can be sometimes. But like I always say, there is no harm in asking.

"I am sorry Harry, but tomorrow is no good," I replied.

It was quiet for a while on the other end of the line. Harry did not like no for an answer. "Right oh, how about the day after?"

"Sorry again but that day is fully booked as well. But the day after that will be good."

"That will work out fine," he said. "Got some bulls to sort out; Eight o'clock in the morning?"

"We will see you then," I said.

At eight, Harry was ready and waiting. The grey mare was tied up in the yard; she was the best horse he ever had when it came to working with big bullocks. I went to work shoeing the mare while Harry went to clean some stuff in his shed but he came back the minute I was finished.

"This bay gelding is a bit young and has got a bit of an attitude. Can you back up your Ute a bit towards that big Macrocarpa?" he asked, pointing to the big tree in the paddock, under which a bay gelding was tied up.

"Will do," I said, and put my tools on the back of the Ute and hopped in to reverse it close to the tree.

Harry continued, "Not really young, about four, but it's about time he is gonna do some work. He was broken in as a two-year-old, I think, and has been ridden on for some time. Occasionally one of my staff used him for a little bit, but now we seem to be short of one horse, so we better make him get used to things in a hurry."

The horse looked in the prime of his life. Well grown and muscled up, he looked incredibly strong. He had been tied up for a couple of hours, but by his looks, a day or two might have been better. He definitely did not look ready to be shod, not a horse who would surrender and lift his feet up on command. Instead he looked as if he would attack anyone who came near him.

Harry brought his nail box to sit on. He was a very big mature man and could not stand for long periods anymore. He must have seen me looking a bit apprehensive, so he said, "Come on, he is not too bad. I rode him for a couple of weeks last year. Forward moving he was, but that helps to cover the ground doesn't it?"

I finished getting my gear ready, and replied that the horse was another year older and a year wiser. With that I approached the horse, which seemed to be very wary of me. The lead rope was tied almost two meters high on a branch. A second lead rope led a quarter ways around this massive tree where Harry was standing and hoping to sit down as soon as the horse settled down.

I touched the horse's shoulder first like normal, then let him sniff my hand, then rub him over the nose, his face and his neck to the shoulder, sliding down the leg to the tendon just above the fetlock. I asked him to lift it up. No reply. I asked again while gently squeezing the tendon. No reply. I told him this time and squeezed the tendon with all my might. Guess what? No reply.

Plan B. I grabbed hold of the chestnut, one of the natural little growths on the inside of the legs, above the knee, front and back. When a foal is growing in its mother's womb, the front legs and also the back legs are glued together so they will not be able to kick around and do any damage. At the moment the foal is born, the legs split apart and all is fine, but these little callus-like growths stay, and funnily enough they keep on growing although they have no function any more. I suppose someone once thought it looked a bit like a chestnut, just to give it a name. On a horse it is as big as a real chestnut, and when I grabbed this one in a fist, nothing happened. So, I squeezed it. The leg went up in a hurry, but the horse was not happy, he told me.

So, it was a matter of telling the horse that everything would be fine and we were not going to kill him today. Gently, but firmly is the way to go. When the horse is good, we are good. When the horse relaxes, we relax.

I cleaned the hoof, cut some of the wall away with the nippers and rasped it nice and flat. Then I brought the leg forward. That was a bit too quick, and the horse went backwards in a hurry until he came to the end of the rope. There was no give in that, so he jumped forward to get away from that pressure, wondering what was going on. I had to start again. This was going to be a long shoeing, I was thinking.

It took a long time to trim this front hoof, but hopefully things would get better from then on.

Harry was happily sitting on his nail box and watching what was going on from half behind the big tree.

Lifting a back leg for the first time can be dangerous. You touch the horse on the shoulder first, move a bit forwards towards his bum, take another step forward, never losing contact, go over the bum and slowly down the leg. If a horse does not like it, they move away from you, kick backwards or come towards you. If the horse does not do anything, like this one with his leg firmly planted on the ground, you have got to reach the tendon just above the fetlock. At all times you have to keep your head out of the way; yet I always have the feeling that my arm is never long enough to safely lift the hoof up. Squeezing the tendon, there did not seem to be a reaction, just like the front leg. The leg was frozen to the ground. With my shoulder I pushed a bit against the top of the leg to try to put more weight on the other leg. Ever so slowly we were winning, and the horse half-lifted his hoof up, only resting on the toe.

Now I had to stretch a little bit more, grab hold of the hoof and lift it up. After waiting a second for this new position to sink in, I took a step further away from the horse so he could stretch his leg far enough backwards so that I could lift it onto my lap and relax. I took a deep breath, shifted my feet a bit so the horse could balance his weight, and told him that all would be well.

I cleaned the hoof, cut the wall and rasped it flat, so easily said, all the while keeping an eye on the horse. This sounds a bit funny when you consider that the only thing I could see of the horse was the hoof and a little bit of his leg. The only thing I had to go on was the bodily contact with the horse through my hands, the top of my legs and my side. I couldn't see his eyes, ears or facial expressions. I couldn't see if he felt happy, sad or scared. All I had was body contact, which is normally enough. I really had the impression that the horse had been trimmed before, as it felt as if he knew all the movements. He seemed to know what was happening, and without any major issues, we had finished the other back leg, which seemed to be alright, much better than the first one. Then there is only the last front one to do. Forever, I seem to go around horses in this manner. This front one proved to be as bad as the other front. But we managed with a lot of patience. When I finally finished, it was time for a breather.

"That was not too bad Harry, was it?" I asked, knowing very well that it was bloody hard work on my part.

"He is a strong horse, he is. I am sure he will stand up to those bulls, not a problem. Let's hope you can put the shoes on all right. He has been trimmed before, but I don't think he ever had a set of shoes on. But a man with your experience will be able to handle this without any problems, won't you?"

"We will have a look," I said, and found a couple of front shoes, one a size four and one a size five, so I could let the horse decide which one he preferred. Or maybe I had got it wrong and the correct size was a six? The horse decided on a size four, and in the back of my mind I remembered Harry telling me a few times to let absolutely nothing stick out at the back of the hoof, so I had better not look for any trouble. I went back and forth between the anvil and the first front hoof. Shaping, fitting, shaping and fitting until I was happy with it.

"Right oh, we might as well put some nails in," I said to Harry, in probably too happy a voice as if to boost my morale.

"Go for it," he said, and not a second later my hammer made contact with the shoe; having not put a nail in it yet, all I wanted to do was to make some noise. It was just as well, because the horse unceremoniously snatched his leg back, snorted at me and started prancing on the spot.

"Are you sure you want to put shoes on this horse Harry? Maybe you should ride him without shoes for a while," I pleaded.

"I think he will settle down in a little while. There is no way he will survive without shoes in the yard with all the rocky gravel. Take your time," Harry said, from the comfort of his sheltered spot half behind the tree.

Try again, why not? I lifted the foot up, put it in between my legs, put the shoe on the hoof and softly tapped the shoe while making reassuring happy noises and giving him a pat on his shoulder. Going incredibly quietly seemed to work. I got a nail, held the nail in the right spot, held both the shoe and hoof in my left hand,

and gave it a couple of soft hits with my hammer.

Faster than I had ever experienced, the horse pulled his leg out from between mine and thrust it forwards so fast that it hit the tree with enough force to send some pieces of bark flying through the air, which gave the horse an excuse to bring his other front leg up as well.

"Don't you mess with me, boy!" his whole-body language was saying.

While catching my breath I had to think, "I am very happy to leave you alone, but your boss wants it done, so you better start behaving otherwise we will both be here all day." I retrieved the shoe, which had been flung a couple of meters away, and resolved to try again. The plan was to make a little bit more noise from the hammer on the steel, so the horse got used to it a bit quicker. I tried to hold the horse's leg in my hand to see what happened. Tap… tap… and sure enough the leg wanted to come up in a hurry. I just managed to hang on, settle the horse down again, and tap… tap… tap. This time there was only half a pull. After a little while the horse seemed to accept that this was the new normal, and I could try for real to put a few nails in.

Tap… tap… tap… and half a nail was in. Rest, relax… tap… tap… wow this was good. One more tap and the first nail would be in. Tap… no reaction, fabulous. I quickly wrenched off the sticking-out bit of the nail and tried nail number two. I did not believe it—the nail was nearly in, and the horse was standing still, even though I could feel his whole body being so tense as if he would explode any second.

He did after the last hit. The nail was securely in but still stuck out on the inside. When the horse pulled his leg back in a hurry, the nail clawed into my leather apron but got instantly bent over by the force of the leg moving forward. That was lucky as I didn't need any more holes in my legs.

I am always happy when there are two nails in the shoe, because the shoe is secure, and it won't be wrenched off when the horse throws a wobbly. Now it was just a matter of time, patience, reassurance and knowing when to hit the nail, waiting until the horse is relaxed and not hitting the nail too hard. It seemed like a long time, but we finally got there with seven nails in the shoe. It was time to bring the leg forward and tighten the nails, which were now suddenly called 'clenches'. Surprisingly, the horse accepted this. It does make you feel good to accomplish putting one shoe on. It means that there is hope that, no matter the difficulty, the rest can be done.

Full of enthusiasm, we proceeded to attack a back foot. The shaping of the hind shoes is generally a bit easier than the front ones, but in Harry's case I had to ensure that there was no metal sticking out at the back.

Warned by the front hoof experience, we knew where the problem would be—the nailing. This was in addition to how the back leg must rest on my lap where it is a bit harder to hang on and possibly more dangerous too.

I placed the shoe on the hoof and tapped it with the hammer, cautious of the horse's likely reaction of pulling his leg forward towards his body. But as you can guess, that does not work when your own body is in the way. But he could pull me forward, and if I didn't watch it, I would be lying underneath the horse. That was definitely not a desirable place to be.

The horse did not mind the tapping much, so why not try a nail? I held the nail in my left hand, along with the shoe and the hoof, and just hammered the nail in with the hammer in my right hand.

At the first decent tap of my hammer, the horse did not want to be there anymore. With an enormous jerk he tried to retract his leg. I was prepared for this; my footing was just right and I could withstand all his force. At the moment the horse relaxed, I could too, so I tapped again.

The same thing happened—with the nail barely secure, and needing a decent hit. When the horse relaxed, I gave the nail a nice whack on the head. Prepared for the same reaction of the horse, I was put completely off balance as he lifted the other back leg and took a step away from me. Miraculously, I managed to hang on, hoping he would not make a habit of this funny move. The nail was still only three quarters of the way in. But the next hit got the nail home, the second nail went in very nicely too. By then I needed a break, so I let the leg go to straighten my back.

The next few nails took some time. The horse did not want to be there anymore, and started anticipating when I was going to hit a nail, and just moved the hoof a fraction before I could strike the nail, which was rather annoying as I kept missing. Tired, with only two shoes to go, I considered that time did not really matter, as long as I was leaving there in one piece.

The other back one was a repeat of the one just done. By hanging on you teach the horse that it is better to surrender or give in than to keep on fighting, as the man will not let go, whatever the horse does. After a big physical workout, about an hour's exercise in the gym, the shoe was on. Now for another challenge, I eyed up the remaining front one.

Shaping the shoe was not too bad. It was the nailing, again, and by now we had something else to worry about—time.

According to the horse, time had just run out. Until that point, he let me do what I did under protest, but now he was at the end of keeping up with all this nonsense. Just in case I did not know, he had things to do. There was grass to be eaten, and there was his paddock mate who needed to be stirred up—so many things to do. So why does this man keep on making his life miserable by putting pieces of steel on his hooves?

That first nail is so very important. If you can't get it in properly, the shoe will be half loose when the horse snatches his leg back. Trying to hold the hoof, the shoe and the nail all with the left hand, I kept giving the shoe a gentle tap with the hammer, and the horse pulled and shifted his leg. I did it again and again to find the happy spot where the horse gave me the go-ahead. After finely adjusting the shoe and the nail to where I wanted them to be, I hammered again, and this time the nail stayed in place, not yet bent. I relaxed and hit it again and again. Finally, number one nail was in. Before number two, I had to adjust the shoe as it had veered off to the right.

After nail number two I could relax a bit more. It did not matter if he pulled back his leg to stamp it on the ground, as long as we got there. I continuously tried to reassure the horse that everything was alright and there was nothing to worry about. When there was a little lull in the horse's movements, the other nails went in very fast. I just had to bring the leg forward, put it on my knee and finish off the clinches. The result would not win any prizes at an equine fashion show or horse shoeing competition. That did not matter, as long as they stayed on, enabling the horse to do his job and make his owner happy.

"Piece of cake," I told Harry, with a smile on my face. This happened to be one of the hardest horses I ever put shoes on.

Harry replied, "You did very well, thank you. I knew you could do it. Let's see if Mum can make us a cup of tea, shall we?"

His wife, whom Harry always referred to as 'Mum', had prepared morning tea for us workers. As soon as we sat down at the kitchen table, she put down a big plate of sandwiches. They were filled with boiled egg, luncheon or cheese and looked to total three quarters of a loaf of fresh white bread. Harry got stuck into them.

"I hope the horse is not going to kill you when you hop on," I said sincerely. "He looks a bit like a handful to me."

"Don't you worry about that," Harry said. "I have been around horses all of my life. I do not think that I will ever be able to understand them, but I do know that they thrive on regularity. I have got five days left to make this horse rideable, so for the first three days I will tie him behind my old land rover and we will go quietly down the road a bit, ever so quietly and after that a bit further. I have done a lot of horses like this before, and remember, this one has been ridden last year, even though it was not long enough."

Harry had to stop to grab another sandwich. I had one, which was nice and filling enough for me as I had eaten breakfast and before not too long it would be lunchtime.

Judging by the number of sandwiches, I was sure some farm workers would be arriving soon.

"The days before the bulls are going to the works, I will have to hop on, won't I," Harry continued. "I will put him behind the land rover for quite some time, and tie him up in the stockyards, together with the grey mare you just did. I will go and have my breakfast and come back some time later with my farm worker who thinks he is the manager. I will put him on the bay and let him walk around the yard a few times, and when all is well, I say thank you and hop on myself, and he can have the grey mare. We'll walk around the yard for a bit and then go for a little trek in the paddock."

Harry stopped to eat another sandwich.

"The day of the drafting will be exactly the same. But when we are finished riding in the yard, the rest of the personnel will fill the place up with bulls. Big bulls. Four and five-year olds—we have to fill two truck and trailer units."

It was time for another sandwich, and Mum made a cup of tea for Harry and a coffee for me.

"When you are sitting on top of the horse in a yard full of bulls, it gives you a good view of the condition of the bulls and it gives you a lot of respect. Somehow the bulls do not want to argue with a horse, while they like taking on a bike or even a Ute, or a cowboy on foot."

Harry grabbed another sandwich and suddenly there was only one left.

"The drafting itself is much easier too. I just worm my way between the bulls, till the one I want is facing the gate. I call the man who mans the gate to open it, and when it's open, I gently push the bull along through the opening."

Okay, I thought, he might as well have the last sandwich; I don't think there are any farm workers coming. He did.

"I have been doing this for almost fifty years," Harry continued, "and it works. The only thing that changed is the one who is shoeing the horses. I used to do it myself, then my manager, but he is always complaining about his sore back. So now it is up to you. And I am telling you that if you have left the shoes sticking out the back, and the horse rips them off, we will have you back immediately as there is a good two weeks of sorting out bulls ahead of us."

I said, "Ok Harry, will do," and kept my fingers crossed that the shoes would stay on for a long time.

With morning tea finished, Harry was writing out a cheque for my services, and I could not help wondering whether this really was Harry's morning tea, breakfast, or morning tea and lunch combined. He was a big man. But still, I have never seen a man eat that many sandwiches in that short a time while explaining the ritual of sorting out bulls.

I thanked Harry and his wife sincerely, told Harry again not to fall off, and went my merry way.

He did fall off his horse, the poor old man.

It must have been two or three weeks later when I heard through the grapevine that Harry came off his horse and broke his pelvis and a few other bones. I heard that he stayed a long time in hospital, as a big mature man would take some time to heal. I never got around to making a social visit. I kept on ruminating that if I had persisted and refused to put the shoes on, Harry would not have got injured. I knew it was a very strong horse, physically and emotionally. It would have taken a superman to get on top of this horse.

Harry could well have been a superman in his younger days, but I would not be lying if I called him old.

I parked the Ute next to the implement shed, hopped out and enjoyed the scenery, looking over the house with two horses on the lawn to a rich green gentle rolling valley in the middle of Northland. I was really enjoying the beauty of the surroundings when suddenly the gun went off.

Once you have heard the sound of a gunshot for the first time, you seem to instantly recognise it ever after. I tried to work out where it came from and why it was fired, but I did not have the time to think about it. The horses did not like this sound and came running up the hill to the implement shed. They were terrified, and both tried to put their faces under my arms, somewhere safe to hide from that unexpected noise. As the lead ropes were hanging on the post beside me, and the horses had the halters on already, these would be the easiest two horses I ever caught. Just after I tied them up—one on a pole of the shed and one on the back of the Ute, another gunshot boomed. The horses got a fright, but not enough for them to pull back. We heard another shot, but it did not raise any reaction, just as if the horses said, *"We are used to this now, heard it all before."*

Looking across the road from where the sound had come, I did see a couple of men under some trees in a stockyard. But what they were doing, I could not work out. If it was a beast for a home kill, one shot would normally be enough, or a second one soon after if the first one somehow missed its target. Then came a fourth shot. I watched the men, but still did not have a clue what was going on. Were they clay bird shooting or something? Whatever was going on down there, the horses did not seem to mind at all anymore, so I thought I might as well start shoeing them. The two nice and quiet old horses were really enjoyable to shoe.

He could not have been better described as 'Rolly-Poly'—a miniature grey stallion, as round as a barrel. His neck alone was gigantic and made him look like a heavyweight in his own right. He had been lying down a lot, the owner told me, too tired to even stand up, let alone walk. It was a typical case of laminitis, an inflammation of the sensitive tissue (laminae) surrounding the coffin bone, also called the pedal bone, or by its Latin name, the third phalanx.

This inflammation is caused by an influx of sugar in the diet, much like what sugar does to a person with diabetes—certain parts of the body shut down. The sugar comes from the grass, formed if the grass receives enough sunshine and water. As there is no magic cure for laminitis, such as a medicine, the best and only way to recover is to change the horse's diet—to take it off the sugar-rich grass and give it hay.

Because of his condition, the horse was very laid back, lethargic almost, so you would think trimming his feet would be very easy.

Quite the contrary; he could barely stand on four feet, feeling there was too much weight on any of them, so when I lifted up a front foot, suddenly the other three had to carry more weight, especially the other front one. But the front ones are by default always the most affected by laminitis as the front ones carry two thirds of a horse's weight. It is basically a hell of a job to trim a pony or horse who has got laminitis.

Lifting a front leg backwards to the horse's belly is one thing, lifting it forward, almost stretched out, is almost impossible as it suddenly puts even more weight on the other front foot, as that seems to be the way physics in the body works. As I say, it is a hell of a job.

But like many times before, we got there.

I gave the owner the advice to take the pony off the grass and give it some hay for a few weeks, but did not hold hope that anything would change. Looking around, there was not a smaller paddock than the one where he was in. It was small already, so he needed a yard, which was nonexistent.

The next time I trimmed the little grey stallion, nobody was there. I walked into the paddock, and when the horse noticed me, I could immediately see something had changed from last time. Today he was a young stallion again, definitely not the sick, slow, debilitated and very old horse relegated to the sick bay. This stallion meant business. He did his best to outrun and outperform me. But as normally happens, he did settle down after a quarter of an hour, as it takes a lot of energy to keep running around in circles. When he stood still after a while, I simply put his halter on. Although still a bit stilted to walk and trot, at least he could move around, which was a vast improvement from last time.

I tied him up, and after letting him sniff the back of my hand, I let my hand slide from his neck to his fore foot and gently squeezed the tendon at the back of his leg, just above the fetlock joint.

Nothing happened. I squeezed a bit harder, but the stallion actually pushed his leg a bit deeper in the ground.

As the pony was not big at all, I tried the physical approach and got hold of the leg underneath the fetlock joint with both hands and heaved the leg up.

Halfway up, he used me as a springboard by putting all his weight on my hands so he could bring his other front leg up with such a force that he had no trouble snatching the leg I was holding. Forward and higher and higher, he raised his front feet in the air, confidently balancing on his back two feet. This was not the time to admire his acrobatic heroics, however nice looking, impressive and powerful, when you are still bent over beneath the hooves.

The front feet were coming down soon, and as there is a mighty spring in those back legs, he could land anywhere his lead rope would permit. He could land with enough force to send me to hospital, and he could be very accurate about his point of impact, slamming down onto whatever, he wanted. If I had stayed there, he would have picked a mark anywhere on my body and come down on target with all his force. Though not a big pony, tiny feet like his could still throw a nasty punch when they come down with his entire weight behind them. Luckily for me, I was not there anymore when the feet came down.

It was time to make the lead rope a bit shorter. If I made it as short as I possibly could, he wouldn't rear up that high again.

But he tried, as I knew he would, not taking no for an answer. With his now limited rearing height, I did feel safer. He would not cooperate, that was simply not in his mind, but as long as I could work safely for both of us, we would be fine. And indeed, we managed although it was a bit scary at times.

Next time I saw the owner, I asked why she would keep a nasty little pony like that, since if he was trying to kill me, he certainly wouldn't be safe around kids.

And that is where I was wrong. He was an excellent pony for small kids, possessing no vices, nothing at all. If there was the slightest chance he would not be suitable, he would have been gone a long time ago. The owner and her siblings had all learned to ride on him and had a ball. Because he was so good and fitted the family so well, he was never gelded. He was a sweet little angel, simple as that.

"And this is our grey pony called Blue," Darren said, on my first visit. "The youngest daughter is riding this one, and they get on very well together."

The first front foot did not pose a challenge, but the first back one did, as I had to get all my wits together to master it. The other back leg was the same. Wow, that was a little workout. The last front one was no problem at all.

Little did I know that this time would be the easiest to trim Blue's back feet for the rest of her life. It just seemed to get worse every time. The front feet were as good as gold. But if you so much as pointed at the back leg, the pony would be off. I suppose the pony was 13 hands high, but she was very strong, her strength coming from being a little overweight combined with an enormous attitude. She was strong and quick, but luckily for me she never 'fought dirty' by kicking or biting.

The next time we tied Blue up really short, and when I thought I had the back leg secure on my lap, having taken a long time to pick it up and slightly push her against the fence, she still managed to worm her way out of it.

When I thought this was as bad as it could ever be, the next time would be worse again. I could not even lift the back foot up, left nor the right. Being tied up real short did not make any difference.

The pony simply said, "Not today, thank you."

And that was it. Plan A and plan B were long gone, and I think we were up to plan K or L. It was still up to me to find a solution for the problem although sometimes I thought, wouldn't it be nice to say, "Sorry, I can't do your horse, find someone else please, and see you later."

I found a soft lead rope, and when the pony was standing still, I threw the end of the rope through the legs. And as she was still standing still, I tried to grab the end with my rasp, gently pushing it out of harm's way and slowly towards me where I could grab it with my hands. You never ever do anything quickly when you do things like this. I assured the pony that everything would be fine, and I slowly got the two ends of the lead rope together and put them in one hand, making sure the rope was between the hoof and the fetlock. When time was right, I pulled gently.

When nothing happened, I pulled a bit harder until the pony gave in. And when she did give in, I stopped pulling and just held her right there, started touching her leg all over and prepared myself to trim the hoof in question.

The pony wised up to the idea very quickly of the rope between her back legs, and simply moved away when I wanted to pull the rope up a bit. This was so time consuming and frustrating that it was not even funny. It must have been during the third or fourth time carrying on like this, when I met Darren's wife Jo, who came to the rescue. "Time out," she said, "we are all getting hot and bothered and not getting anywhere. But I have got an idea."

Now that sounded good, I thought. We had just tried all we could come up with and now you found the solution? I was curious, so let's hear it please.

"What if I pick up the front leg and hold it up for a while, so you can put the rope around her back leg and gently pull it up. When you are all set, I will just let her front leg go," she said with a smile on her face.

"It sounds so simple it might just work, you know. That's the best idea I've heard in a long time. Let's try, shall we?" I said.

Jo lifted the front foot, and her pony was very relaxed. I put the rope in between Blue's back legs, picked the rope up and put it in position just under the fetlock. I picked up a little slack and said to Jo that she could let go of the front leg. I pulled the rope up a bit more so that the leg was well off the ground and the pony was just standing there very relaxed wondering why I was not trimming her back foot while it was up in the air.

Since that moment, whenever the need arises to put a rope around the back leg where the horse tries to dodge it, I can now say, "Let us do it Jo's way. Foolproof, believe me."

As the seasons came and went, Jo had to let go of one of her old horses. She postponed the decision for a long time, but when the horse lay down and did not want to get up, it was obvious that the horse's time was up. The vet came, followed not much later by the drain digger who just happened to work across the road.

I was very surprised to find a new horse in the paddock next time I visited, a yearling Gypsy Palomino with a bit of white in colour—a very nice-looking young gentleman.

"He is not a replacement for the one who died not long ago, he is here to replace the other quarter horse, the broken down one, over there, whom I had great hopes for. But unfortunately, he developed this condition and he will never be ridden. Well you know, you trimmed his feet, the front legs are as stiff as boards. So this one is going to be my new riding horse. Maybe you can trim his feet today," she said.

"It will be my pleasure," I said and all went well.

Then there was the time that the grey pony was not there anymore. It is always sad when a horse passes away, this one of old age suddenly just giving up on living. It was hard for the youngest daughter; she had totally outgrown the pony by now, but for years the pony was her best mate.

Next time I was there she had purchased another grey, a fifteen-hand high Thoroughbred gelding.

As the daughter did a lot of riding, I put shoes on him for a few seasons. Jo was riding one of the older ones, and that one had shoes on too over the summer.

Then Jo bit the bullet and bought herself a nice riding horse as the Palomino was still too young. The new one was a black and white Pinto, still young but not stupid. After Darren finished doing up a horse truck, they were off to pony club, ribbon days, beach riding and the odd A&P show. Life was good.

"You know all that rain we had a couple of weeks ago? My old riding horse ended up in the drain," Jo said, when I arrived for the next visit. To put things into perspective, if Jo talked about a drain in her area, it was something so big you could easily hide a tractor in. The catchment area in Waiotira, in the middle of the island, was massive, with some of the nicest up and down country you will find anywhere, so the drains, streams and rivers are wide and deep. The water level can come up very quickly, and sometimes whole areas stay flooded for weeks as the water just can't get away quick enough.

"When I come home from work, I stop at the last little rise before our place to do a head count: one missing. I worked out which one is missing—it's the old boy, well, he is only seventeen but I always call him the old boy. He is retired for a while now.

"Anyway, I come home, park the car, get changed, grab a halter and oh, better take some hay as it is time for their evening feed. It was not long before I found him, and it did not look good. On the edge of the drain he was lucky to have some footing to get some of his torso out of the water. The marks on the side of the drain showed that he had been trying to get out for a while. Once, I had the fire brigade to pull a horse out of the drain, but that was on the other side. Darren was not coming home for a little while yet, and the neighbour's who have a tractor were on holiday. You know, it's always like that isn't it when things go wrong.

"As the other horses were munching their hay, it was more than fair that old Ben would get some too. Carefully, I put some on the bank in front of his nose. He hoed into that, which is a good sign. I wondered how long he had been in there. The water cools them down so much, it is not even funny. But it looks as if he still got some fighting spirit in him.

"'Let's go and find out,' I said to myself. I put the halter on and gave it a brisk pull to see if there was any spirit left in him. There was life left in him, he wanted to leave this wet and cold place. The left foreleg was doing well, but the right fore seemed to be incredibly stuck somehow. I wondered if I could somehow help him by lifting it out of the sticky yellow clay. The horse did not have to go far; a couple of steps further along and the bank was almost level with the water.

"'That's where we will have to go, old boy,' I slid in the water next to the horse's right foreleg, and got the alarming feeling I might get stuck as well. With nobody knowing where I was, this was a bad place to get into serious trouble. So I told the horse that we better get out of this together, both of us without any injuries, otherwise we are both in big trouble.

"'Now, what is wrong with your right leg? Broken? Stuck? Just tell me, will you?'

"I pushed his neck away as far as I could, which helped lifting his right foreleg. I tried to get some fresh dirt from the bank and put it underneath the hoof. It showed a bit of promise as the horse put his weight back on that leg. We will do that again, I said to myself, and I did. I pushed his neck for the third time but he gave way very suddenly so my hands slipped from his neck and I found myself taking some sort of a dive, hands first and then my head and torso as well in the cold muddy water, but my legs were firmly stuck so I could not go that deep or far. In fact, I could not go anywhere.

"'Time to get serious now', I said. I managed to free my legs by pulling myself onto the bank.

"With a lot of yelling and screaming to indicate to the horse the highest urgency, I pulled the rope tight until he would need it himself for balance. He took a leap, the front feet both came up and planted themselves a little bit more forward than they were. I slid back into the water trying to free the rear legs. Pushing against one hip, I freed one leg a bit from all the mud. Then I would wade to the other side and push on that side of the hip to free that leg a bit and give his legs a bit of a rub to generally try to install some positiveness in a hopeless situation.

"Back to the front and the halter; I told Ben he could not lift his front legs this time, he had to use his whole hind and bring it forward. But no, Ben had to use his front feet first again, and amazingly they found a bit of solid ground a bit further on the side of the bank. He literally sighed, took a deep breath and started to put more and more weight on his front feet, like using them as anchors to pull the rest of his body forward.

These back legs were so stuck; he had a hell of a job. The suction of the clay and the mud, it was phenomenal, but he managed. It was a slow-motion business as anyone who has ever been stuck in mud will know. There is no way you can get out with a quick mighty pull.

I could see both hind feet now, but the horse was on a mission: he did not want his hind feet getting stuck in the sticky clay again and used this ever so small motion forward to leap forward with his fore feet, grunting as he did. The hind took the weight but as they started to sink in the mud, the impulsion urged the whole back end forward, and with one more stride the horse was on the dry.

After we both caught our breath, I urged him on, and he willingly followed me home. I cursed as I had lost both my gumboots in the mud. But I would be back the next day to retrieve them; after all it was my favourite swimming spot. In the summer that is.

"I rinsed him off as well as I could while looking for any injuries: but surprisingly, none. It took a lot of towels to dry him, but after all that, the only thing Ben wanted was food, to get some warmth and energy in his system. He got a good feed and heaps of nice hay, a warm cover and a stable for the night.

"And here he is... doesn't he look good?" she said, with a big smile on her face.

"He certainly looks very happy and healthy," I said.

The time had come to break in the young gypsy horse. Just don't talk to Jo about 'breaking in'. Call it 'starting up' or anything you like, as Jo did not like the breaking in words or philosophy. As it turned out the horse was going Warkworth way, to one of Jo's friends.

Jo wanted the keyword surrounding her young horse to be 'easy' and there would be no doubt that she would get an easy horse back—easy to catch, float, ride and anything else. He was already good with his feet, a breeze to trim, we made sure of that.

It did not take long for Jo's friend to ride him. She basically just hopped on his back in a very confined space and generally progressed from there. He was almost a boring horse, as everything went without a struggle. But to make a balanced horse out of a youngster, they need riding and lots of it. Nothing fancy, nothing strenuous, just walking. Anyway, Jo's friend would put the miles in the horse, as some people call it.

On my next visit I would hear about the progress. I shod the grey for the daughter, the Pinto for Jo and finally I asked about the progress on the Gypsy horse.

"Dead," she said. "He was going so well and my friend was so happy with him, it was so sad. It still is sad—it was only four days ago. They reckon he had a stroke, and that was it really."

"I agree, that is rather sad and sudden. You had great hopes for him," I said.

"Maybe it just was not to be," she said. "Maybe I should just concentrate on my Pinto and be happy."

"You will be," I said. "He is a nice horse."

A few more horses to trim and I was finished again.

Next time, as there always seems to be a next time, the Pinto was gone. I did not realise as the head count was seven, like normal, all tied up on the railing of the arena. I shod the daughter's grey one again and was waiting for the Pinto when Jo came with a nice young-looking Palomino. She always caught them for me and tied them up on the Ute.

"Shoes for this one, please," she said.

"You booked in two for shoeing," I replied. "What about the Pinto? Are you going to take his shoes off?"

"You won't believe it, but he died as well, a week after you shod him. I had them all tied up around here, like now, and rode both of the horses for a change, and let them all go again, back in their paddock. I was cleaning up around here when I heard a commotion from the other side of the house, where the horses were in their paddock. Somehow you can hear there is something terribly wrong. There was.

"By the time I got there the Pinto was dead. Just like that. Heart attack or something. I felt so sorry and sad. First, I thought I might have overdone the riding a bit that day. But I did only half of what I normally would do with him as I wanted to ride the grey as well. Never mind, it's all part of life I suppose. Here is a new one for you. He is young, but I have to ride something."

8
Whangarei

When the Pohutukawa tree flowers, you know that it is Christmas time—summer is here. The time it takes for your skin to burn in the middle of the day in full sun is estimated to be only five minutes. While many people go out to enjoy their holiday, horse people seem to stay home and enjoy their horse and wonder when the farrier will come.

My phone started ringing the day after Boxing Day with people wanting to book in early for the New Year. On the second day of January, fifty people were booked in, so it was time to return to work.

After a break of ten or twelve days, it is actually good to do a bit of physical work, but the heat makes it pretty hard. The full sun in the middle of the day is unbearable.

A cloudy day is something to appreciate when you work hard outdoors. A windy day is good too. Rain, on the contrary, is bad by definition as work is almost impossible. You don't have to watch the weather forecast anymore unless there is a tropical cyclone coming, but by then everyone is talking about it so you will be well informed. There is nothing worse than the TV weather presenter saying that tomorrow will be a nice day with temperatures around twenty-eight degrees.

That is not nice when you are working outside. It will be a killer day, a long hard day, and when you survive, you consider yourself lucky.

She got up before I did—the sun. At breakfast she was frivolling with anything that gives shade. Small beams of colourful light shone on the kitchen table, broken by the numerous trees around the house. When I closed the kitchen door behind me to start another working day, I noticed it was still relatively cool and enjoyable. But the sky looked a pale blue with not a cloud in sight. There was not the slightest sign of a breeze. Like a conspiracy, they seemed to work hand in hand—no clouds and wind gave her the mandate she craved—to make this place as hot as could be.

By the time I reached my first customer of the day at eight in the morning, the shadows kept on receding, quicker as the day went on. Unfortunately, there was no shade at the first place. She still can be called my friend as she warms my back, which seemed a bit stiff that morning. By the end of shoeing the first horse of the day, it was warm, with the owner complaining it was hot. My singlet had some wet patches on it already.

Ten years ago, I did not have a worry in the world. The sun could shine all day long, and I worked under it every minute and loved it. But now I longed for the shade of a century-old oak tree, the nicest shade one can find.

As the day progressed, the shadows got smaller in a hurry, until at one o'clock they were at their smallest, and then the shade slowly crept in from the other side. She is burning down on me with a relentless vigour and patience. She is definitely my friend no more. She is a cruel enemy and it is best to stay out of her way. In the shady places it is still hot, but at least that burning sensation is gone. The Christmas holiday was a distant memory and there would probably be two more months of this weather coming, so I had to accept it.

And all the while she is smiling at this little world of ours and the animals that live on it. "I will get you, you little buggers. Frying is the word. I will burn you so hard that tomorrow you will be redder than a beetroot and sore as hell. Because it is me who is calling the shots here, don't you ever forget it with all your wisdom. I am melting the ice on the poles, causing droughts all over the world, and instigating bush fires through the land. The only thing you can do is hide. Hide in your homes and offices and turn on the air conditioning. Because if you stay outside you will fry—that is my job and I love it."

She does not show compassion, even if the horse owners do, but somehow they still want their horses shod, thank you. At lunch time I was hot and bothered and wondered why I did not stay at school a bit longer to get a real job. I drank more than a litre of water already and two cups of coffee, and it felt as if I could have drunk another ten litres of water.

That summers day, like so many others, felt like a marathon, although I have never run one. This marathon started at eight in the morning and finished around five in the afternoon.

It was a matter of hanging in there and pacing myself.

Don't get angry, don't get mad, was my advice to myself—it costs energy and there is nothing you can do about the heat or the sun. Go slow. Concentrate but relax at the same time. Try to make every movement a good one, not to waste precious energy. Hang in there, you know you can do it, put your mind at ease, think about your next movement, don't slack off, don't make mistakes, and don't take shortcuts. Don't think, 'She'll be alright, mate', because then you will stuff things up.

When the sweat crept into my eyes and the saltiness made me all blurry eyed, it was time to wipe it off with an old shirt easily found in the back of the Ute. I drank a bit more water, but too much was no good either.

What was the time? How many more to do? How many more

customers? How many horses? There was no way I could do all that, maybe I could cancel one, some or all. I opted to finish this one first, and then I would make my mind up.

I hopped in the Ute, which was bloody hot. But driving soon cooled things down a bit. With coolness the logical thinking came back—that was not too bad, was it? A bit hot maybe, but surely I survived, so I could easily do the next customer. I didn't want to come back another day, did I? No, that was for sure. Well, I had to get on with it then. The next customer might even have some shade.

The next two customers did in fact have a bit of shade, and I felt some energy coming back to me. The second lady had a beautiful oak tree growing in the middle of the turnaround. She told me that she had specially planted it thirty years ago for the sole purpose of giving shade to the farrier, and thoughtfully called it, 'The Farrier's Tree'. She was a darling and a heroine. I was as close to Heaven underneath the tree as I was to Hell outside in the sun.

At four in the afternoon I arrived at the last stop for the day, just outside Maungatapere, hoping it would cool down a bit. But of course, it did not, taking until eight or nine that night to get milder.

I was hoping there would be a bit of shade, but when I looked at the owner's beautiful courtyard, there was neither a trace of shade nor any hint of a breeze. There was only one tree, but the branches hung so far down that only a miniature horse could have fitted underneath.

The sky still had the same pale blue look as it had in the morning, and the sun, who used to be my dear friend, made herself my personal enemy number one. How dare she upset my whole day, making my life miserable. The lady came out of the house just in time to stop my sun-hating mindset.

"Just the usual, thanks," she said, with a smile on her face. "Bit hot, isn't it?"

"It is a bit," I had to admit. Number one was a big pony who was straightforward to do, and next was a little pony who would give me the run around sometimes. But today she gave in pretty quick. The sweat was pouring out of me though. It felt like the hottest it had been all day. Wasn't it supposed to cool down around now? The third one took the last ounce of strength from me, so somehow I had to regain some energy and composure to trim the last one, which was normally a handful. It took a few minutes before I had my breath back. It just seemed to disappear in the heat and humidity.

The last one was a big horse the owner had rescued—big, bold and strong. Just what I wanted, for the end of the day. One had to be so quiet around this horse; one quick movement or sharp noise and the horse would just lose the plot. But even if you were quiet as a lamb, he would still find a reason to snatch his leg back. I knew that what the horse needed was some good old-fashioned roping up of the legs to teach it some manners and respect. But here I was trying to hang on to a back leg of a horse that was maybe eight times stronger than me, not to mention the speed he could kick with.

And the heat was stifling. The last sweat was pouring out of me, and it felt as if there was nothing left. I just tried to hang on until there was a change in attitude and the horse would let me do my job for a few seconds, when he snatched his leg back. I had to pick it up and start all over again. I was managing, but there was still one front one to go. I did not think I had the energy; it was so hard to just breathe. I just could not get enough air.

My body temperature must have been at a dangerous level, I was thinking, when I made an effort to lift the last leg off the ground.

Secure between my thighs, I started dressing the hoof and started to count down. There was no reason in doing all this anymore. This was cruel. But the end was in sight. The marathon was nearly finished.

I took just a couple of seconds break while holding the hoof in place to catch my breath. I put it on the hoof stand and dressed the outside of the hoof. Things started to get a bit blurry, and I thought it was the salty sweat again in my eyes. I didn't think about it, and carried on. Nearly there; the lady said something, but it did not register, and asking what she said would take too much energy and time. Quick, quick now, I compelled myself, before the horse started to play up again.

I let the hoof drop to the ground before saying, "Done!"

I picked up my toolbox, walked to the Ute to pick up my water bottle and went to the sole tree. I dropped the box underneath it and sat on it.

Did I notice the slightest bit of a breeze? The feeling of not having enough air started to hurt. I took one sip of water, breathing as if I had run a marathon. I had to slow it down before something nasty could happen. Breathe in, relax, breathe out, and relax. Repeat. Drink. Put some water over my head. Oh, it was hot. Oh, I was tired.

This was close. Man, this was close. As I slowly regained some of my better brainpower, I started to realise how close I came to a complete collapse caused by overheating. Sunstroke, blackout, whatever they call it, I knew there and then that I came very, very close.

Breathe, sip, breathe, relax, it took some time. I found that since plunking on my toolbox, I had not moved one millimetre. I stretched my legs a little, and it felt as if they belonged to someone else. I kept on moving a little bit to make everything work again.

It took a few more minutes before I was completely restored and felt strong enough to stand up. I felt as if that body of mine was somehow thirty kilograms heavier. But that sensation went away after a while, so I concluded I was fit enough to drive home. I said my goodbyes to the owner, who was oblivious about what happened since she was putting the horses away. I stopped a few minutes down the road in the shade of an old warehouse where I enjoyed a cup of coffee out of my thermos, and it tasted really good.

Rangi was a good old Maori horse not fazed by anything, a good all-rounder who needed some shoes to go to Pony Club camp. In the middle of the summer, the pony club joined with a few more around Whangarei to form a huge pony club camp. The very first day was always a killer, as the ponies walked for a few hours over rough metal rural roads and farm races. The advice, close to a prerequisite, was for horses and ponies to be shod. The owner booked me in almost two weeks before camp to make sure I had the time.

Putting the shoes on the front feet was a breeze. Trimming the back feet was good too, but putting the back shoes on was near impossible.

Rangi did not like it one little bit. Why, I just did not know. Once you know what the problem is, you can do something about it. We just knew for sure that Rangi did not like the hammering bit. With a lot of persevering, I did manage to put the near shoe on. It did not look too bad, really.

But the off side proved so much harder. It was a struggle to just hang on to the leg, let alone try to put in some nails. I did manage two nails, one on the outside, one in the inside of the hoof. That always makes me feel good. It was time for a breather. If the horse threw a wobbly it would be unlikely that he would lose that shoe.

I tried a couple more times, but whenever my hammer even slightly touched the shoe, Rangi would move sideways. And if he could not go any further, he would go forwards or backwards, basically any direction to evade the shoe hammering. Desensitising is the key word. I would just have to find a way to let the horse get used to it, in as short a time as possible. Of course, one cannot be and should not be in a hurry when working with horses, but by the same token, to make a living out of shoeing horses, one has to keep moving along.

I put a strong halter on the neck and tied it up loosely on the neck strap only. Then a soft rope went around the horse's leg, above the hoof and below the fetlock. The soft rope was what they call a vet rope and has got a loop on one end; by putting the other end through it, it forms a beautiful soft loop which won't do any harm. I normally do not do all this as it is not really my job; it is the job of someone starting up a young horse.

As the owner was my daughter and the rider my grandson, I felt obliged to at least try my very best.

As all was set to try it out, it was time to pull on the soft rope, gently, until it was far enough from the ground so I could work on it. I pulled the rope around the halter, and with a half hitch I made a quick-release knot.

The exercise was complete—we had a three-legged horse. Now all we had to do was desensitise the hammering on the shoe. I plainly touched the steel of the hammer to the steel of the shoe. The horse did not like it, so he took a step aside. Another touch with the hammer resulted in another step. When the horse reached the side-stepping limit, he stepped forwards and backwards until he was back where we started. He could now go sideways again, and again, and then forward.

It would be so nice if the horse gave up with this theatre performance. He did not look overly upset in any way, or frightened for that matter, not at all.

It was more like being overly defiant, as if Rangi was saying, *"Bring it on, you won't get me, I will win as I have got far more patience than you will ever have. I can handle this, you know. But if you think that I will let you put in any more nails in my hoof, you have got another thing coming."*

I was waiting for the horse to give up his silly behaviour, to give in and accept me as master. Rangi was waiting for me to give up the hammering, give in and accept that he was a free spirit who wished to be left alone. This standoff I called a personality clash. To put that shoe on, one of us had to change.

I could not change the fact that the shoe had to be put on. I supposed I could make some slight changes in my approach or handling of the horse. Yet when I tried the very nice approach, nice, cool, and calm and all the other things, where did it get me? Nowhere, so I was going to put a lot of emotional pressure on the horse—he was the one who had to change his attitude.

If I had the time, he should have stayed there tied up for as long as it took. I would come back every half-hour and tap his foot. If he was quiet, I would put some more nails in. If not, I would come back in another half an hour. I am sure that it would work if we took the time factor out of the equation. But I did not have any time. I never seemed to have any time in early January, the busiest month of the year. While I discussed the options with my daughter, I kept on tapping the shoe in question, with the predictable result. The talk seemed to have a lot of 'What if…' in it. Indeed, it was hard to know what to do.

Rangi made it clear to me that he was not going to change his attitude in a hurry, rather wanting me to change mine and set him free. To cut a long story short I said to my daughter, "Ok, if you can get a vet here the day after tomorrow to give him sedation, I will put the shoe on. I don't think those two nails will hold it on for that long."

As she agreed I took the halter and rope off Rangi to be on my way to the next customer. I really made a point of not looking at Rangi, as I did not want to see the big smile he would have on his face saying, *"Ha-ha, I got the better of you, didn't I?"*

A couple of days later, there was still no way I could put the shoe on. I had to try of course but after a while decided to wait for the vet who arrived soon after. He gave Rangi a sedation, and we waited five more minutes for it to work. Five minutes later the shoe was on.

I asked the vet if I could have some of that sedative for future problem horses. Although he was very sympathetic, the answer was a simple, 'No', of course.

The camp at Whananaki went very well, of course, as the ingredients for a perfect camp were all there—sea, beach, estuary, stream, ponies, children and beautiful weather. The highlight of the last thirty years was swimming with the pony in the estuary. Whenever I relate this event, I sincerely hope that the children realise how incredibly special this is, as there are not many places in this country, or anywhere in the world for that matter, where you can do this. Having fun with your pony in the water is something unique and very special.

That year, for the first time ever, a complaint was written to the editor of The Northern Advocate daily newspaper. The writer had no worries with ponies and children on the beach and estuary. If only the horses would not poo in the water, he would be very happy.

A few months later, Rangi got sold to the sweetest of all girls, who simply loved him to bits. Sometime before the sale I took his shoes off, and remarkably Rangi did not seem to mind taking his back shoes off at all. It is always amazing how a horse adapts by being in work, being ridden almost every day; they seem to accept everything you throw at them. I trimmed Rangi for the new owner in Paparoa at a place I visited regularly. The girl's mother got hold of a horse too, and luckily she had found some grazing on the other side of town, and that's where I trimmed both of their horses next time.

The girl said that Rangi was a bit grumpy with his back feet. It was not until the mother told me that Rangi had come from my daughter that I finally recognised him, so I tried to think of the best way to teach the girl how to handle a pony as strong as Rangi.

"Is Rangi good to ride?" I started.

"Oh yes he is. Once I am in the saddle, he does anything I ask from him. And I don't know much about riding yet—I am riding for three months now," She said with a smile to confirm her absolute happiness.

"She sure is doing very well," her mother added.

"So, the only thing you have trouble with is lifting his feet and cleaning them out?" I asked, already happy that the riding part was all good.

"Indeed," she replied, "he can be so grumpy, and sometimes with his back feet it can be a bit dangerous. That's when I get a bit scared and I have the feeling that Rangi feels that too. But at Pony Club they say that we always have to clean the feet out before we go out riding." The poor girl lost a bit of her spark at that point in the conversation.

"When you are riding," I began, "Rangi accepts you for being the boss and he does whatever you tell him. On the ground, Rangi is saying, *'I am the boss now and I do what I like.'* To become the boss and lift his feet up you have to take a deep breath, make yourself twice as big as you are now and lower your voice as low as you can go, ready to growl when he does something wrong."

I started lifting the front foot up, and almost instantly Rangi snatched it back. He sure was a strong-willed pony. I growled at him in a low voice, "No Rangi, we are the boss now," and lifted the leg up, and since the action went well, I trimmed his hoof.

To the little girl I repeated, "Make yourself as big as you can, and at the moment something goes wrong you growl at him. If you are not happy to lift his back feet up, my advice is simple: Don't do it. Ponies like this one don't care if you never ever clean their feet out. But I know that you will get there one day."

I picked up the back leg and almost instantly had to growl at Rangi as he tried to get away, big time. But that growling was just enough this time. I trimmed the hoof with a lot of difficulty. Rangi sure was a strong pony in body and spirit. After the other two feet I felt like I'd had a good work-out.

"Don't worry about the back feet," I advised. "Every time before you go out riding, try and clean the front feet. But if it's too hard, again don't worry. Sometimes he doesn't mind after you have ridden him. Keep trying, but play it safe, won't you?"

I felt rather inadequate about the advice I gave her. But there was always hope that things would go well.

Another day, another new customer. It is still amazing how many new customers one needs. Of all the new customers, there is a big number who never book in a second appointment, and you always wonder what the reason was. Did they soon tire of the novelty of owning a horse? Did they move away? Did they find another farrier because someone told them to, or did they not like the work I did, or maybe just did not like me? From some, I heard that as soon as the owner hopped on their new, freshly shod horse, the horse bucked them off, they broke a bone and the horse got abruptly sold.

At Sophie's place in Maungakaramea, I had to wait some time while she dragged the first horse out of the steep paddock. It was not really a nice lifestyle block. Though the house did not look too bad, the land was poor and too steep for comfort.

This first horse was retired and a bit stiff in the old bones, so I took my time and made sure that the horse was comfortable at all times. As Sophie insisted on holding the horse, it took another little while to put it back and drag another one out of the paddock.

This was going to take ages, I thought, but luckily I was not in a hurry that day. This next horse had been rescued, or in other words saved from a nasty time at the last place she was. She was not too old, and seemed like a nice pony club pony. I could not find anything wrong with her.

The next was her daughter's pony, a real cutie. After that was another old retired one, a pony for the other daughter, followed by another rescue horse after that.

Six horses on eight steep and rough acres is very hard going, especially in the winter, and Sophie told me how much hay and hard feed the horses went through. To top it all off, she was a solo mum with three school-age children and a full-time job, too. In the winter, after work, she picked the children up from her mum who lived near the school, rushed home, fed the horses their feed and hay, and then spent almost an hour picking up horse manure and bagging it up to hopefully sell to gardeners. Picking up the poo is a good habit as it reduces the risk of horses picking up new worms that cause all sorts of problems in a horse's guts. On steep land it is a hell of a job.

Sophie had not asked me how much I charged for trimming a horse. From the talk about her situation I could feel that she was not rolling in money, and I predicted that she would ask for a discount regarding her financial situation and the fact that some of the horses were old and rescued.

Indeed she did, and I did give her a little discount. But I told her that the most logical thing to do was to reduce the horse numbers.

I said, "Believe it or not, there are people who would just love to look after an old horse or a rescued one. I have a few customers who do just that. And as far as one of your rescue ones goes, that one would be very happy on a farm doing an occasional ride.

Apart from the fact that these horses are costing you a considerable amount of money in hay, hard feed and covers, there is also the time that you are running after them and a considerable amount of stress in the winter. Fewer horses means less work, less stress, less money spent on them and guess what? More grass!"

She agreed with what I was saying, but she did not think that she could let go of any of them.

I thought I came close to overstepping the mark by voicing my opinion, and I would not be very surprised if I did not see her again.

She did call me a couple of months later, and she turned out to be a good customer for many years to come. One rescue horse was gone, and I complimented her on a great achievement. She had found a good home for the horse, and the new owners were happy to finally get a nice-looking lawn mower on their lifestyle block.

Following the road east out of Whangarei, I meet the east coast at Ngunguru with its beautiful estuary and sandspit. Following the road over the hill to Tutukaka I found a marina and a nice-looking apartment building. After a couple more hills I turned into, what I hoped from directions given, was the right driveway, which turned and twisted through a few gullies and over a hilltop.

I parked the Ute to take in the scenery laid out in front of me. The driveway veered off to the right to a cute little cottage, but straight ahead was where the action was. East coast waves were pounding a tiny rocky island probably only fifty metres from the rocky coastline which formed a little bay. The coming and going of these waves was never a dull moment. There was another cottage on the left in which the owner lived, as I heard later. The paddocks were all sloping towards the water, and the donkeys I was supposed to do must have had the most beautiful view of all the donkeys I have in my book. They sure were spoiled, and I hoped they appreciated it. But come to think of it, where were they?

Just then I heard a motorbike start up at the cottage on the left, and after a few minutes the owner appeared. After our introduction, Fred picked up a plastic bread bag from the bike with almost half a loaf left in it and walked into the paddock, calling his donkeys. Sure enough they responded, and the first two became visible just on the horizon, having an even better view of this magical place. In time they all came down; the calling was probably a sign that there might be a bit of old bread.

In the middle of the paddock there were four gates tied together with one of them left open, and this was all the yarding there was. I had serious doubt if all eight donkeys would get in there, but Fred was not worried at all. Once they were all very close by, he started throwing slices of bread inside the enclosure, and in their quiet way all the donkeys wandered in for a slice of the action. When they were all in, Fred lifted one end of the open gate and brought it to a close. Eight donkeys in a pen in the middle of the paddock, just like that. I could hardly believe it.

Fred put a halter on one of them, and I trimmed its feet, after which we let that one out to make a little bit more room as it was rather cramped. As none of them put up a fight or tried to kick me, this was a really enjoyable experience.

As everything went well, I did not mind coming back next time and a lot of years after that. After a while, Fred did get a bit tired of those stupid gates that formed a pen as they were falling to bits, and I couldn't agree more with him. The donkeys got spoiled with a state-of-the-art stable complex, complete with a solid outside yard and a dry and cosy inside area to nibble some hay when things got too wet outside. The whole building was a replica of an old Sheriff's office of the old Wild West and was completed with a jail with solid steel bars. To add his own personal touch, Fred made sure there was a layer of topsoil on the roof so that grass could happily grow there. The donkeys were happy before, but now they were super happy, especially with the rough rocks in the outside yard which was very good for their feet.

As it took a while to trim these donkeys, it was inevitable to have a yarn about anything which had come up on the day. In fact, it is these talks with customers which make my work so very interesting and enjoyable. I had to ask Fred, of course, how he ended up having eight donkeys.

"I always liked donkeys, simple," he expressed. "My wife was not too keen about them, so things went on the back burner for some time. As you can see, we got the room for them here, the rough ground and pasture are really suited to them, but somehow I never got around to it. Then my wife had to go overseas for a couple of weeks or so, and I started to look around. I found this Australian donkey and Toby, the one over there. My wife arrived home one evening in the dark, but in the morning I took her outside and said, 'I have got a surprise for you.'"

She came for a little walk and at the corner in the driveway I stopped and pointed half way in the paddock to where the two donkeys were.

"'You got two donkeys,' she said, a little surprised. 'I don't know if I like donkeys.'

"'But I do,' I said. 'And here they are. And I think they will add to our place. It just looks like they belong here already. They look very happy and content.'

"'You really like them, don't you?' my wife asked, just to make sure, I suppose. 'Indeed, I do like them, and I am sure you will get used to them,' I told her."

Fred was silent for a little while, but I did not want to say anything as I felt there was more to come.

"And then they started to bray," he went on, "the loudness completely disturbed our peaceful place, it seems to go through everything, especially because it is so incredibly quiet around here apart from the noise of the sea breeze and the waves, but we are used to that.

"And like roosters, they really like to let their presence be known very early in the morning. The donkeys both came from the same place, but I think they just missed their mates terribly. They kept on braying and braying—day after day.

"My wife kept her composure but I could feel she was not happy with this disturbance of our paradise. Just when I thought she could not take this braying noise any longer and would say something like me having to make up my mind and choose between her or the donkeys, they suddenly stopped braying after nearly seven days.

"I can't tell you what a relief that was. Now you hardly hear them. As it turned out, one of them was pregnant, which we did not know; another Jenny. We borrowed a Jack from somewhere and before you know we had thirteen of them. We sold one or two, gave one away I think, a couple died and we are down to eight, two of them being old; one of those is very old and likes lying down a lot."

Indeed, the old Jenny was lying down outside the yard. As it was very hard to trim their feet when they were lying down, we tried to get her up, but she just did not want to. It took quite a lot of persuasion, but we finally got her standing on four legs. Still, lifting any of the feet proved to be a challenge as she needed all of them to keep her balance; she just could not spare one of them.

"I can remember the old Jack dying of old age," I said. "He was like this old girl, wasn't he? He became very light, lost all his weight, had trouble with his balance and liked sunbathing a lot, too. But one day he just never woke up."

"Indeed," said Fred. "You must have been coming here for a while then. It was a few years ago now."

"I hope this one will pass away in her sleep as well. And with that I must say they are all done again. Thanks, and see you next time."

The intersection was new and very big, and I had to stop for the red light. There was plenty of room to come or go to Whangarei, Kamo, Hikurangi or Auckland. On the far side of the intersection a horse and rider approached, walking leisurely along the footpath and the green verges, heading for the bench that was often occupied by pensioners who watched the traffic go by. There was quite a bit of lawn around the bench, and there the rider stopped the horse. Not only that, but he also made the horse sit down so the rider could comfortably step off the horse. The rider had gotten off to stretch his legs, and I noticed he had a severe limp in his right leg, almost as if the whole leg was as stiff as a board, and I remembered seeing him before.

As the lights finally turned green, the man was sitting on the bench, the horse was sitting on the lawn and I was on my way to another customer.

Probably two years before, we met the man, named Bob, who came to have a look at a nice Appaloosa my wife had for sale. The way he walked with this stiff leg of his, made it almost impossible for him to ride a horse, let alone a young horse. Pepsi, the gelding, was three or four and professionally broken in, but still needed a lot more riding under his belt to make him safe and trustworthy. He was an eye catcher of a horse, totally black with a white backside on which were sprinkled some black spots, a desirable colour for an Appaloosa. He had a nice temperament as well, so there would be no trouble selling him. But would you sell a nice horse to a man who never has ridden a horse in his whole life and has a bung leg? We put the saddle on and his bridle, but there was no way Bob ever could get up without an oversized mounting block. At one stage he managed to lie over Pepsi's back and both seemed very happy with it. For a total beginner he had a very good understanding of the horse. But unfortunately, we could not get Bob in the saddle. This however did not dampen his spirit—he still wanted to buy the horse.

What Bob needed was a twenty-year-old plodder who had been here and there and done just about everything and was looking for a quiet retirement place. I told him so, but this made him even more determined to buy Pepsi. It was not the first time that we had refused to sell a horse to a prospective buyer when we thought it would be totally unsuitable. Bob kept on stroking the horse from head to tail. He managed to pick up all of his feet, found a brush and started to brush the horse all over, with Pepsi enjoying every minute of it.

When the time came to put the horse back in the paddock, Bob simply had to do this himself. When my wife and I saw him leading the horse to the paddock, we both knew that Bob had a special way with horses, or at least with Pepsi.

"What are you going to do?" I asked my wife. "He can't even get on the horse with his bung leg; green horse, green rider—a recipe for disaster."

"I agree with you there," my wife said. "But he has got something there… he sort-of understands the horse. I can see him overcoming his hurdle of his stiff leg and being able to ride Pepsi one day. But I will have to cover my butt. I will make out a little contract stating to be aware, this is a green horse and consequently things can happen. And if it does not work out, I would like to have the option of buying him back, if he is not too spoiled by then."

"Sounds like a good idea," I said

When Bob came back from putting the horse in the paddock, he looked sincerely happy. "I would like to buy that horse, please," he said in a firm tone.

"Normally we would not sell a horse to someone who can't ride. But for the last couple of hours you have shown us that you care for the horse, you seem to understand him and I think that Pepsi likes you too. But I will write down a little contract to state that he is only just broken in, meaning that you should be aware that he can change his mind any second he likes. Horses do that sometimes," my wife explained.

"Thank you," was all that Bob could say, but it came from the bottom of his heart.

I made a cup of tea while my wife wrote out a sale agreement, and Bob gave us a brief look into his life up to now. He had been heavily involved with a motorbike gang, used and sold numerous types of drugs and was close to being a terrible alcoholic. Then he had a near-fatal car accident that resulted in his leg being the way it was now. Ironically, he said that he was sober as could be, having no money at all to buy a drink or any drugs for a few days, but the other driver was in fact as drunk as could possibly be.

While in hospital for a couple of months, he changed his ways— he had no choice, really. He managed to wean himself off the drugs, the alcohol and the motorbike gang, and the reward was huge—he had his life back and kept his wife, who was just about to leave him before the accident.

"That was almost two years ago. I am as clean as a whistle since, but now I need something else in my life, and I decided it had to be a horse. I need a new challenge, something to occupy my mind, something totally new and exciting." With that he finished his abbreviated life story. Having listened carefully, I responded. "I have heard of people with one leg confidently riding a horse. I have seen a video of someone who had no arms riding a horse, so I suppose everything is possible. But it would be so much easier if you would choose a horse who knows it all, a horse that will be able to teach you. A nice old plodder," I told him again earnestly.

"I have got the time, I can spend a full day around him, day after day, and I am sure it has got to work out just fine. At the same time, I am not that stupid as to not further my knowledge of horses, as well as getting some riding experience at a local trekking place. They were willing to help me along at cheap rates, as long as I come early in the morning, which I am willing to do. I just need a new purpose in life, and Pepsi will be a good reason to keep me out of the s#*!," he said.

I did not have to say anything to that as my wife came back with two pieces of paper, one for Bob and one for us, that outlined the sale agreement and the 'Please Be Aware' notice at the bottom regarding the freshly started nature of the horse.

Laurel and Bob signed the papers, Bob paid for the horse right there and then and no one could be happier than Bob, who was by now only worried about the fact he had not arranged transport.

We managed to keep his enthusiasm up by offering to deliver the horse in a couple of days for a reasonable charge. He was over the moon, although the next day would have been better.

Over the next few months a few phone calls came our way from Bob, who encountered little problems here or there. One of them was Pepsi kicking out at him. He could not understand how a horse could be so ungrateful after all the things Bob did for him. After feeding, watering, brushing and generally caring for the horse, Bob regarded it as an insult to be kicked by the horse. The first time, he was taken by surprise, but the second time, he instantly kicked the horse back, and that seemed to have been the last time the horse ever kicked.

He explained to my wife how he was busy training the horse to sit down so he could easily slide his good leg over the saddle and then slowly make the horse stand up. The next phone call was to say that the horse got up a bit too quick and spooked a bit so that poor Bob came off and broke his wrist. That slowed him down a bit.

The calls became less frequent, and we were hoping everything was alright with horse and rider when we did not hear anything for over a year.

But then we spotted him in the Northern Advocate newspaper, which showed him riding his horse on the beach. It was a beautiful photo of a horse and rider on the wide beach with big waves in the background. Pepsi was enjoying a nice canter by the looks of it and seemed very happy, as did the rider. On closer inspection it became clear that there was no saddle and no stirrups to put his bung leg in. There was no bridle either. The bit-less bridles had been introduced a few years ago by that time, but there was simply no bridle. I have seen plenty of people riding around home just using a halter, who use the lead rope as reins. But Bob even had to go one step further; there was no halter either.

Within two years Bob had come so far that the green broken horse had accepted his rider for the full one hundred percent. That was no mean feat. My wife was already on the phone to congratulate him on his achievement. Bob was over the moon really and said that all his work finally paid off and that they both were having a wonderful time and enjoying each other's company.

Bob told her, "This is what I wanted to achieve. This is what I dreamt of in hospital such a long time ago. And everyone said that I was mad and that it could not be done, that I was unable to steer the horse or worse, could not stop him. I coached him a little bit with my good leg and with my hands on his neck, but most of the commands come out of my mouth. Pepsi is such an incredibly good listener, picking up the pitch and the tone of the command words and reacting accordingly. He is such a cool dude."

9

Waipu

There was a lady grazing her horse on Liam and Emma's farm and once or twice a week she came over to ride there. Just before she rode off, we had a little yarn.

"It is about time I go a little bit further today," she said. "The horse is ready for a good workout, I think. She must be in her prime by now. I don't think you will see us back for a few hours. I am so excited to finally have the rest of the day off to ride my horse, time to relax and put all the frustrations of this busy working week behind me," She looked as happy as could be.

I wished her well and hoped that she and the horse would enjoy the ride.

It was time for me to relax too, to likewise put my worries behind me and shoe a few horses. I was sure I would get a buzz out of doing just that.

Out from the shoeing bay I could get a clear view of a couple of hundred metres of farmland before the track wound up into the bush. I finished shoeing the second horse since the lady left, and while straightening my back, I had a look at the beautiful scenery. There was something strange going on in the distance. I could see a horse, alright, being led at that. But the one leading the horse looked like a strange creature, or somebody with a humpback. There were not many of those around here.

It was so hard to decipher in the distance, I decided to carry on and move a couple of horses around to get ready for the next one to shoe.

When I looked again, the pair had covered enough ground for me to see what was going on. The horse was being led not by a humpback, but by the nice lady carrying a big western saddle on her head.

Something must have happened, I thought. But she was not yelling or waving, so I decided to take the first shoe off my next horse. She came into the yard looking totally exhausted, so I dropped my tools to give her a hand, which was just as well since she could not hold the western saddle anymore. It slipped off her head, and I caught it just in time. She was out of breath, so I thought it best to let her settle down a bit before asking what the hell happened out there. I took the reins, took off the bridle, put a halter on and tied the horse up. The horse seemed fine. After the lady had a good drink of water, she found a place in the shade to sit down on the bench. It was a rather hot summer's day. "What happened?" I asked in the nicest way possible.

She had gained her breath and half of her composure, so she answered quietly, "We were going just fine; we were having a ball. Then the horse went slower and slower and eventually stopped and there was no way I could make her go again. So I thought I better lead her for a while. That was a hell of a job too; she just did not want to go anymore. I turned her around as if to go home and she slowly went off again. But not for long; I thought maybe the saddle was not fitting properly or that it was too heavy. Maybe I was too heavy too. So, I took the saddle off as well. It took forever and a day to come back. I don't know how many times I crossed that bloody river. And all the horse wanted to do was stop and eat a bit of grass here and there. Well, everywhere. Do you know how hard it is to lead a horse if they don't want to?"

"I got a fair idea," I said. "It can be rather frustrating."

"I kept on thinking that there might be something wrong with the horse or something. She is not normally like this, you know. Maybe I should ask Liam what the problem is and how I should fix it."

"That is your best bet," I said, "Liam knows a lot about horses," giving the horse a pat. The Lady went to the smoko room or the toilets, so I asked her horse, "So what was all this about then?"

In a soft but steady voice the horse spoke:

"We set off all right. The lady was keen to go for a big walk. She told me. But half way through she stopped telling me where to go, she stopped urging me on, she just stopped giving me directions and forgot to ride me. Now, I could not just take over and go where I wanted to go could I? She obviously did not want to be my boss anymore, but I could not just take over and be the boss myself, could I? I could have easily, don't get me wrong, but then I would get a bad name for myself and I heard from my mates that some people take exception to that. So I just stopped, awaiting further instructions. I ate some grass, and I must say there is some nice tasting grass out there, all along the trek. The lady half-heartedly tried to make me do things but I just ignored her. I suppose that will give me a bad reputation too. She hopped off and started leading me, see if I care. I don't. But even at that she was not very forceful so I ate a bit more grass. She kept on pleading with me, 'please do this and please do that' instead of making me do things. It's not the way I have been brought up really.

"Then she even took the saddle off, and I felt sorry. It is much easier for me to carry that heavy thing than it is for her. But if that is what she wants, it's fine by me.

"I ate some more grass on the way home and that is about all I know really. It's a bit sad really that it turned out this way. You might not believe it, but I am actually very submissive. Just tell me

what you want done, mean it, make me do it, and we will be just fine; we both can have a ball. Just don't ask me to be the tour leader and the mode of transport as well. It does not work. Eh, the lady, is she all right?"

"She will be fine a little bit later I hope," I said. "I think she still has a lot to learn about how you think and work. Maybe you should try telling her."

"That will be a hard thing to do. Ever since I was a foal, I could do in the paddock as I pleased. But I learned very quickly that as soon as someone puts a halter on my head that I should be one hundred percent under their command... simple really. And with the right handling or riding I can surely thrive and enjoy myself. If only she could have a bit more guts about her and really make me do things, we could form an awesome duo. I have done it before, you know."

"I will tell her to see Liam. He will be able to help her. As for you, maybe you could try to be a little bit more obliging next time. It would make her day, you know."

"I was a bit blunt I have to admit, but can you blame me? But for her sake I will try a bit harder next time. She is a good sort really," the horse said.

With that I had to go back to work and hoped that horse and rider would work out their differences.

Finally, we were on our way, Liam, Emma, an exchange student and me. We were heading to Kerikeri for an introductory course in barefoot trimming. Apart from the student, we were all excited. Liam and Emma were thinking that it might fit in well with their natural training methods and maybe save themselves a lot of money. For me it was simply a case of learning what I could. Gaining more knowledge is at all times a good thing.

Barefoot trimming had suddenly appeared, out of nowhere only a couple of years before. Prior to that, the only trimming of horse's feet was done by farriers, normally. And to become a master farrier took four years in a proper apprenticeship. Yet all of a sudden, this barefoot trimming was proclaimed to be the only way to go if you wanted to take proper care of your horses' hooves. I was keen and willing to learn how they did it.

Our tutor first explained how he handled his herd of around thirty horses. Every day one of his workers would make the horses go around the decent sized track for an hour or so. Although reasonably flat, the surface changed a few times from very rough stones to finer ones and small gravel, while the rest was mainly coarse sand. Apart from getting fit, the exercise was good for the hooves as there is a lot of blood going in and out of the hooves while at work. The different grades of stone and sand gave the horse good balance as well as hardened the soles of the hooves, he said, while at the same time wearing off the wall of the hoof.

I would have thought that this was enough trimming of the hooves, but the man told us that every second week he would trim each and every hoof so that it could withstand the vigorous life of a top show jumper.

Then he proceeded to give a beautiful slide-show about the workings of the hoof, what a good hoof should look like and a few case studies of hooves in a terrible state who only became presentable after a few trimmings. And as if to establish an anti-shoeing motion he finished by showing slides of some of the worst shoeing I have ever seen. There was one picture of a shoe completely grown in the hoof which was not a pretty sight. Most of the shoes had just been on way too long, which made things look awful.

After the slide show, followed a lot of testimonials, of people having had bad experiences with either farriers themselves or with the job they were doing. Each one seemed incredibly anti horse shoeing and proclaimed the barefoot trimmers as their saviours.

These fellows, by their account, performed miracles. The pony that could barely walk, suddenly found the energy to walk for half a day after a barefoot trim. They fixed lame horses and donkeys, but above all, the horses were so much happier for not having to wear shoes anymore, they declared, as nails driven into the hoof wall poisoned horses considerably. How humans could ever have invented horseshoes was beyond them.

"Who came up with the idea of putting shoes on horses' feet anyway?" a man in the audience of about thirty asked our tutor.

"I will answer that, if I may?" I said. On a nod from the tutor I proceeded.

"It was the Romans who started shoeing horses in a big way. They conquered most of Europe and established some major highways. One of them, the Via Apia, went from Italy to Germany, France, Belgium and Holland. A branch went all the way to England. Couriers on horseback were used to relay messages and found that the horses could not cope with the enormous distances travelled. The hooves just wore off too much, leaving them very tender. They tried canvas bags and leather boots, but even those wore out too quick for the work the horses were doing.

"The Romans were very proficient in forging all kinds of weaponry out of steel, so it was not a big step for them to forge some horseshoes, and with a few nails they could nail them on. This enabled the horses to go further and quicker with less downtime due to tender feet and stone bruises. Even in those days, time was money. The sole purpose of the horse shoe was, and still is today, protection of the hoof."

I did not expect an applause, but what I heard was close to a 'boo...' Little comments resounded like, "How dare they," and "How stupid they were." They carried on for some time about how good the barefoot trimming was and that horse shoeing was on a par to cruelty to horses.

When things settled down a little bit, in a quiet moment I asked the tutor,

"I have a little girl as a customer who has a pony to visit her grandmother every day after school. She completely wears the ten-millimetre-thick steel horseshoes down to nothing in a matter of six weeks. How much hoof would have been worn off if the pony did not have shoes on?"

"The problem in this case is the prolonged effect of a monotonous walk on the road," he said with a smile on his face, "probably metal or tar-seal. It is advisable to ride on the grass verges, which is better for the hoof. Apart from that the hooves probably need to be trimmed every two weeks to take some of the sole away to let the wall grow a bit faster. No worries there."

I honestly could not see that taking more sole away from a hoof which was worn down to nothing would be beneficial to the hoof and the horse's wellbeing.

I could not believe that the profession I chose and believed in was so totally rubbished to the point of being almost the cause of all evil, that I thought it best to keep my mouth shut and let these people have their opinion.

I knew there was still a very big demand for a farrier.

Over the years I occasionally bumped into the results of some bad barefoot trimming. They were so bad sometimes that the horse could not walk anymore. Then the owner of the horse had a change of heart and asked if I could possibly fix it.

"It is unfixable," I said. "Sorry. But this is going to take some time. The vet can prescribe some painkillers, as we can see that the horse is in considerable pain. Have you ever cut your fingernail too short, or did you ever have a piece of fingernail break off too far up into the sensitive area?"

The owner nodded and flinched at the thought.

"That is exactly what happened here, too much sole taken off, too much toe taken off. Accidents and mishaps can happen, but this was no coincidence as all four feet are too bare to walk on," I said.

"But the trimmer came highly recommended," the owner replied, "and he showed me all the certificates he had. He looked so professional, how am I to know?"

"You just don't, that is the problem. But I am very sorry; there is nothing I can do. I can't even put a shoe on. The feet just have to grow again. I know it is not much help, but every day will get a little bit better. Try and keep him off the sharp stones, the last thing we want is a stone bruise. Put him in a nice soft paddock. Good luck."

"My barefoot trimmer is on holiday. Can you please come over and give my horses a barefoot trim?" the lady asked.

"I can give your horses a trim," I said, being careful not to mention the word 'barefoot'. I would not have even bothered going there, but she lived very close to a customer of mine whose horses were booked in already.

"The trimmer comes," she started, "and then for two weeks I cannot ride my horses as they are lame. Then I can ride them for two weeks, and then he comes again and the horses are lame for two weeks again. The trimmer explained that this was normal. The horses are doing very well, he said. And I must say that when we are riding, we are having a ball."

"I will trim your horse's feet today, this morning actually, and as soon as I am gone, you can put a saddle on any one of them and take them for a ride, permitted that you won't go galloping on the road, metalled races or limestone tracks. Not good for their bones either," I said, and started my job. There was not much to do. It had been only five weeks since the last trim, but I looked busy for a while.

On completion, I said, "The feet are indeed in very good condition. I recommend you give them a small trim in around six to eight weeks. In the meantime, just enjoy the horses; they are a pleasure to be around with."

She thanked me and paid me, and that was the first and last time I saw her.

"What kind of trim have you given my horse?" the girl asked. "A farrier trim," I answered.

"That is a pity, now I can't ride my horse. If it was a barefoot trim, I could ride him. If I only knew; I suppose I should have asked when I called you," the girl sighed, looking rather sad.

"Contrary to belief, it is perfectly safe to ride your horse after a farrier trim. I guarantee it," I said.

"Really?" she asked. "For sure," I said.

It was in Waipu, towards the cove, that I first met Louise. I was having a bit of trouble shoeing a pony for the young girl who had found the pony somewhere in the neighbourhood and bought it very cheap as it had not been broken in. She spent the time with the pony, and started to ride it. Now it was time to put some shoes on, so she could do some road riding to get the pony used to everything. And then she would sell the pony to make some money, since she would need it when she started university after the summer. There were only two more shoes to go on when Louise arrived—a mature lady of slight build going back into riding, or maybe even starting to ride. She seemed to have a bit of money as she arrived in a pretty expensive car.

The girl did tell me that a lady was coming to have a look at the pony that morning—I just did not realise she was an older lady. And this was a young pony. If not young by age, it was certainly young by experience, as I think the girl told me that she had only rode it around ten times or so.

Young horses are not ideal for the more senior ladies, who need an older and more experienced horse. Louise, however, seemed very relaxed around the pony and sounded knowledgeable too, so maybe I got it all wrong. Maybe this time my gut feeling was wrong. I am here to shoe the pony, I reminded myself; I am not here to voice my opinion about what I think is good or bad, right or wrong. I finished shoeing the pony and wished them both well, thinking I would see neither of them again.

How wrong I was.

It must have been around six weeks later that Louise rang me to re-shoe the pony called Chester. On a little peninsula on the way to Tinopai, stretching out into the Kaipara Harbour, Louise and Peter had the ideal waterfront lifestyle property. In their retirement they managed to make something cosy out of the place—a nice house, a big shed, new fences and a nice garden. Chester had to be re-shod. No barefoot riding went on around there, as the block was too small to ride. So, it was road riding, and the roads around there were not very kind to the horse's feet.

Louise told me she was getting on not too bad with Chester, she had only come off once, but she more or less expected that as the pony was only young and just broken in. It was quite often that she went riding along the road, and as she had a bit of trouble putting in a bit, she just rode him in a halter. With support from her friend Heather, she would be sure to get there.

"I am a bit in a hurry you see. For years I longed to have a horse of my own, and if I don't do it now, it might never happen. Of course, Peter and the kids are a bit worried, but what the hell, I have got to do what I want to do—simple really. Yes, Chester is a bit frisky, but hopefully everything will work out fine with a bit of work," she said.

Heather introduced Louise to Twilight Show Jumping at the Paparoa Showgrounds, not that they would jump, but it was good for a horse and rider to socialise. When the season came to an end, the hunting would start. To get in the swing of things there were a few social rides the hunt club organised to get everyone together and slowly get their horses fit. Heather took it as her duty to introduce Louise to these rides as well, and they immensely enjoyed themselves.

And after these rides came a few little hunts to let the hound puppies have a taste of hunting, to show them what it is like and what would be expected of them in later life. Louise and Chester enjoyed these too.

Then Opening Hunt came along with all its glamour, hype, and above all, busyness. You have a very special horse if it can stand still when 60 or more horses are galloping past. The adrenaline created by the excitement normally rubs off on the young and new-to-hunting horses. It does something to them. If a horse and rider survive the first eye-opener, there is hope—if they manage to follow the herd pretty closely, they are on their way to becoming hunters.

Louise never survived the first hurdle. The sheer number of

horses caused her horse to freak out and buck her off, which is not a great feeling for a mature lady.

Luckily, she was all right, and Heather managed to catch the horse later on. Louise then hopped on again and followed the hunt from a distance.

Louise tried and tried, but Chester basically stayed a young horse who did not want to mature. He remained pretty good at plodding around home, but highly excitable when going out. The horse definitely knew that Louise did not know.

Louise came off the horse a few more times before she made the decision to part company. What made the decision easier was that she was offered an ex-hunter, mature and not too big. What a lovely couple they made. The horse, Jock, had absolutely no vices, and did not have to be at the front of the hunt either, nor did he have to jump, he was very happy to stay at the back and go through all the gates. Louise was a very happy lady.

At the next shoeing she told me how happy she was with Jock.

"Just as well," she said, "as I am in a hurry. I am not getting any younger, and as I wanted to ride horses all my life, finally my time has come, and I have to make the best of it. I will be doing really well in a couple of years when I have a big birthday coming up, and I will be riding my horse."

My simple reply was, "You are doing well already, Louise."

Some people are lucky when it comes to horses and some people are not. Unfortunately, Louise was not. After only two seasons, Jock basically gave up. He was suddenly an old horse, and Louise had to let him go.

To find a new horse proved to be a nightmare. By now Louise knew a lot of horse people, and some knew of a nice pony here or there. Louise would go and have a look only to find it was unsuitable.

"It's got to be small, otherwise I cannot get on. It's got to be friendly, good for me to ride and good to follow the hunt. It does not have to jump, as I won't, but it's got to be safe. 'Simple,' you would say, but not really. It is not just a saying, 'It is hard to find the perfect horse.'"

On the east coast near Whangarei, the Wilson sisters were making a name for themselves, especially after their TV series, 'Keeping up with the Kaimanawas', and dealing with New Zealand's wild horses.

They had been involved with horses all of their lives and had now suddenly become famous, not only here in New Zealand but in Australia and the United States as well, where the oldest sister Vicky competed successfully in some stallion challenges.

The girls came across one pony from way up north. They put the pony to work to see what it could do. Their forte is show jumping, so when the pony is fit enough, they put it over some jumps, hoping that it will be a natural jumper. A pony that can jump is worth quite a bit of money.

Unfortunately, the pony did not want to know about jumping. He was not the slightest bit interested, and when pushed a little too hard, he would rather go through the jump than over it.

Louise was very happy with Cary. He looked like a bush pony. Overweight and a little out of proportion here and there—there was nothing refined about him. But he looked strong, very strong.

"I have been riding him every day, and he is really good. We are having a lot of fun even though he is a bit frisky when I first hop on him. But I am sure we sort each other out... and he came from the Wilson sisters, so he should be fine."

Vicky Wilson was also very good at shoeing her own horses. "Cary was no trouble for her to shoe, she told me, so we should be fine," Louise said. Cary had front shoes on, so I believed what Louise said, "We will be fine."

Cary felt like a little firecracker when I first lifted one front foot up, ready to jump in the air if asked anything too quickly. Continuously, he tried to snatch his leg back and shook as if treatment like this had never happened to him before. There was no way I could put the front leg in between my thighs. No way. My admiration for Vicky Wilson was great. How did she do it? How am I going to do it? If I had any brains, I would tell Louise, "Sorry, but I cannot shoe this horse. You will have to find someone else."

But I did not. I just stood there holding the front leg, the hoof in my hand, trying to get a feel of this pony. When I tried to put the leg in between my thighs, it would disappear away from me. Well, at least that was good—better than coming towards me. But how was I going to remove the shoe, trim the hoof and put the shoe back on with one hand when I needed the other hand to hold the leg?

What was needed was a hell of a lot of patience and a hell of a lot of acrobatics to put my body in the most awkward positions to take the strain away from the pony and try not to upset him. Above all, it was to take time. The hardest action was the rasping with one hand. After the first front leg, questions began to form on what the hind legs would be like to shoe. I knew it was no good worrying about it, speculating or predicting. I just had to try and find out in a hurry. Cary did not have hind shoes on, but I knew Louise would love it if I could put some on.

Lifting the hind foot, while anticipating hell to break loose, was like a breeze. It was easy to clean, rasp, change position and do more rasping and the pony still felt good. I could not work this one out at all. The next hind one, what would it be like? As good as could be.

By then I felt sure that the last front one would be a problem foot like the first one. Indeed, it was. It was terrible how nervous and stroppy Cary could be. And now I had to do it all over again and put some shoes on these feet. Surprisingly, the front feet were a little bit better, so that was good, even though I didn't know why.

The back ones were just fine. But Cary remained a strong pony looking for a fight all the time when I was shoeing him.

During the next couple of times, Cary learned to kick with his back feet... real nasty.

I told Louise not to lift his back feet any more to clean them as it would be too dangerous for her. It was dangerous for me too. Something had happened, somewhere somehow, to make lifting the back feet very dangerous.

This carried on for a whole year. He was very dangerous sometimes, but now and then there were a few good times too. Riding-wise Louise found that Cary responded well to lowering the amount of grass eaten, especially in the 24 hours before riding. If he had a little bit too much grass, Cary would be totally unmanageable and almost out of control. If he was put in a starvation paddock, he turned into a little angel. But it was hard to do. As Louise had fallen off a few times, it was time for her to buy a new-age body protector vest. You put it on, and tie a string to the saddle. When you come off, the string breaks, activating a little gas cylinder which inflates the body protector in no time, like an air bag in a car.

Once, she told me she came off the pony and ended up in a shallow drain, with the protector fully inflated. It felt like being in a giant balloon, with no way of getting out. Unable to turn around or get up, she could not help but laugh and wait until the gas emptied out of the balloon.

Then, all of a sudden, Cary went strangely lame in his left hind leg. One day it would be so bad he could hardly walk on it, and the next seemed to be as good as gold. Of course I had a look, but I could not find anything obvious. To make sure, I put some copper sulphate (bluestone) on the hoof, covered it with a pad made from an ice cream container lid cut in the shape of the hoof and then put on the shoe. This did not seem to make much difference as the lameness seemed to go on and on. The local horse vet had a look and could not find anything either. 'Just keep on riding and see what happens' was the message.

Amongst all this, Louise's husband died. Though not totally unexpected, it was very sad and upsetting all the same.

But the pony needed to be reshod, because ride we must. At least Louise had something to hold on to. But sadly, Cary kept on going backwards, and another vet examined the horse. After a lot of deliberation, it was more or less decided what the illness was and that there was no hope of fixing it, the prognosis being that it only would get worse.

So poor Louise had to send poor Cary to the hounds, which was one way of saying thanks to the hounds for so many years of hunting, just what Louise and Cary loved to do.

A few weeks later Louise rang me to see if I could shoe her new horse. Amazingly, she had found another one, I heard through the grapevine, which in the horse world sometimes sounds like a fog horn. I did not want to spoil Louise's happiness and joy and her little secret of not telling me who the new horse was until I got there.

"Look!" she said. "Here he is. It's Midas from Lesley Barlow. Am I not lucky? I have been riding him for a couple of weeks now, and we are getting on very nicely, thanks."

I was so happy for her, as ride she must. I put the shoes on Midas with not a problem and hoped that Midas would not run away with Louise. When the shoes were on, I wished Louise all the best, especially with the hunt season just around the corner.

I reshod Midas six weeks later, just before the opening hunt, and that was the last I heard of her for a long time.

Early in the hunt season, she fell off, and it took some time for her injuries to heal. As a new summer was approaching fast, she called on me to put the shoes on again. The horse would go to an experienced trainer to get fit and gain a few manners. I called in on the trainer to shoe another horse there and asked how the horse was getting on.

"I can get it fit all right, but I still don't know how I can make it quiet enough for Louise to ride," she said.

"That a good challenge for you, it won't be easy," I replied, as we both knew that Midas was not an easy horse. Strong and knowing it, might have been a good description.

After a few weeks, Midas came back home, and I supposed Louise had been riding him as she called on me again to re-shoe Midas. It was during the last week before Christmas, but I managed to fit the job in. I was running rather late, so when Louise left a voice message on my mobile phone at some stage, I never retrieved it, as I thought she was just wondering where I was.

When I arrived, I could see that things were not well at all. Louise and the horse were on the other side of the gate and Louise was crying, trying to bury her face in the horse's neck. The neighbour, Heather, approached me, so I stopped the Ute and politely asked what was happening. She said "The vet has just been and found that the horse has colic. She pumped him full with all kinds of medication and will be back in an hour or so to check the horse again. Louise is not coping very well."

"Anything I can do?" I asked.

"Probably not," the neighbour said.

I got out of the Ute, as if just saying hello might help Louise feel a little bit better. "I left a message on your phone," Louise said.

"I thought you were wondering where I was. I am running late again," I said. "Colic is it? Poor Midas."

"If only we could get him off the driveway onto the grass I will feel a little happier," Louise said, wiping the last tears off her face.

"Let us try," I said, and picked up the lead rope. I put a little pressure on it, and a little bit more, and a bit more again, as we were dealing with so much emotion that quietly would be best. Heather, a horse woman in her own right, put all her weight against Midas's backside and slowly he took a few steps.

"The vet would have loved him in the stables, but I do not think we will be getting there," Louise said.

"I don't think so either, but we will give it one more go. The front feet are on the grass, we are nearly there," I said, and started pulling the rope again. The neighbour put all her weight against Midas's backside, and slowly he moved a few steps until all feet were on the grass. That was where he stayed. He had done enough, having been severely doped up, and now these people wanted to move him.

Louise had had enough worry for a little while. She unclasped the lead rope, while I patted Midas one more time to cheer him up. He was in the best of hands with a really experienced horsey vet looking after him, so he would pull through, I was sure of it. I wished Louise well as she and the neighbour went inside for a cup of tea, and I said that I would be back early in the New Year to re-shoe Midas.

I did not have to go back. I heard a couple of weeks later from another customer that the vet had to put the horse down when she came back later that afternoon. There is no cure for a twisted bowel—poor Midas, poor Louise.

Everyone was keeping their ear to the ground. A couple of people had a spare horse, but was Louise willing to carry on, or would she simply throw in the towel?

Then the news was out. There was no way she would give up now, she had no time to lose, she lived a life long enough without horses, and now was her time to ride them. She only started riding in her late sixties and reckoned she still had some riding years left in her. Soon everyone in her circle of horsey friends knew about it. News travels very fast indeed nowadays. The offers of people willing to lend Louise a horse for a while came in quick, from close and far away. There was a two-day horse trek coming up down the line for which she and her friends booked ages ago. She had settled on borrowing a nice little pony and already had her first ride.

But then the people who had schooled Midas not that long ago contacted her. They had a nice Palomino pony for her. Their kids had had heaps of fun on her, but had unfortunately outgrown her. So maybe Louise would like to come over for a ride?

She did come over. She went for a ride. She took the pony home and never looked back.

10

Mangawhai

"You did tell me you were looking for some more business, didn't you? I have got a nice German couple coming over this morning to check you out," Liam said with a smile on his face. "They came over here a couple of times for some lessons and to pick my brain, I suppose. But they are not very happy with the farrier they are using at the moment, and asked me if I knew of someone good and reliable."

"That is me I suppose, but I wonder what went wrong with the present farrier. Probably something to do with the human relationship, I suppose," I said.

Over the years, Liam and I had talked a lot about horses and their owners, and came often to the realisation that good people go hand in hand with good horses.

"We will soon find out I suppose. Where do they live?" I asked Liam.

"Somewhere in Mangawhai, I think. They asked me to go over there soon to give them a hand with one of their horses who does not like to go in their brand-new float. It will be interesting. Like we say; it's all about people."

I was happily shoeing one of Liam's horses when a heavily German-accented female voice asked, "Good morning, do you know where we can find Liam?"

Before I replied I thought I had better turn around and face the one who was asking the question.

"I am sorry... I don't know where he is. He has been coming and going the whole morning, so I assume he will be back soon. I am just here to shoe some of his horses, and I am loving it here. The horses are all nice and quiet, and we seem to make a lot of tourists happy by enabling them to go trekking in the bush. Anyway, my name is Frans."

And with that, I extended my hand to this mature Lady who shook my hand, said that her name was Amelia and introduced me to her husband Johan, who was a little shorter than her.

"We have a few horses of our own, and Liam will be coming over to give us a hand soon. We are looking for a new farrier, and Liam told us about you. He is very pleased with you," Amelia said with a smile on her face, believing I must have been something special.

"I have been coming here for a while now," I said, "Hard to know how long really."

"Where did you learn your trade?" Amelia asked in a sort of job interview voice.

"In New Zealand," I replied, "Pukekohe to be exact, at Earle Adlington's Forge. He is probably the best farrier in New Zealand. The Horse and Pony magazine had a few articles about him a while back and Country Calendar, that's a TV program, had an episode about him. He is about as famous a farrier as can be."

"Right and how long have you been shoeing horses?" she asked.

"That will be around ten or twelve years now, I think. Best job I ever had," I replied, fearing that this interview could carry on for a while.

"Liam told us that you are very quiet with horses. We are having a bit of trouble with our farrier. He is a bit hot-tempered really; he does not seem to have any patience at all," she said, looking a bit worried and looking at her husband for a bit of help.

Johan did. "They are big horses. Youngish, but well behaved really. I got no trouble at all picking all their feet up and everything. But this farrier always seems to be in a hurry," he added.

"Dressage," Amelia said. "We specialise in dressage. We first bought two New Zealand Stationbred horses, and not too long ago we imported two beautiful warm blood horses from England. They are beautiful. So now we have four of them, but at least we have a few acres to play with, we managed to build them some stables and we have a bit of concrete for you to shoe them on."

"That sounds all very good," I said. "And they have all got shoes on?" I inquired.

"Two at the moment, just the Stationbreds. The warm bloods are not quite ready to be taken out anywhere. They are still young, you see," she said.

"How old are the young ones then?" I asked, as there is always a lot of variety in people's perceptions about being young.

"Six," Johan said, as if he knew what he was talking about. He believed that six years was pretty young while to me a young horse is a two-year-old.

Just then Liam came to the rescue, and after some small talk he invited them over to the arena where he would show them how he was starting up one of his two-year olds.

Amelia came back just as I finished shoeing the horse, and I could see in the way she was striding towards me that she meant business.

"Johan and I talked it over and we would like you to shoe our horses for us. Would next Wednesday morning, 8 a.m. be all right for you?"

"I better have a look in my diary," I said. I knew for sure there was actually not one booking for the whole of next week, but I had to play the game that I was very popular and consequently very busy.

After I consulted my diary in the Ute, I told her that she was lucky and that next week would be just fine. All I needed was her address and her phone number, as you never know what happens. After a few more pleasantries, she and her husband left, and I grabbed myself the next horse to shoe.

The two Stationbreds, both beautiful and black, were ten and twelve years old, and had plenty of handling and riding under their belts. They both had shoes on, and within a couple of minutes I knew what was going on here. These were spoiled horses. Spoiled with too much kindness and not enough discipline. You just feel it when you are handling them. I did manage to shoe these Stationbreds, and a lot of times after that, and each time they became a bit better. They really needed a tune up, but in this environment it was better to be a bit more tactful. And it is possible to teach the horse what is acceptable and what is not when you are putting the shoes on.

But sometimes things do go wrong. Almost a year later, I had just taken a back shoe off one of the horses, cleaned the hoof, trimmed the wall and decided there was still a lot of hoof left. In my wisdom I used my hoof knife to take off some of what I thought was excess sole around the toe area. There was no excess, and there was not too much sole. The hoof only looked long. The knife took off way too much sole, exposing the sensitive tissues, and resulting in heaps of blood. No customer ever asks for a farrier to cut a hole in the hoof to make it bleed. It was a mess.

Luckily there was no one present at that time, which gave me a little time to think about what to do. There were not too many options, best one being sheer time, since the bleeding should normally stop by itself as I did not cut an artery or something, but it could take a while. I could bandage it up for some minutes, but would still have to take it off again to put the shoe back on, and it would probably start bleeding again. I rummaged through the Ute to find my emergency roll of toilet paper. From my emergency tool box I grabbed the roll of duct tape. With the first wad of toilet paper I quickly cleaned the hoof. The second wad I held tightly on the hole and its surrounds to make it as dry as possible for the duct tape to stick. Almost as soon as I took the bloodied paper off, I put the duct tape on and immediately put another strip on, overlapping the first one, and cut the excess off with the hoof knife. As it was close to the frog now, there appeared a gap which I filled with a bit of paper, and for good measure I attached another strip of duct tape. With the mission complete, I was now hoping for the best. With the remaining toilet paper, I cleaned up the puddle of blood and made a mental note to replace the roll as I might need it for its intended purpose one day.

I carried on shoeing the horse, keeping a wary eye on the injured hoof, expecting a puddle of blood to appear any moment. But all went well until I had to put the shoe back on that hoof. Just then Amelia appeared, and before she noticed anything, I explained what happened and how I was planning to fix it. She asked if it was necessary to call the vet, but I told her there was no need for that and that everything was fully under control.

She trusted me a hundred percent, and I was grateful for that, hoping that I could put the shoe on over the duct tape without disturbing the bloody hole. The end result was not that of a nicely shod hoof, but the shoe was securely on.

It was time to relax and hope the horse would not develop an infection in the foot. There is not, however, a lot of time to relax in this job. One more horse had to be trimmed, the pure-bred warm blood from England with a very long name and pedigree.

Well-bred and well fed she may have been, but it had not had enough handling yet. I took my time to let the horse get used to me. I had in mind to treat this horse as if it were the first time ever someone handled her feet.

But my, oh my, she was strong, and Johan holding her and

looking like a midget, just did not have the experience to deal with a horse this young and powerful.

I had to look out for the horse, look after Johan and preserve myself as well. It was no mean feat. The horse came close to rearing up a couple of times, which would have been the end of Johan. Disaster struck at the third leg, the near hind.

I had put the hoof nippers in place to cut the wall off the toe when the horse moved backwards without warning and slammed her foot, with nippers in place, on the concrete floor. It happened so quickly that I did not have time to take my nippers out.

The horse realised something was wrong the second the hoof hit the ground, so she immediately lifted it up to kick backwards, narrowly missing me, but shooting the nippers through the air.

Johan could not see what just happened, but soon got worried as a puddle of blood appeared underneath the hoof.

Two, in one day... what a mess. As I needed a breather, I informed Johan about what had just happened and like Amelia, his first reaction was to call the vet.

Like the earlier mishap that morning, I was sure that the flow of blood would slow down heaps, given a bit of time. Oh, what a disastrous morning, not what the owners had in mind really, was it? Out of my horse First Aid box I grabbed a bag of cotton wool, some bandages and a bit of copper sulphate. It took a while before the horse was willing enough to let me pick her foot up. The hole from the cutting edge of the nippers was deep, on the wrong side of the white line, right in the middle of the toe. Blood was flowing freely, making a mess on my hands and apron.

I put plenty of cotton wool on the toe area, a sprinkling of copper sulphate on top to stop a possible infection, and then the bandage. It had to be rather tight to form a bit of a pressure bandage to try to stop the flow of blood.

As if the horse knew that bad things might happen if she would not stand still, she stood like a lamb when I trimmed the last foot.

After I gave my heavily reduced bill to Johan, he filled out a cheque for me, and by that time I was sure what I had to do.

"I am very sorry Johan, but two mishaps in one morning is too much. I hereby resign from being your farrier. I think that you and the horses deserve a better treatment, and I don't think you will have any trouble finding another farrier. Thank you."

Before he could take it in, I was in my Ute. He said something like thank you and that it was not my fault or something, but I was gone. I had seen enough blood that morning to hopefully last me a lifetime.

The first thing my darling wife told me when I walked in the door was, "He won't let you resign."

"Johan just rang, did he?" I asked.

"He sure did, and in a most beautiful and formal way. After our introduction over the phone he said something like, 'I simply cannot and will not accept Frans's resignation. We will not allow him to resign, and we would like to see him at our next scheduled appointment.' And if I would relay this message to you. I promised I would. So, what was all that about? What happened?" she asked.

When we sat down with a cup of coffee, I told her the whole story.

She thought that the first injury was a bit stupid on my side, but did not think that the second mishap was my fault at all. I agreed with her reasoning but I still could not help but think that I should have got my nippers out of harm's way.

"But there is no resigning for you," she said with a smile on her face. "You will just have to go back and do things better next time."

I did go back six weeks later. In fact, I spent a lot of years shoeing their horses, apart from two short breaks. In the first one they wanted to try barefoot trimming to see if their horses would benefit from it. They did not. The second spell came when one of the horses developed a crack in one of the hooves. They decided to get a master farrier in for that one, to see if he could fix it. He managed to reduce the crack a lot, but they simply could not handle his unreliability.

Once, my Ute had a little breakdown, so I was running ten minutes late. My mobile phone rang to see if I was alright, as up until that time I was never late.

I was there when they had problems with one of the black horses. For over a year I kept on telling them that the horse was too heavy. Now the poor horse had developed an unexplained lameness. A very good vet specialising in horses came to take some x-rays which basically showed that there was not a lot wrong with the hooves, and the coffin bone was close to the perfect angle. The vet gave me proper instructions as to how to shoe the horse for the near future, which I followed. A few months later, another specialist came with the newest in heat detection in relation to chronic pain, lameness and things like that. Of course, the local vet came by as well to take blood tests which came up with nothing. The last to be called upon was an equine herbalist, who prescribed a range of herbs and spices.

It was at our next appointment that Johan confided in me. "You know what? I think all these experts are not completely honest with me. I think they just like the money they charged me. Out of all these expert opinions there is not one who could pinpoint what is wrong with the horse... except for you."

Now he had me worried.

"You were the only one ever to simply state that the horse is too fat, carrying too much weight for her feet to carry. If she would lose a lot of weight, she will be much happier and healthier," he said, and I simply had to agree with him.

She never did lose a lot of weight, but she somehow managed to outlive the other three. While I was on an overseas holiday, they had to put one of their English warm bloods down after complications from a simple stone bruise. I so wish I could have been there as I had a gut feeling that the decision to put the horse down was rather premature. Stone bruises and infections in the hoof can sometimes result in a couple of weeks of lameness, sometimes longer, but almost all of them survive.

The other English warm blood developed colic. The first time, they managed to save her and take her to a horse hospital near Auckland. The second time, only a few months later, proved fatal.

The other black one was diagnosed with emphysema, the first horse I had ever come across with this disease. The likely cause was dust, either from the sawdust in the stables or the hay. The sawdust was replaced with shredded cardboard, and the hay would be cleaned by a specially designed steamer to make it virtually dust free. It was too late for the horse however, who sadly joined the other two.

I closed the gate and drove towards the house as the dashboard clock told me I was on time, as I really liked to be, especially for new customers like today. So I kept my eyes open to see if I could spot the ponies somewhere. They were not in the front paddock and not around the house, which seemed very quiet. Surely, they heard me coming, but there was no sign of life anywhere.

The nice little cottage sat on a section with a few peach trees in an enormous flat paddock at the bottom of the Pakiri hills. After ten minutes I heard a farm bike, which was a good sign. Someone was alive in this very quiet place.

The man on the bike held out his hand, we introduced ourselves and engaged in the normal small talk about the nice weather, the beautiful place and what have you, to finally come to the reason for my visit... where were the ponies?

"They are on top of the hill. If you like you can hop on the bike with me, and I will take you over. And I hope you got a bridle as I can't find mine. The ponies belong to my landlord, I just look after them."

Luckily, I had allocated some extra time for this first-time customer, I thought, as I gathered my tools, making sure I got them all, as having to go back would not be a very smart thing to do.

With my apron, tools and halter I settled myself on the back of his four-wheel bike. Not a machinery man myself, I appreciated the careful and slow driving style of my new customer. The track must have been made many years ago and would have originally been wide enough to take a decent size tractor up the hill. Somehow it had fallen into disrepair with the pampas grass and gorse getting totally out of control, making the track very narrow in places.

There were some holes, ruts and little washouts in the track, but my driver seemed to know every one of them. We were getting higher and higher and the view of the coastline was becoming very beautiful indeed. I told my driver afterwards that if this place were ten minutes out of Amsterdam, people would have loved to pay him hundred dollars to be driven up the hill like we did, for the thrill, the experience and the view. He did not believe me.

With all our travelling I still could not see any ponies. At times the hill was rather steep, and I really hoped there would be some flat land around there. Just as I realised that all this country was one big paddock, the driver stopped and looked all around him. "They were here this morning," he said, "I made sure of that."

The steep hillside was covered in gorse and big clumps of pampas grass. The driver told me there were fifty acres here, home to two ponies and twenty-four weaner steers, but none of them showed their face. If I didn't come there to work, this place would have been ideal to relax and enjoy the view. It was postcard material with here and there some Cabbage trees, Totara and a few flowering Flame trees a bit lower down the hill where there must have been a house at some stage. I estimated we were only half way up the hill and imagined that the view from the top would be really spectacular.

As we were contemplating what to do, only twenty meters away and a bit below us, a little grey pony appeared from behind some bushes, happily grazing, soon followed by the other one. The man was obviously happy he found them as a big grin appeared on his bearded face. He told me the names of the two grey ponies, which I immediately forgot as they were rather strange and ill-fitting for these two bush ponies. I would refer to them as 'the big one', about twelve hands high, and 'the small one', about ten hands high.

Then the man told me they were not broken in or anything, but assured me they were good to catch. He was not sure if anyone had ever lifted their feet up, let alone trimmed them, and since he was waiting for an important phone call, he wished me well, hopped on his bike, promised to pick me up soon and drove off.

Perplexed, I was left there standing on the side of a steep hill in the middle of nowhere with my tools on the ground and the ponies twenty metres away. I hoped that I would not be there in three hours' time still trying to catch these ponies. Or that they would kick me in the head, leaving me lying on the slope for a few hours, waiting to be found.

Oh, what was the use of worrying? Just do it, I resolved, and in this case… rather quietly. Talking quietly to the ponies, I managed to get closer and closer. They certainly did not seem to mind me or the noise from the motorbike just gone. I managed to pet the first one and slowly put the halter on. But now what? There was no flat ground. The flattest piece was where the bike turned around and that had a big slope on it too, and it was rather open, leaving nowhere to tie the pony up to.

The ponies were standing in series on a little cattle track on the side of the hill, a flat streak just wide enough for one cattle beast, as it was cattle that had formed the tracks all along the hill over many years.

Maybe I should just try to trim their feet right here where they are happy? Maybe they will just stand here long enough. They might have been unbroken ponies, but someone must have spent some time with them, as it was very easy to lift the first leg as well as trim the enormously overgrown hoof. The hardest part was finding my balance, which was harder when I did the two feet on the upside of the hill. I did not want to turn the pony around as that might have upset it or the other, who was standing close by.

When I finished the big one, I slowly started to walk towards the small one but it slowly started to back away. I stopped walking and hoped the pony would do too. It did. So I edged a bit closer, and the pony walked a bit backwards. This would have gone on for hours, so I went downhill to the next cattle track. Small one walked forward to park just behind its mate, so I went uphill again, emerging at the pony's shoulder, and after a pat I was able to put the halter on. The feet of this one were even bigger, so there was a lot of chopping going on. As the bigger pony walked forward, the other one wanted to move as well while I was still trimming its hind feet. Luckily it was a longish lead rope, and I had kept hold of it while busy with the back feet, and with a gentle pull, the pony stopped moving. The uphill side was worse with this one as the small pony was a bit too short for comfort.

As I gathered my tools and admired the view again, I heard the bike coming to get me, surprisingly, everything went like clockwork that day.

For a couple of years, I trimmed these ponies' feet and learned a little bit about their history. The owner of the place lived in Auckland, and he had bought the ponies a few years ago for his grandchildren, who by that stage were coming over every weekend. As it happened, the children got bigger and stopped coming, so the ponies were left to their own devices. There was nothing wrong with that so far, but every time I saw them, they were getting fatter and fatter. Instead of grazing on the hill, they were now grazing the lush flat paddocks. There were no facilities to lock them up, and although the man who looked after the ponies really liked them, he was not really interested in the almost impossible task of controlling their diet.

Just before my last visit, the owner had rung me, feeling very worried about the ponies, who could hardly walk. He needed me to please fix them. I told him they had both developed laminitis, that it was a long time coming and that they had to go on a strict diet. Four months in a small pen with nothing but a little bit of hay and water would put things right.

He could call the vet if he liked, who could give them some pain killers and tell him to lock them up for a few months with a little bit of hay and water.

"If you want to keep them here, you will have to build some yards to lock them up. Apart from that, you will have two more options." I said. Without waiting for a reply, I continued, "You can send them to the hounds, where they will be used for dog tucker, or you can give them away. A couple of years ago, when they were looking really good, they might have been worth some money, but I do not think anyone would want to pay anything for them the way they are looking now, sorry."

The man had some decisions to make, so I left him to his thinking and trimmed the pony's feet, which had deteriorated a lot since last time. I did not need to use a halter with them anymore as they certainly would not run away. They could hardly walk, the poor things.

Two days later he rang me, asking if I knew someone who would like to take them on. They had to go together and their names were not to be changed. As it turned out, my grandchildren loved the idea of having a couple of new ponies, but there was no way any child would call these ponies the names they were given. The odds that the ponies and the owner would ever meet were very small, so I agreed to the terms and picked them up the following Saturday.

They could hardly walk when they arrived at my daughter's place. But two weeks later we could see improvement in their mobility, and consequently they enjoyed life more. The ponies could not help but transform from obese to good looking... from lame to galloping around. It is still amazing what starvation and riding can do. I mentioned to my granddaughters that the ponies were probably not broken in, but within a week the kids were on the ponies' backs. The ponies could tolerate just short periods of time as they were still too sore, but they only progressed from there.

The bigger of the two, now named Shadow, proved to be a very good pony club pony. Good bones, hardy, still solid but fit, he looked like an old-fashioned farm pony with a really laid-back personality.

After attending only a few pony club rallies, it was time to go to a ribbon day in Waipu. The youngest granddaughter Aimee would ride Shadow in the flat classes in the morning, and the older granddaughter, Monique, would jump him in the afternoon. He proved he was fit and ready to go.

After the halter classes, where Shadow did not get placed as he was not a fine, sleek, top of the line show pony, it was time for the dozen or so ten-year-old girls to hop on their mount and walk, trot, canter and whatever else the judge told them to do. Shadow was incredibly relaxed on his first ridden class at his first ribbon day, mostly due to the super relaxed Aimee who put on her lovely smile.

They got placed, and then again in the next class. While the judge handed out the ribbons to the first four, the other riders were leaving the ring. One of these girls, somewhat disappointed at not being placed, came out of the ring and walked her beautiful show pony to the two ladies next to me.

"We did not come all this way for you to fall asleep on the job," the mother started. "You will have to do better than this, otherwise we are going home."

"Fancy us spending ten thousand dollars on your pony, and you are not getting anywhere," added the grandmother.

I felt very sorry for the little girl with so much pressure put on her young shoulders. She was nearly in tears, and with the attitude of her support crew, she was definitely not enjoying herself.

When I picked up the ribbon from Aimee, I said "Well done. Whatever you do, have fun and keep that beautiful smile on your face."

She had a ball. Years later, when she was almost twenty-one, we were having a family gathering, and, like often, we talked about ponies and horses.

"And when we took Shadow to his first ribbon day, Opa told me to put a smile on my face, which I did. We ended up with a lot of ribbons, but I had a very sore jaw that night," she said to all present. (My grandchildren call me 'Opa', which is Dutch for Granddad.) Monique had fun with Shadow in all the jump classes in the afternoon. Shadow really enjoyed this. You can see if a pony is happy, and this one was truly very happy.

The girls loved their ponies very much, but as nature dictates, they were growing too big for their ponies. The little one was soon too small, but a lovely home was found for it with a very young girl who developed great riding skills.

It was sad to see Shadow go, the girls had to admit, but again he went to a good home and developed from a reasonable show jumper to an excellent one and gained pride and joy as he went to the Horse of the Year show twice and made a good name for himself.

"There is something wrong with my pony's feet. Why didn't you tell me last time you were here?"

This welcome was like thunder from a summer's blue sky. What is this lady talking about? I looked at the grey pony tied up to the rails, its winter coat just gone, the four black feet at a glance in very good condition, and could not work out what I was supposed to say to her about the pony having something wrong with its feet. There was only one way of finding out, of course, "Why do you think there is something wrong with your pony's feet?" I asked politely.

"Well, I tell you. We just had an exchange student over, and she is adamant there is something wrong with the feet," she said.

I did not get very far with this explanation, so I asked, "And what would be wrong then? Did she say what is wrong with the feet?"

"Oh yes," the lady said, "the colour of all the soles of the hooves are white, and they should be grey. That's what she reckons. She reckons it's probably a lack of some minerals and vitamins or something like that."

For the life of me, I never ever considered the colour of the sole having any meaning at all. To me they are the colour they are given by so many generations of breeding.

Consequently, I never take any notice of the colour, just the condition of the sole. After I had trimmed the feet of this nice-looking pony, I had to agree with the lady that indeed, all four soles were white, simple as that. And from experience I could also say that some other grey ponies with black feet have grey soles.

But how come the exchange student was so convinced that they all had to have grey soles? Because she grew up in an area or environment where they had a lot of grey ponies with only grey soled feet, I thought to myself. And then the penny dropped.

"The student," I asked, "she would not be from southern France by any chance?"

"Why, yes, she lives somewhere close to the Pyrenees, and she showed me a few photos of all the ponies running wild around there with the mountains in the background."

"I have a few photos of them too," I said. "They are beautiful, I managed to spend a holiday there a lot of moons ago. And that basically solves the mystery."

The lady, however, was none the wiser, so I had to explain a little bit more.

"Your student grew up with these ponies that she regarded as the norm—all these grey ponies in southern France had grey soles. So, she concluded that all grey ponies with black feet had grey soles, but somehow it is just not true. Different breeding, different continent, oh well, so many variables.

"You can rest assured that there is nothing wrong with their feet at all. No genetic defects or mineral deficiency; just normal. Just enjoy your pony."

With that explanation, the lady was happy, as there was nothing wrong with the feet at all.

Mel found herself a new horse, a nice and quiet chestnut Thoroughbred. She already had six or seven horses, but this was her first race horse. As she was doing a lot of road riding, the horse needed some shoes to make him cope better on the surrounding rough rural metal roads. And we were doing very well, trimming all the feet, ready for fitting the shoes. It was oh so quiet. The other horses were grazing on the other side of the fence. All was good. That was until the first hind one. It was as if the horse suffered a complete meltdown. Like a meltdown just before an explosion, there was no way the horse could stand still anymore as it was sure something terrible was going to happen in the next minute or so. The sky was falling down or ten tigers were creeping up from behind a bush somewhere.

The horse was going backwards, forwards, sideways, up in the air at the front, up in the air at the back, indeed anything but standing still. The amazing thing was that she was still there, as the lead rope was only tied to an old piece of bailing twine. It just showed that this horse was beautifully broken in. When horses get excited like this, they work up a sweat out of fear and fright, and it got so bad that the horse was actually dripping sweat from her coat all over her body. White foam patches started to appear on the coat of the neck and chest and soon on the flanks and especially around the mouth: the horse worked up a lather, the worst I have ever seen.

While I was looking at the horse, dripping wet and white with lather, I came to the conclusion that I should better tell the owner, so she could see what her horse was doing. And maybe I should do it quickly—the horse might even overheat so much that she would have a heart attack or something like that. Walking behind the shed, where the cottage was, I came across the other horses happily grazing there. Instantly I realised what a fool I was. The horse missed her mates terribly... this was the only reason why she got so upset. I jumped the fence, got the attention of all the horses and herded them back around the shed to where the horse was tied up. This caused an instant metamorphosis. Trying to jump out of her skin one minute, she now was standing docile and looking at her long-lost family and practically saying that it was not her who was playing up. It took a couple of towels to dry her of the beautiful strong smell of fresh horse sweat. Within a couple of minutes the horse was ready to resume being shod. I seemed to learn the hard way all right. I could not understand why I did not pick up on it sooner, but never again will I forget the strong power of horse bonding.

It was a beautiful foal. Then again, they are usually, if not always nice looking. This was the first foal that Kathy had bred, and like most people, she thought it was the nicest foal in the whole wide world. When the foal was three or four months old, I had the privilege of trimming his feet for the first time. I take great pride in doing foals for the first time, since if I do it well, they will be good for life; simple. The foal was nice and easy going for the first time and the second time. The foal turned into a yearling, and I told her it was time to geld him, to castrate him or as some people call it—chop off his balls, as he was turning into a strong horse. She said that she might want to keep him entire, to keep him a stallion. To have a stallion just for fun can be dangerous, comparable to bulls and stags.

Basically, there are too many hormones involved, which can make the animal out of control. It is not uncommon for people to get killed by them, even some very experienced people who have worked with them all their lives. For some reason, the animal can sometimes lose the plot and turn on the owner or handler with no other purpose than to try to kill them. When we think of getting killed by animals, we instantly think of lions and tigers, meat eaters. We just don't think that these grass eaters would have it in them.

The colt was a year and a half old now and getting frighteningly strong. Again, I advised that it would be a good idea if she gelded her horse as he was getting really big and too powerful. She still reckoned that all was fine and that he was a real gentleman and that, when she was handling him, he was fully under her control. I may have been no expert in dealing with stallions, but I heard a lot about their behaviour and I have seen all the precautions the professional people take in handling them, so I felt it my duty to warn Kathy about what might happen.

"One day," I started, hoping it did not sound like once upon a time, "you walk into his paddock, and the stallion takes an interest in the smell of your deodorant, so that all common sense goes by the wayside. Or out of the blue, he will just try his luck and see how far he can go. His primeval instinct takes over, and he gets stuck into you."

"No, he won't," she said. "He loves me." This, of course, really got me going.

"One of these days, when you least expect it, he will pick you up at the back of your neck with his mouth, like they say, by the scruff of your neck, lift you up, shake you around a couple of times to make sure your neck is well and truly broken, and then throw you a few metres away like a rag doll. To top it all off he will ceremoniously plant his front feet on your dead body, arch his neck to show himself off to anyone looking as if to say, *'Who's next?'*"

"He will never ever do such a thing. I will make sure I will stay on top of him and will always be his boss," she said.

"I sure hope so, as they can kill people, you know. Don't you ever turn your back on him, it's basically inviting him. Good luck, we will see you next time," I said, and left.

The next time proved to be the last time. After trimming a couple of her other horses, it was time to do her stallion, which was then almost two years old. She had taken him to a local A&P show to a couple in hand classes and came back happy with the right-coloured ribbons.

"And how was he to handle in public?" I asked, not meaning humans, but his equine companions, especially fillies and mares in season.

"Very easy," she said, "I put heaps of Vicks on the inside of his nostrils so he would not smell a thing."

"That's very clever," I said. "Anyway, shall we have a look at him? Where is he?"

"I tied him up on the other side of the house to get him away from the others. Don't worry, he will be fine," she said with a big smile on her face. In her mind, her boy could not do a thing wrong.

That gave me a lot of encouragement. It was good to see the horse being tied up, but it was tied to the top deck of a two-storey house. Kathy went around the house the other way and ended up on the deck, where she got hold of the lead rope.

"He will be fine," she said, "He is used to this."

That might well have been the case, but I was not used to doing it this way. "I hope you got control of your horse from there. It seems a long way away."

"I've got him fully under control," she said.

With that information in hand, there was no other way than to start and see what happened. Once I touch a horse I can feel if we can carry on or not. The reaction I got from the first touch was a bit nervous. So okay, I lifted a leg up like normal, put it in between my thighs and started my work. It felt absolutely horrible. It felt as if at any split second, something could explode. That feeling overpowered me so much that I started making every movement as quiet and smooth as possible, like walking on eggshells underneath a 400-kilogram horse.

Before I started, I knew that relying on Kathy would be a big mistake if something happened, so I continuously kept thinking about all the different escape routes along the way. At this particular stance, if the horse did this, I would go there, but if the horse did something else instead, maybe jumping that way would be better. One would have to be a computer programmer to try to work out all the different scenarios. But still, one has to be prepared for the unexpected, even though I would not have a clue how to do that.

It just didn't feel safe, with the horse arguing that he didn't want to do what I wanted him to do. It was as if he was saying that he was much stronger than me and that I couldn't make him do things he didn't like. All I had, apart from the lady up top who could hardly see me anyway, was the feeling I got from the body contact, and that told me that the horse was waiting for a good moment to get me.

For the next hoof, I tried with all my might to define how unhappy the horse was. Should I make up a chart to gauge when a certain feeling occurred that meant it would be time to bail out? For now, shall I hang on or let go? What will be the consequence of either action? I will need a computer again. Is that a sigh of relief? Are we nearly there? Is it only one more hoof? Was Kathy right all along? Is it me who is living on a different planet? Why is the horse still not cooperating or giving up his fight, or giving in, or surrendering or whatever you want to call it? *Why?*

I did get there. I did. And the horse did not get me; that was a big bonus. I gave the horse a slight pat on the neck while watching his mouth, and then retreated with an enormous feeling of relief.

We met again beside my Ute. "Sorry Kathy," I said, "This was the last time. This was totally irresponsible. I will not be doing this horse again, thanks. He was just so close to having a go at me it was not even funny. I could so feel it when I had to rasp the front of his feet and be underneath his face. I had to be so on top of my nerves and tell him off a lot of times by slapping him on the nose or with my sheer psyche. And when you tell him off, you have to be prepared for the reaction you get back. The reaction I got from him makes me scared, sorry, I can't help it, I won't be doing your horse again."

Looking at her, I realised that we were on different planets. She had no idea at all what just happened down there; she had no idea why I was scared of what could have happened. I suppose she was thinking that I was going nuts in a big hurry. It actually did not matter what I told her, as the horse was her baby darling who couldn't do a thing wrong.

Politely, well, I like to think it was, I told her I would not be back again. I took the money and wished her well. I would not see her for a great number of years.

Unfortunately, I heard that within a year, the young stallion attacked her and put her in hospital. I never heard exactly what happened and it probably would not matter anyway.

Half a year after the accident I heard that the stallion had put her in hospital a second time. Again, I felt very sorry for her, but at the same time I felt very lucky that it was not me. Not very nice thinking, I know, but one cannot argue with the hormones or behaviour of a stallion.

11
Kaiwaka

Not too far out of Kaiwaka there was a girl in her last year of high school who knew just about everything there was to know about horses. And there was a rather big horse, probably a Stationbred, according to the size and shape of him, who knew all there is to know about his owner.

While the girl thought she was in control of the horse, the horse knew for sure he was in control of the girl.

The first time I got there, the girl was standing in a paddock with the horse on a lead rope a good thirty metres away from the gate. I do like walking, but with my apron on and tools to carry, it would have been much easier if she came to the gate with the horse.

"Can you bring the horse to the gate, please?" I asked.

"I can't," she said. "He doesn't like it there. Over here he is happy, if you don't mind?"

I did mind, but if I could make the customer happy by walking to the horse, I supposed I could walk.

I had only just got through the gate when the horse started snorting, moving around a bit to have a better look at the man who dared to come into his grassy domain, of which he was Lord and Master, and tell his boss what to do. The girl just smiled and said, "He always does this, you got to be very quiet and slow moving, please."

The closer I crept, the worse the horse became, and I would not have been surprised if he were to jump out of his skin soon. The girl was just loosely holding him, smiling and probably thinking this was a hell of a joke. She really was thinking that she had the horse a hundred percent under control. It was only by the horse's good nature that he was still there.

"Just tell him to cut that out. That snorting is a sign of bad manners," I said.

"But he is only young, I don't want to tell him off just yet," she said.

It was all good and well, shuffling for the last ten metres and finally coming within arm's reach, but how do you get hold of a horse like this, how do you ever get to touch him?

The closer I got, the more the horse moved away, around and around the girl who, it must be said, had the patience of a saint.

After playing merry-go-round for three rounds, I stopped and asked the girl, who was not embarrassed or worried in the slightest, to stand on the other side of the horse to stop his sideways movement.

"Oh no, he might get me bowled over!" she said.

"I can't get hold of him if he does not stand still, sorry. What if we bring him alongside the gate so he can't go sideways?" I asked, getting a little bit frustrated by now.

"But then he might get a fright and never go through a gate again," she replied.

"What about next to the show jump, over there, that will be a good idea," I said.

"That's a really bad idea, he might never want to jump over that one again in his whole life," she said.

"So, what do you suggest, how do I get hold of this horse?" I really did not have much hope with this attitude.

"He will give in," she said. And when the horse stood still for a moment, she took a step forward and in one motion lifted a front foot up.

"Stay right there," I said, and quietly moved next to her to take the hoof out of her hands. But the horse smelled me and probably did not like it, and off he went again. The only good thing was that he always moved away from me. So, I tried and I tried to get close enough to touch him, and finally, out of the blue, maybe feeling a bit bored of the game he was playing, he let me touch him on the shoulder and he was at ease. I let him have a good sniff of me and proceeded to let my hand slide from shoulder to hoof, which I even managed to lift up, put between my thighs and start trimming. Wow, I could not believe it. We had a slight hiccup, as he slammed his foot down when I wanted to bring the leg forward. I had to start again from touching the shoulder after another couple of merry-go-rounds. But I got there and was rather pleased.

I would have loved to leave the back feet for another time, but they looked such a mess that I shifted my attention to the nearest one. If the horse would only stand still, if only there was some kind of a barrier on the other side so he could not keep moving away, if the girl would only tell him off... oh, there are too many variables with this type of behaviour. But out of the blue, the horse stood still again, and I managed to get hold of the leg. He was surprisingly well behaved again when trimming his hoof, but I was careful not to give him any reason to perform again.

We managed to do the other foot, and I was incredibly thankful when we were finished. The girl, however, seemed to think there was nothing wrong at all with his behaviour, let alone her inaction. I hoped I would never have to go there again, that she would find someone else who would be able to understand her horse a bit better.

No such luck. The second time was, if it were possible, even worse than the first time. The snorting and performing started before I even got near the gate. And not once did the girl try to growl at him, to reprimand him, to tell him off, to yank his halter—just a total nothing. If the horse wanted to back up, she let the lead rope gently slide out of her hand, to take it in a little bit when the horse would stand still.

With a change in her attitude she could have made a nice and well-behaved horse out of this unruly character.

Once again I managed, but it took some guts and perseverance. I felt like telling this girl how it should be done, what she should be doing and when. But when you are exhausted from this very demanding trim and feeling hopelessly frustrated about the whole affair, it probably wouldn't come out very nicely. By the time we reached the Ute, I was settled down enough to politely tell her that this snorting business had to stop, and that she simply had to tell the horse off for doing it. It was just plain bad behaviour.

I am sure I was polite and truthful, but I did not see her for quite some time.

Once I had a yarn with a fellow farrier who trimmed this horse a few times as well and he could not understand the horse's behaviour either. I told him that the horse's snorting and mannerism was a learned trait that the girl had instilled in him and nurtured. The girl had simply lived a very sheltered life and not really seen or experienced what other people could do with their horses and how they handled them.

The farrier took a little while to digest my opinion, and to clarify my point of view, I said, "All she has to do is yank the halter directly after he first starts snorting and really growl at him to tell him to cut it out. This she has to repeat a couple of times, and the horse will be as good as gold."

"You sure about this?" he asked.

"Positive. The problem, however, is telling her in a nice way. I have the feeling that if I am too blunt, direct or forceful, she will crumble and start crying," I said.

"There is no way I will ever go back there; it is almost ridiculous," he said.

"I like to think so too, but I am afraid she will be running out of farriers soon," I replied.

Sure enough, she sent me a text a while later. "Can you please trim my horse? He is well overdue."

This time I allocated even more than the extra time I normally took. Today had to be the day that I would get it in the girl's mind that snorting and playing up is not a desirable trait in a horse.

I put a smile on my face, took note not to lower my voice as I did not want to scare the rather timid girl. I put it in my mind to listen when she said something, and wait before replying... and not to be rude, as I didn't want the girl to cry either. I got out of the Ute, grabbed my gear and walked over to the gate. Before I reached the gate, I could hear some snorting going on.

At the gate I could see him, and he started snorting and performing with abundance now that he could see me as well. With a smile on my face and with what I thought was a happy and casual tone in my voice, I said gently, "Now is the time to tell him off, please. Jiggle the halter, get his attention and tell him to cut it out."

She sort-of did. She seemed scared to put too much pressure on the halter. Maybe he would get a hang up about that, maybe he would never allow a halter to be put on his head again.

Surprisingly, the horse stopped snorting, and I got myself on the horse's side of the gate. Then he started snorting again, and I can honestly say that this was the only horse I have ever come across who did this.

"Tell him off again, growl at him," I said, and I had trouble not to lower my voice too much.

I did not hear her say anything, but the horse went quiet. Maybe she whispered something in his ear, I do not know. I took a few steps and the horse started snorting again, this time even pawing the ground. I stopped but did not say anything, carefully watching what the girl was doing.

She was actually doing totally nothing, which you could admire as being non-confrontational, but for the horse's sake it reinforces his thinking that whatever he does is alright. She waited until he stopped again, me too. When he did, I walked a few metres more before the same thing happened.

I had the urge to yell at her, "Yank the lead rope and tell him off: this is so bloody rude it is not funny."

But the girl still thought it was funny and had a big smile on her face, still thinking that she was the boss of the horse. I just had to wait until he was quiet again.

"Next time he starts snorting, you will have to tell him off. I don't care how you do it. We are at the end of the road now," I said, trying to remain as friendly as I could be, while still ten metres away from the horse. "If the horse does not behave, and if I choose to leave him and go home, you are in trouble as none of the other farriers around here want to come here again."

"I know," she said in a very soft voice. "They told me already."

I could detect a shift in her confidence and hoped she could keep it together.

"What this horse does is not normal for horses to do. It is a learned behaviour—he knows he can do it and get away with it. I want you to relax, I will take a couple more paces, and the second he changes his attitude you have to tell him off by growling at him and pulling hard but short on the lead rope," I said, becoming a little frustrated.

"I understand," she said. I sincerely hoped she did.

I started walking, and surely enough the horse started his horrible snorting business again. To my surprise the girl yelled at the horse at the top of her voice and gave it a short pull on the lead rope.

The horse could not believe what was going on. He did not even react by going backwards or sideways in a hurry, he just stood there wondering what had just happened. "That was well done," I said, and took the last few steps to stop next to the horse. He was still just standing there, trying to take it all in. When I tried to pat him, he suddenly woke up and took a few steps backwards in a hurry. I grabbed the lead rope as she let it slide out of her hand, and the moment the horse stopped, I gave a mighty pull on the lead rope, the horse reacted by going backwards again but I followed. When he wanted to stop, I pushed him backwards another ten steps, and when he stood still, I patted him.

Then I walked back again to the girl, with the horse gently following me. She was just as surprised as the horse at what just happened.

"Sorry," I said, just to keep the peace, as I was not sorry at all. I gave her the lead rope and said, "He will be all right now."

And he was. I trimmed his four feet in a real good time, and the horse did not put one foot wrong.

As the job was done, it was time to evaluate things a bit. I had to leave on a good note and try to instil the notion that the horse would not change his behaviour until she changed hers. I left her with the remark that he was much better behaved than last time. The next time, however, there was a big improvement and I was able to walk undisturbed up to five metres from the horse before he snorted. Remarkably, she growled at the horse in a low tone while jiggling the halter, and the horse stopped.

I was full of praise, "Well done. I knew you could do it. He is almost a horse now."

I don't know where that last bit came from; it just came out of my mouth, yet it seemed to make perfect sense. Trimming the feet was not difficult at all. And eventually, yes, he felt like a horse now.

"New horse?," I asked Carl, the Cowboy, as I call him, but not to his face, as he always wears a cowboy hat. I do not remember a lot of horses, but I had been putting the shoes on Carl's horse for a good number of years and could not help but notice that this one was new. "Yes," Carl replied, "borrowed it from the lady down the road. The other one was getting a bit too old really. But the problem is there are not many horses for sale."

This was news to me as I always had the feeling that there were way too many horses around.

"There is not a single decent Quarter horse or Appaloosa for sale on this side of Rotorua. Either people are not breeding them anymore or if they do, they are not breaking them in. And for some of them, if they do break them in, they seem to break their spirit as well.

Remember the guy who lived down the road here for a while? He moved to the South Island I think, but anyway, he was so hard on his horses I would not want to give him my wheelbarrow to break in."

"Is that right?" I asked, as indeed I knew the person in question.

"Or what about that fellow down Dargaville way? The poor horse died in the process of being broken in. I could not believe it."

"You will do it yourself anyway," I said, as I knew he was very capable. "How is that young horse of yours getting on then?"

"I had to shoot it," Carl replied. "He turned nasty."

"You chopped his balls off did you not?" I probed, as this makes them more docile.

"I sure did, but this one just turned nasty. It was not a matter if he was going to kill me, it was a matter of when. Oh well, he is gone, still looking for another horse if you hear of anything."

"I will keep my ears open." I replied. "I suppose you could always buy a horse from John Wayne in Taupo? At least it will be bomb proof."

Carl's face lit up. "You are right there, if they don't make the grade, he turns them into dog tucker. Only the very best will ever leave his place, and consequently he wants a lot of money for them. I did give him a ring, and he only had one for sale, but he wanted thirty thousand for him so I told him where to go. Some rich lady will probably buy him just to ride him a couple of hours a week. Funny, I only rang him a couple of months ago but can't remember his proper name now. John Wayne will do, he enjoys it really, and he thinks it is an honour to have a nickname like that."

"How did you get on at the last show?" I asked.

"Oh well, seeing I just borrowed this horse, I did not compete. But something funny happened at the last introductory weekend. I better tell you, you will like it," Carl said. He told me a lot of yarns over the years while I was shoeing his horse, and I learned to allocate a little bit more time so we would not be rushed.

"There were four of us, three ladies and me," Carl started. "It was on the Saturday, which was our instruction and introduction day for people new to western riding. The show, like a ribbon day really, was on the Sunday. Anyway, we were just standing with our horses on the lead;, the day was finished. Some learned a lot, some would never learn, that goes for riders and horses."

Here, Carl had to laugh at his own joke, and indeed it sounded really funny.

"They started petting their horses and telling them how good they had been today, and then the first lady started, 'When we get back to the float, I will give you some nice carrots because you have been very good today.'

"The second lady said to her horse, 'When we get back, I will make you up some of your favourite food and I will cut up a few apples and hide them in between the food as you have been such a sweet little girl.'

"The third lady was obviously very happy with her horse too as her horse would get some nice horse food as well as a carrot, an apple and a slice of bread with some electrolytes on it, because the horse did a fantastic job today.

"After that, the three ladies looked at me, and the last lady, the pommy one, asked me in her most proper English accent, 'And what do you give your horse, Mister Carl, as he has been very good for you, I did not see him put a foot wrong all day long?'

"I just could not help myself," Carl carried on, "This borrowed horse of mine just did a lambing beat of six weeks of eight hours riding every day. He is just a horse, a stock horse, and that is what they are supposed to do. Today was just a little outing for him, a bit of fun really. All the other horses probably only get ridden a couple of hours on a Sunday and that is it.

"So, yes, I could not help myself, and I said, 'I will let him live.' The ladies were all so shocked about the simplicity of my answer that they all disappeared to their floats in a hurry to attend to their horse's wellbeing."

Carl was laughing, and I had to agree it was a hell of a joke, but for the poor ladies, I could imagine it would have been a bit harsh.

It was only a couple of weeks later when I met Carl again. One of my other customers close to Carl's place asked him for a hand one morning as a lot of horsey things were happening. There were a few people in the covered yard working on a horse, and Carl was holding a horse for me to be shod a little distance away where the driveway was nice and flat, when suddenly it became very quiet in the stables.

As I looked up, I could see the group was having a quiet chat over the body of the horse lying sedated on the stable floor. The owner, her friend and the vet were there to geld the horse. They all looked a bit worried, but what the heck, I was there to shoe the horse.

While I was underneath the back of the horse nailing a shoe on, the friend came over to inform Carl in a very quiet voice, "The vet just cut off the horse's penis. She mistook it for a testicle."

Carl was quiet for a little while, and then said, "Just shoot it."

He could not believe it. I couldn't. Nobody could. The vet would not be pleased about it either. Nightmare stuff that was, something the vet would regret doing for a very long time. The vet managed to divert the urethra to the outside, under the anus, so the horse would piddle like a girl, but it would work quite successfully. After all, there is nothing wrong with trying.

Whoever said that shoeing horses is a boring job is definitely wrong.

The first time I shod a horse for Neville was the first time I got kicked seriously. It was a real beauty, dead-smack on my thigh. Of course, I said it did not hurt, not that much anyway, but it did immensely, and it turned into a nice blue black and purple swelling, staying sore for most of the week.

The kicker was a mature dun coloured horse, Neville's hunter for a few years, being solid in legs and body and as strong as an ox. I had just lifted a back leg up, but he snatched it back and cow-kicked me as quickly as anything.

There were horses coming and going all the time at Neville's place. He used to break them in, ride them on, buy them and sell them. This new horse I just started to work on just could not help himself, never standing still, always trying to get away from whatever I wanted to do with him.

From the previous owner, Neville got the advice to put a fence batten on his forehead, from the nose to between his ears. No banging on his head, just hold it there. We thought it worth a try, so we did it. The result was an instant submissiveness, and the horse was a breeze to shoe.

Almost finished, Neville took the batten off the horse's head out of curiosity, to see what would happen.

The horse reverted to its usual unmanageable self. The batten went back on, and the shoeing got finished without any problems.

The big Clydesdale cross bred was a different story altogether. He was incredibly strong, and he knew it, yet he managed to use his strength in the most refined manner I ever came across.

The front feet were just fine, though maybe a little bit heavy for a Clyde cross but still good to work on.

The backs were a different story. Most horses with trouble back legs tell you directly that they don't like it, and some start playing up the second you touch them, like the dun who kicked me. This one told me that he did not mind anything, that he'd had shoes on a thousand times and that nothing would ever bother him.

So, I was nicely relaxed underneath the back end of the horse doing my work when the horse slowly decided that he he'd had enough of it for the moment, thank you, and gently but surely lifted his leg up and backwards. The instant reaction is to hang on as tight as you can but when your feet are off the ground, you realise that this horse is not going to give in.

When I thought that he couldn't lift the leg any higher, he still did and added a tiny kick, which made me gently fly through the air. And when I was airborne, he just shook his leg a bit to make sure there was nothing else hanging onto his leg any more before slowly putting it down.

Because everything seemed to be in slow motion, the landing was easy, but I had to go back and do it again, even though I could see the horse smiling and thinking, *"That was fun, shall we do that again?"*

Twice more I floated through the air in slow motion before the horse somehow gave in as if it was no fun anymore. He was probably getting bored with me, ready to do the same to another guy double the weight of me—that would be a real challenge for him.

Dairy farmers tend to live a very busy life, and Neville's was even busier with his show jumping commitments and the handling of other people's horses. He was lucky in a way as he managed to surround himself with young people who lent him a hand with either helping run the farm or helping with his horses, or in some cases both. He had a lot of time for teenagers when it came to anything to do with horses. But something had to give way, and that was tidiness in and around the shed where the horses were handled and shod. There were all sorts of machinery and bits of pieces lying around, which sometimes made it tricky to handle or shoe young horses.

The big grey was a prime example. Youngish, not keen to be shod, she pulled back when the first nail was driven into her hoof and took a couple of steps backwards towards an old engine with the bare bolts sticking up, which managed to puncture her leg just underneath the hock. There was blood everywhere, and the horse was in total distress with someone attacking her from the front and something attacking her from the back. She was a lost soul.

As the flow of blood seemed to stop by itself, I prized myself lucky and hoped she did not have any permanent damage. But in the meantime, I thought I might as well try getting the shoes on. Somehow the horse realised that she had better cooperate, lest more bad things would happen.

A lot of farriers don't care what happens with the nails they pull out of the shoes. Or the pieces of nail they twist off the end to prevent potential injury. I like to know where every nail is and what happens to every off-cut. Shoeing in a paddock might be an excuse for some to litter the place with old nails, but a horse, cow or sheep does not notice a nail stuck in a mouthful of grass. But that nail could do some serious damage anywhere in its digestive system. I never look for any trouble.

Shoeing on a metalled area or concrete looks very safe from old nails. But when the hoof is just being trimmed, it is still possible for an off-cut of the nail to penetrate the sole and cause an abscess.

Then there is the chance of my Ute having a flat tire. Consequently, I like to be very consistent in putting the old nails and bits in my shoeing box, a simple and nice habit, really.

But it does not matter how careful you are, bad things happen sometimes.

When it was show season, I came to Neville's place almost every week to shoe a couple of horses. This time he presented me with a horse I had shod the week before, a big Chestnut who was as lame as could be, and I must say that I felt sorry for the horse. A horse being lame a week after being shod does not sound good. Maybe a nail went the wrong way, which can happen of course.

After cleaning the hoof as good as I could, I could not see anything obviously wrong, so I put the hoof testers on the horse and started applying pressure all over the hoof with no result.

That was strange. Horses don't make things up. It would be no good taking the shoe off if the pain was not under the shoe. But where was it? In the heels maybe, or the bulbs above the heels, or the frog? No... all good. No pain.

Out of frustration I put the wire brush on the hoof again to give it a real good clean, and then I saw something shiny in the middle of the frog. It had the same sheen as a horse shoe nail and the same shape as the head of a horse shoe nail. In fact, it was a horse shoe nail. Before I pulled it out, I drenched the frog in Iodine, trying to minimise the chance of infection. Apart from the most important bone in the horse's body, the pedal bone, or coffin bone as some call it, a horse's hoof contains a hell of a lot of sensitive tissues, and an infection there will cause a terrible mess. I pulled the nail out and drenched the hoof again with Iodine, then simply but whole heartedly hoped for the best. That was the best I could do, I suppose, other than praying, of course.

As it turned out we were bloody lucky, the horse never had any ill effects whatsoever. It did, however, leave the big question about how the horse managed to step on the nail, and a new one at that.

When handling a total of seven tools to shoe a horse, there is a lot of tool changing in and out of the tool box, combined with the four shoes taken off the hooves going in and out of the box. On top of the toolbox I have two little boxes to hold the new horseshoe nails, each about the size of four matchboxes. And it does happen occasionally while changing tools or putting down the used horse shoes, that one of the little boxes gets disturbed and a nail manages to jump out to land on the floor.

So far this has never been a problem, as I always found them and put them back in the box. The cleaner the environment, the easier it is to spot a lost nail. In Neville's case, however, a nail must have jumped out of its little box and landed in a pile of horse poo, as there were a few around the yard most of the time.

The nail must have landed with its head down, and the horse had managed to put one of his feet right dead smack on the pointy end of the nail so that it would penetrate the frog. We were oh so lucky that the horse was sound and well.

On another occasion there were quite a few people around. The owners of a horse called Whoopy were there to have a look at how their horse was getting on. Neville was breaking her in for them, but she required a bit more of his attention than normal. I did not know they would be there, and neither did Neville for that matter, all I knew was that Neville had a young horse who needed some shoes on for the first time so that he could ride her a bit more.

Barry, my biggest customer at the time, another real horseman, was there as well, so between him and Neville there would not be any concern in dealing with young horses. Whoopy was not by definition young, being already five years old, but only recently did the owners decide to do something with her. A well grown and well-fed filly, she was consequently full of beans. I knew the horse as I had trimmed her feet for the last three years or so, but for some, putting shoes on seems to be a completely different matter.

All seemed to go smoothly, with the feet trimmed and the first shoe shaped according to the horse's hoof. I only had to fasten the shoe with six or seven nails and the job would be done.

Just before I put in the first nail, I slightly tapped the shoe with my hammer to see if there was any reaction from the horse. There sure was: in no uncertain terms the horse suddenly needed her leg back to stand on because this whole affair was ridiculous. Somebody banging on her hoof with a hammer and a bit of steel was not normal in Whoopy's constitution.

Before I jumped to conclusions, I had to try again to see if this was just a one off, or a more serious problem. Lifting the leg was not a problem, and putting it in between my thighs was not a problem either. Putting the shoe in its place was just fine. One little tap with the hammer on the shoe was barely acceptable. A second tap proved way too much.

"Rope her up Neville," Barry said in his normal relaxed manner. "That should fix the problem. You have got some leg straps, haven't you?"

"I sure have, and she is pretty well used to it, she even had them on only yesterday," Neville said as he disappeared into the shed to get them.

The concerned lady owner asked Barry, "This roping up you were talking about... it does not hurt the horse, does it? I heard so many bad stories about it, so I am not sure that I like it."

At this point I thought that this was going to be a very long and drawn out shoeing job. The balance of power was shifting. Neville asked me to shoe a horse, and the two of us would have been just fine since we had handled horses like this before. Barry, who was just visiting, was giving a hand and advice, and no one would say no to that. And now the lady owner was having doubts about roping the leg. Next thing you know, the lady's husband was going to put his two cents in.

"The horse will be just fine. I have done a few hundred of them. There is just no way the farrier will be able to shoe the horse, like she is behaving now," Barry said with his normal patience.

"I just don't want her getting hurt, that's all," the lady said. "Suppose she is a bit special as she is the last horse we bred. Then again, her mother was a right tart as well, and we had a few dramas putting shoes on that one too for the first time."

That is really nice to know, I thought, and I wondered why someone would want to breed from a mare like that in the first place. Luckily, Neville returned with a bundle of heavy-duty soft ropes and leather straps with heavy duty buckles on them. Now we just had to see how Whoopy would take to all of this.

Not very kindly did Whoopy accept all this carry-on. She just did not want to be there anymore, clearly preferring to be in the paddock she came from.

Now, with a big strap around her front leg, there was no way she could put it down to the ground. She could still move around, but after a while she settled down, trying to make sense of it all.

It was up to me to put the shoe on without upsetting Whoopy.

It was a bit of a mission to get her leg in between mine with the strap in place. A couple of slight little taps on the shoe later to tell the horse that it was all right, she could just hold herself together. I supposed I might as well try to put a nail in with some small little hits with the hammer.

I thought that Whoopy would explode any second, yet slowly but surely, the first nail went further and further in until it was securely in place. Number two nail was on the opposite side, being pressed in by tiny little hits so as not to upset this big hunk of dynamite ready to explode. I could feel by sheer body contact that the moment of detonation was coming closer. The fuse was getting shorter and shorter, but there were two more strikes to make with the hammer before the nail would be safe. I managed one.

As I had just enough warning about the things to come, I managed to get her leg out from between mine just before the horse reared up with all her might. Back, going back, as fast as I can, the horse was thinking, *"Run away from these mad people, Barry and Neville—who was holding the lead rope, but above all, this guy who is so mean as to put nails in my hoof!"*

She took a couple of steps backwards before her front end came down to the ground again, but her momentum forced her to go back even more until her back legs came to a stop against the open back of my station wagon. Though her legs had stopped, the backwards force was so great that her backside continued and she managed to sit right in the back of my station wagon, whacking her head or neck on the open door, causing a massive dent.

She just sat there for a few seconds rather uncomfortably, contemplating her miserable life. YouTube missed out on this one as it had not yet been invented.

The lady owner was beside herself. The trauma put on her darling horse was way too much for her to cope with. She would have a nervous breakdown before the horse did. Barry and Neville were equally embarrassed, as they had never experienced something like this before either. As for me, I was worried about the big dent in the door and hoped that it would still close. It looked rather buckled, and I was lucky the glass was not broken.

After a while, Whoopy decided she better get up and settle down a bit. When I approached her again, I just tapped the shoe with my hammer and got no reaction whatsoever. Did the horse learn a lesson or was she playing with me? I had better try and put a few more nails in. As if by a magic spell, she stood as still as a lamb.

The blood pressure of the lady dropped considerably, and Neville and Barry were happy with the outcome too. It did not take long to put the nails in, take the strap off and finish clenching the nails. We had a little struggle with the back leg, but after a while the horse settled in with a classic total surrender. The other two feet did not cause too much trouble. Whoopy learned her lesson pretty quick—*it is easier to do what these silly people want than to fight them and end up with a rope around the leg and jammed into the station wagon.*

'Storm' would best be described as very strong willed. He used to be called Stormy when he was a bit younger, but somehow it just sounded a bit too sweet for this 14.3 hand high pony. Dark bay in colour, he had a couple of white feet and a rather big blaze. A solid wide chest made his front legs stand apart, and with his head held high on a very strong neck he seemed to say, *"Come and get me if you like. Whatever you want to do with me, I will find ten reasons why I do not want to do it."*

I always find it amazing what horses can tell you if you are willing to listen.

"This one is going to be trouble, I feel it," I said to Neville, who just appeared from the farm, having closed the gate of the paddock where the cows were grazing.

"I thought so too, that's why he has been tied up here for a few hours now. I just got the cows in this morning and Storm was leaning over the gate, so I grabbed him and tied him up so that he will be nice and quiet for you. Well, that's the plan anyway. This is going to be one hell of a show jumping pony if we ever can get on top of him. We have been riding him for a few weeks now, but he finds his feet a bit tender on the farm races and does not want to go forward anymore," Neville said.

"He might appreciate a set of shoes then," I replied, hoping indeed that Storm would appreciate it if someone put some shoes on his feet.

Storm might have been tied up for a few hours, but he had not been happy about it. He had been pooping a lot and scattering it all around him. Underneath his front feet was some nice clean concrete where he had been pawing the ground. He looked at me with utter contempt, "Don't you come near me; you just leave me alone."

This was a case where it was wise to wait for the owner to approach the horse first. So when Neville touched Storm and told him all was well, it was my turn to approach him. I aimed for his right shoulder to touch him there first. When Storm saw me coming, he moved away as far as he could until his left side hit the wall. Can't go any further now, we both knew.

I gently touched his shoulder, but to Storm my touch was like an electric prodder so he shot forward, trying to jump over Neville who was caught off-guard and had to take a few steps backwards to prevent being run over. It was lucky then that Storm found the end of the lead rope, but this caused his bum to swing away from the wall towards me, so it was my turn to take evasive action.

That was a good start.

After trying a couple more times, Storm finally stood still long enough for me to touch his shoulder properly and tell him that everything would be all right.

He did not believe me.

After rubbing his shoulder for a while, the time had come to go a bit further and touch and rub the top of his leg. I could feel he did not like it, but he did not make a move as yet.

So, my hand slid lower to the fetlock joint, where I stopped to rub his bottom leg all over. Now it was only a matter of gently squeezing the tendon just above the fetlock joint between my thumb and first two fingers. As there was no reaction, I decided to use a little bit more force.

As fast as lightning he whipped his leg up so that his hoof literally hit his chest, squashing my hand in the process. Such a jerk of a movement like that gave me a hell of a fright—time out. I checked if my hand was still working like it should. Luckily for me, all was well, but only after a while

Neville commented that Storm had a very strong will and that he proved to be one of the hardest horses he had come across when it came to roping up his legs. As for the quickness in lifting up his leg, he said that Storm always did this, so I better be prepared. As Storm was getting used to me, it did not take long to come to the point of lifting his leg up. To prevent crushing injuries to my hand and wrist, I had to be so careful, especially when it came to the squeezing bit. Just as well I took precautions, because the leg came up like a tight spring released every time. When the hoof was up against the chest, almost in neutral mode, I grabbed it, and when there was no resistance, I stroked and patted it to see what would happen. Nothing did.

But his hoof was still tight against the chest, and I needed it in between my thighs. But there was no way Storm would release his hoof. For all I knew he was swearing to be left alone.

I had to use all my strength to pull it sideways, talking to him to reassure him that all was alright. I managed and rubbed his hoof against my apron to get him used to another new thing, after which I tried to get the hoof in between my thighs. But Storm thought I was going to kill him again and leaped forward with no respect for Neville or me, only stopping when the lead rope got too tight. At least something was working.

I tried again and again, until finally Stormy said, "OK, I will let you do whatever you want to do to me, but if I don't like it at any time, I will tell you by jumping forward again."

In a relative truce, I managed to clean his hoof and started to nip a little bit of the wall away. There was not a lot to remove as the horse was in work and had worn a lot of it off already. I was a little bit too forceful with the rasp, I suppose, because Storm took a mighty leap forward again, saying loud and clearly, "I told you to take it easy. Better still, just go away and leave me alone."

I was back to settling the horse down again, lifting the hoof up and this time slowly rasping the bottom of the hoof. Done... with a deep sigh of relief. Now, in slow motion the hoof had to go forward to rest on my knees so I could rasp the front and sides of the wall. Slowly does it, with no sudden movements or noises, and we would be just fine. Fine indeed was the result, and we were pleased to have one hoof dressed, ready to be fitted with a shoe. The clock told me that this one hoof took just over half an hour, so at that rate it would be two hours before I was able to put the shoes on. Though I had no other appointments, that day, something needed to change, because carrying on at that rate was just not enjoyable.

After the initial nervousness, the right back leg did not seem that badly behaved, as if it had a mind of its own. But pulling the leg forward to put on my knee while my backside was touching his belly was not Storm's idea of having fun. As quick as lightning he pulled his leg back and gave a beautiful kick in the air. Guess what, we would have to do it again until I could shape his foot into a nice-looking hoof. We tried a couple more times until Storm said that he would allow me to do it.

He became a little bit better with the third hoof to be trimmed, the left hind one. He still would put up a fight, just with less power. Alas, he found his old self again when I tried the left front one. I just had trouble getting near him. Forward, backwards, sideways...

he would move any direction to get away from me. If all else failed he would jump in the air as far as the lead rope would let him.

But eventually he seemed to get a little bit tired of playing this game and settled down enough for me to try and pick up his hoof. I was careful, knowing he might bring his leg up in a hurry like the other one. Indeed, this leg was just as fast, ending up hard against his chest, so I had to pull it away from his chest again and try hard to get it in between my thighs. We managed, but this still was incredibly hard work.

I reached for my stack of horseshoes to find the right size to put on his foot. To shape the shoe, I have to put it on the hoof to see if it fits. If not, I have to shape it on my anvil until it does. This time I had to go to the anvil only twice before the shoe was shaped according to the hoof and was ready to be put on. It was easy really —just put six nails through the shoe in the wall of the hoof and it would be done.

Before I put in the first nail, I tapped the shoe resting on the hoof with my hammer lightly just to see what happened. Exactly as I suspected, Storm snatched his leg back, reared up with the front feet as high as they could go, and when they were about to plunge down, it was like they were aiming for me. This was an unnerving experience to say the least, so I got out of the way in a hurry.

"Right," said Neville. "I have been thinking and have come to the conclusion that he misses his mate. His mate is next to the house, and there is a big latching rail there where I can tie Storm up to and put his mate on the other side. What do you think?" he asked.

"I think I am ready for a change. But you might have to bring your roping gear as well, as I fear I might not be able to put the shoes on without," I replied. I should have thought of a mate much earlier on when he was so unsettled after being tied up for a few hours. That might have saved a lot of hassle. I packed my gear away and drove the two hundred meters to the house while Neville led Storm with one hand and carried a bag in the other full of all the ropes and straps.

One welcome surprise was Neville's wife Lucy, who just came home and offered to make us a cup of tea. That would go down well. After Storm was tied up, Neville went to get the horse's mate and came back soon with his big grey hunter. Storm was happy to see him, and I fell in the trap of thinking that all would be well from now on. You would not believe that such a quiet pony could give us such a hard time. After a beautiful cup of tea—the harder the work, the nicer the cuppa—we went back to work. Neville shortened the lead rope a bit more, hopefully preventing the horse from rearing up. I left my shoeing box out of reach and grabbed the shoe and the driving hammer and put a few nails in my mouth, hoping I would not choke on them.

I picked up the hoof, placed the shoe in position and after just one light tap, the horse went berserk, trying all different directions to get away, except for pulling back. At least he had respect for the lead rope, which was almost an inch thick and probably the strongest one Neville could find.

Again, and again, I picked up the foot, placed a shoe on it, and gave it a tap and the horse started all over. The big grey solemnly looked at the spectacle unfolding in front of her eyes and decided not to get involved. She thought it rather boring and focused her attention on watching the grass grow.

Neville was getting a bit tired of it all too and very embarrassed, so he offered to put a leg strap on the foot in question.

"Yes please," I said, "we will have to do something else because this is going to take a long time. Desensitising is what we are trying to do, but it will take a long time as he can always get away, I can't hold him, he is way too strong for me."

It did not take Neville long to put on the front strap as Storm seemed to know the drill. With the leg firmly in place, I lightly tapped the hoof with my hammer, and to my surprise nothing happened. So I did it again but a little firmer; all good.

On went the shoe, the hammer tapped it and Storm went up in the air. When he returned to the ground again, I repeated the process half a dozen times, always making sure that I was standing safely away as Storm could cover ground in the strangest directions.

Finally, Storm gave in. That is to say I could hammer a shoe held loosely on the hoof without any flinching by him. You would think that putting in a nail would now be just a formality, that it would be nice and simple, really. Wrong. This is Storm we are talking about, and whatever I wanted to do with Storm would take ten times as long as any other horse. He did not like the first nail being driven into the hoof wall. Storm said that it was completely different than the previous hammering, and although it did not hurt physically, it really hurt him psychologically. He could not see why I could not understand him and stop what I was doing.

Poor Storm, and we still had such a long way to go.

Putting in a nail is relatively easy, permitting that the hoof is nice and still and you hit the nail exactly in the right spot. With every hit Storm flinched. He even started to anticipate the hit from the feelings he got from our body contact, flinching just before I hit the nail, resulting in a noisy miss which caused another flinch.

By sheer perseverance I managed to get all the nails in. Normally I would bring the leg forward to finish off the clenches, but to Storm that would probably be unacceptable.

I folded the clenches from this unusual position, and for good measure I ran the rasp over it to make it all feel and look smooth.

Neville undid the front leg strap and I asked him to put the back one on straight away as to try to get some routine going. It took a little bit of doing as Storm was not really inclined to cooperate with the strap being put on his back leg. Luckily, he was not a kicker; otherwise I would have given up a long time ago. He just did not want to stand still. He just did not want to be there. The relief of having his mate close by wore off the second we wanted to do something with him.

With the back-leg strap securely in place, I started the process of hammering a loose shoe on the hoof after taking some time to get hold of the leg: it was still amazing how much he could move around with one back leg tied up. It was one little tap with the hammer that sent him flying far away from me against the hitching rail. With his shoulder and bum against the rail, Neville and the lead rope at the front, and me on the side and the back, there were not a lot of places left for the horse to go. It was the ideal spot and situation to shoe a horse for the first time. Not to spoil this opportune moment, I did everything in slow motion with heaps of patting and nice words. But then again, the inevitable still had to happen. I decided to start the first nail, which I pushed in with my fingers as far as I could. Two quick little hits, I decided on, to be followed by a little break.

I managed to hit it once, and the second hit missed the hoof by a whole foot. Storm was on the move. The easiest way, he thought, was up in the air, and at his highest point he lashed out with his free back leg, hitting only air luckily, as I had darted away.

The shoe was dangling from the hoof, with the first nail only a little in the hoof, so we just had to try again. I lifted the hoof up, concentrated, and gave it another little tap.

Miracles do happen, I thought as nothing happened; another tap.

"That's it!" Storm said, "That is enough of this s#*! Just leave me alone will you?" and he started to push me around.

Neville had his hands full, making Storm behave. He shortened the lead rope a bit more until there was only a foot of rope for the horse to play with.

For a moment I had this weird vision that by the time we were finished, there would be a hundred ropes all over the horse to tie him against the hitching rail, and Storm would still escape them all like Houdini. Try again, we had to, though we could not afford to be angry or short-tempered. This was a marathon, not a hundred-metre sprint.

When nobody invaded his space, Storm was not too worried really, just standing there, almost sulking. When I approached him, his head rose up a bit higher, his muscles tensing up, ready for another fight. But we were winning. The first nail was almost home, so I decided to put in the second one. I had three goes at it and was happy with the result—two nails, we're now home.

It was time to relax, and by this I mean leisurely standing next to the horse, just tapping the shoe with my driving hammer and ignoring all the little tantrums, pulling away and the walkabouts.

I wished sometimes that horses like Storm would read the horse manual where they talk about desensitising and that it only takes a couple of minutes. Yeah, right. I could have had another cup of tea by now. I do believe, however, that horses do give in at some stage. Or you can call it 'give up' or 'surrender'. And Storm did just that after probably a quarter of an hour.

Suddenly, there was no reaction to my tapping with the hammer. It would be unwise to carry on doing this, so I lifted the leg on my lap and put another four nails in, just like that, and managed to change position to clench the nails as well.

Two down, two to go. Neville was getting excited too at the prospect of having all four shoes on. The odds were in our favour as long as we kept our cool and kept on trying.

He took the strap off the back leg, shifted the strap on the neck and tied up the other back one. The leather strap went around the leg, just above the hoof. The soft rope got secured in the shackle from the strap, and the other end went to the shackle on the wide leather strap around the horse's neck. Then it was only a matter of tightening the rope and putting a quick release knot in it. It was very safe for the horse and me.

I took the third shoe, put it on the hoof and slightly tapped it. There was no reaction from Storm, which I thought a bit odd after all we had been through. I took a nail and placed it in the right spot as the shoe seemed to fit pretty well to the hoof. I gave it one reasonable tap this time, expecting the worst, but again there was no reaction to speak of. I hit the nail again, and like before, nothing happened. I knew there was more to come, but for now the best philosophy was to take things as they were, so I relaxed, putting the nails in one by one, just like a normal horse. We were having a really good time until the last nail. Storm gave me a split-second warning, just enough time to wake me up from my relaxed state. He let fly with the tied-up leg, which did not really work well, so his other leg tried to join, which was no good as he nearly fell down. He regained his composure and started hopping from left to right like he had done all day long. It is hard to change habits.

The second he stood still I wandered over, picked the leg up, put the nail in and finished the clenches. Just like that. We are making good time now. After Neville put the front strap on the leg, I approached the horse again with a new shoe in hand to do the same old thing again. First, I checked if it fitted... almost, but not good enough. So I went back to the anvil to hammer it into the right shape and check again. The shaping was a bit overdone, so it was back to the anvil. This time it did fit, and all I had to do was put in the nails and the ordeal would be over.

"I might as well see what happens," I said to Neville. "We haven't got a lot to lose, have we?"

Neville agreed wholeheartedly. "I think he will be all right now.

I certainly would give up by now, I think."

"Yes, we would, but hey, we are not horses, are we?" I replied, as I put the first nail in place and then put the hammer to the nail, prepared for the worst. Since no reaction happened, I relaxed a bit and put the other nails in.

But Storm would not do his name justice if he did not do something. The second to last nail was almost completely in when he threw a wobbly, not with all of his might, but still scary enough. He tried to lift himself up on his back legs, but the lead rope was too short. He changed tack quickly to shy sideways into me while I was retreating. He then pretended to get a fright from me and shied the other way. It's hard to be a horse. When he settled down, I hammered the last nail home and put in the final nail and finished the hoof. In record time the last little bit was finished.

Neville was ecstatic now that the shoes were finally on. Lucy was over the moon as well and praised my patience; a job well done. She gave us a beer to celebrate that the shoes were on. Because of all the hard physical work, the frustration of handling a horse with an enormous attitude, a horse that can't stand still and caused us many scary and dangerous moments, it must be said that this was one of the finest beers I ever drank. I enjoyed every sip immensely and was very happy and relieved this ordeal was over, but kept on wondering if Storm was happy. He just stood there quasi-relaxed, contemplating life, so I thought he would be alright.

Shoeing Storm improved quickly in the next half year, but he would always stay a strong-willed horse. Neville's son did very well show jumping Storm, and later took him out hunting. After that, Lucy started to ride him for pleasure and continued to hunt him for many a year. To Storm, I was the only one ever to shoe him, from his first shoe until his retirement. All in all, shoeing Storm was the longest time it had ever taken me to shoe a horse (not counting Fella, the first horse I ever shod) three hours in total, the cup of tea break not included. This record would stand for the rest of my career, and the feat has been brought up many a time while shoeing for Neville and Lucy.

12
Wellsford

Marianne and her husband Bill were proud owners of a Hereford stud near Wellsford. They had a runoff down the road, but it was a bit hard getting around there with the quad bike or the tractor. So that is when the horse came in handy. When working stock, the horse was in her element. Sorting out the bulls, some would be going to the works; she was as natural as a Quarter horse. Because she was a Thoroughbred horse doing a lot of road riding, she had to have some shoes on. Marianne was a mature lady who loved the pretty cruisy farm life, as they were well under-stocked, and she enjoyed her golf as well as her horse riding.

When there was no stock work to be done, she rounded up two of her neighbours. "Come on, let's go horse riding." And off the three of them went, hurried on by Marianne, who liked to cover some miles. The other two horses were barefoot and very picky where they put their feet. Once in the paddock they were all in their element.

Once I was a bit early; it happens sometimes. I watched Marianne walk in the paddock where the horse was, but I could not see a horse anywhere. She moved around the trees in the far distance while I got my gear sorted. They would be a while, I thought, it looked like a big walk.

To my surprise they were back very quickly. Marianne was riding her horse, cover and all, bridled up (I think she did not even own a halter and lead rope), and they both looked very happy.

"Wow," I said, "that did not take you long, did it? How in hell did you manage to get on?" I asked.

"Not easy," she replied. "The days of jumping on are well and truly gone, I'm afraid to say. She likes being caught, so all I had to do was to park the horse next to a log or bank and then hop on—easy really."

Not a rider myself, I wondered about the word 'easy', but then Marianne would have had a few years' experience, no doubt. While shoeing her horse, she revealed that her big 80th birthday was coming up that weekend with a bit of a get together with family and friends. Eighty, and still riding up hill and down dale, urging her friends on to keep up with her, though they were many years her junior, Marianne can be an inspiration for us all.

Whenever Marianne called (she did not have a mobile to text) I would be there as soon as I possibly could. There was no way I wanted to stop her from living life to the fullest.

She was a nice and quiet horse, I put shoes on her feet for years now, but today there was something terribly wrong. She was a mature Appaloosa mare with a sweet laid-back nature. But today she just would not stand still. Anything I asked of her was too much.

She did not like any of her feet picked up, let alone trimmed and reshod. I battled on, thinking she would give in soon as they normally did. The owner Desiree, a sweet and kind lady herself, could not work it out either.

"You know what?" I asked her. "What if you make us a nice cuppa tea? Maybe a little time out will help the horse settle down, and besides, we could do with a break as well."

"Good idea, I will make it right now." Off she went inside the house just a couple of steps away.

I never ask the owner for a cup of coffee, that's just not me, but in this case, I wanted to find out if the owner had something to do with the behaviour of the horse. I carried on for a while and came to the conclusion that the owner had nothing to do with it. The horse still played up. Even if I did nothing, the horse still was not happy, moving the legs all the time without trying to get away with a bit of head tossing and twitching of the skin around her chest. It was a total mystery to me.

Desiree came back with a cup of tea. "Did you change her feed suddenly?" I asked.

"No, the feed has been exactly the same; she did not even have a fresh paddock or anything like that. She certainly behaves as if she had too much tucker or something: she seems to be full of beans," she said, sounding and looking very worried. "I don't know what it is," she said, but she is definitely not her own usual self. How are you getting on?"

"I can manage, but it will take a little longer, that's all," I replied. After the cuppa I was back into it, trying to be as quiet as I could. I did manage, and I expressed the hope that the horse would soon be well again.

By chance I met Desiree a week later at the local Four Square in Wellsford.

"You would not believe what happened," she started. I was going to say something, but before I could, she continued.

"That evening, just after seven I think, I thought I better go and check on my mare. Just as well: She was lying on the ground thrashing around. After watching that for a little while, I knew there was something terribly wrong so I rushed inside and rang the vet. I rushed back out to see if I could put a halter on my mare and try to settle her down a bit. The vet did not take long, I did have a halter on the horse, which finally stopped thrashing but was still lying down. The vet went about his business rather thoughtfully and thoroughly. But he could not do enough while she was lying down. He asked if we could try to stand her up, and surprisingly she was eager to stand on her feet again. He took what I thought was a very long time asking all sorts of questions. Then he was silent for a while, and finally he said:

"I think, but I am not completely sure, she has got an acute selenium deficiency. The most severe case I have ever seen. It affects her nervous system; most horses are a bit low in selenium as there is just not enough of it in the grass. I will give her a dose in her blood now to make her feel better very quickly. After I have done that, I want you to check her again at (looking at his watch) ten o'clock and if she does not improve, I will come out and give her some other drugs to get her through the night."

"I checked her at ten and you will not believe it—my old horse was back again. You know she is always pretty well laid back, never in too much hurry. No nervousness or spookiness at all like before. Oh, I was so rapt and thankful to the vet," she said. She looked so happy.

The barber rang me. He used to have a beautiful looking, well-mannered Percheron gelding. Some horses seem to make such an impression on you that when you close your eyes for a second, you can see them in all their glory. This was one of them.

It was a few years ago since he had sold the horse, and I wondered if he had bought himself another horse. But instead of the normal horse talk, he talked bull.

"I have got a lame bull, and I think you are just about the only one who can fix him," he said.

Of course, it is a compliment, but wait a minute, I don't have any qualification as a vet. And come to think of it, the last cow I trimmed I cut off too much of the toe and made it bleed, so I can't really see why he wanted me.

"Why don't you call the vet," I asked. "They can give them some nice painkilling drugs and some antibiotics and what have you."

"I can't get him in the yard, he is that fricking lame that he spends the whole day lying about, and I am getting a bit worried really. The vet won't come unless he is in the yard. Occupational Health and Safety act, you know."

"I don't want to get killed either," I said.

"Look here," he said," I won heaps of prizes with this bull, I have been to a lot of A&P shows and he has never let me down. I really would appreciate it if you could have a look at him. I live in Wellsford now, not far from the main road."

You would not believe it, but I was just going to Wellsford the very next day, so I gave him a time. As he was busy that whole day, and he did not really stop for lunch either, I said I was going to have a look by myself.

The bull was big, huge, enormous, as purebred as can be, Hereford, with a record of his family history of probably a mile long. He would have looked even bigger if he was standing up, but luckily for me he was lying down. Well, actually it looked uncomfortable as he seemed to be somewhere between sitting up and lying down against a little rise no more than a foot high. You would be amazed at how much difference these little things can make. The yard was on the other side of the paddock, too far for a lame bull to walk.

There was only one chance, and that was trimming his feet right here and now while he was sitting up / lying down.

But I would have to do the sore one first; otherwise I would run out of time. But which one? Did the barber tell me? Did I forget? Why do things like this always happen?

It was plain obvious that it was the front left. It had to be the left as the bull was lying on his right side. The back right was sort of stuck against a little lump, enough to push his left shoulder off the ground a bit to help ease the pain.

Left front, so obvious.

It was time to get close and personal, so I finally got into touching distance and held my hand in front of his wet nostrils so he could have a smell of me. This was one big head full of curly white hair, and although the bull seemed friendly and quiet, I still had to be prepared for the unexpected, so I planned my escape route. Bulls, stags and stallions—respect them and watch them all the time.

Before I touched the foreleg, I was thinking what would be the easiest and quickest way to find the problem. I could not make up my mind what exactly should be the sequence of my actions, so I just lifted the hoof up gently. Wow, that was one big foot with two enormous toes with nails just way too long.

That made my mind up in a hurry: Just trim the nails of both toes and then put the hoof tester on it and see where he was sore. We did not have to wait very long. As I was cutting the wall with my hoof nippers, I must have touched the edge of a stone bruise, as a wet spot formed on the outside of the outer toe. So with the hoof nippers I cut a little V where the spot was and a lot of pus oozed out from the pressure behind it. Immediately the bull let out the loudest sigh in the whole wide world, which gave me such a fright, that I instantly let go of the leg. The bull must have felt an enormous relief as the throbbing pain suddenly stopped and he sighed a few more times which almost sounded like a thank you.

If I don't do anything else, I still can be pleased with myself.

I managed to open the hole a bit more and rinsed it with a syringe of water and Iodine. At least I was prepared. The first part was done.

The other front leg was firmly wedged underneath the big red body, but the hoof was just sticking out far enough to allow his excess hoof to be cut off. It was simple, really. But then I was on to the back feet.

Have you ever been to a rodeo? Did you see how many people and clowns there are to take the bull's attention if someone is in trouble? All I had was the word of the barber that the bull was quiet. One kick of the back hoof in my face and I would be a goner. He could have stood up within two seconds, in which time I could not be at the nearest fence to jump it. Have you ever seen a bull charging a human on foot like in Spanish bullfighting? All the things you can think of when approaching the back feet of a 800 kilogram five or six-year-old bull lying down in the middle of a paddock just outside of Wellsford, with no neighbours in sight and without modern aids like cell phones.

To go back to basics, all I had was feelings, the feelings I get from the bull by observation and touch. They, like horses and maybe a lot of other animals, release stress signals in their body that can be picked up by our body by sheer physical contact.

I touched the bull's left hind leg first and did not feel any anxiety or fear, so I managed to get those overgrown toenails cut off. I had the feeling that the bull regarded me as a saviour—the one who took the pain in his hoof away. The right hind one was half tucked under his body. I managed to do the inside toe not too bad, but the other one was too far under his belly. By scraping a little hole in the dirt underneath the hoof, I managed to do the outside toe as well. The whole time, the bull did not move. He really must have appreciated the opening up of the feverish abscess.

I straightened up, said bye-bye to the bull and wished him an early recovery.

On the way back, I looked over my shoulder a few times, just to make sure he was still lying there and not chasing me.

13

Warkworth

There was a pony waiting to be trimmed, tied up next to the shed a little past the house, but the lady stopped me way before I got there. It was the first time I had been there, and after introducing each other I was ready to go. But she wasn't yet. She talked about how nice a day it was, how long I had been doing this job, whether or not I enjoyed it and she just kept on going.

I soon got the impression that I was being vetted, to see if I was good enough to trim the feet of what was probably her pride and joy.

At the first lull in the conversation, I asked, "Shall we have a look at the pony then?"

"I want you to create a good bond with Polly the pony," she replied. "The last farrier and the pony did not get on together at all, and the farrier before that either. I would like you to have a good understanding of the pony, to take your time, to make it an event very relaxing for her. I hope that she does not get stressed or excited or angry as she did with the last farrier," she said.

"Like I said on the phone, I will have a look and take it from there," I said, and wanted to go over to the pony, but still had no such luck yet.

"I have got a little bucket of baby carrots here, maybe you can give them to her to create a nice bond for the two of you?" she asked.

"When we are finished, I would love to give her some carrots," I said. "When we are finished."

She looked a bit disappointed with my reply but finally, I was allowed to walk in the direction of the pony.

Polly just stood there, relaxed as if she had been there tied up for half a day. Probably ten hands high, chestnut with a good woolly coat of hair as winter was on its way. When I was ten metres away, she slowly turned her head around so she could look at me with both her eyes through her overlong forelock. After five more metres, I slowed my pace considerably and stopped beside the pony.

Even though Polly did not seem to take any interest in me, she watched every move I made, every step I took and listened to my voice. She did exactly what her owner did a few minutes ago. She checked me out. She put all the information she gained about me in her computer brain and simply concluded that I did not pose any danger to her.

With my right hand I touched her right shoulder, and I felt that she would let me work on her feet. I let her sniff my hand and knew that all was well.

Polly felt my touch on her shoulder and interpreted it in a positive manner. The smell of the back of my hand probably told her more than I probably could imagine.

The smell told her that I was a male, did not wash my hands since seven o'clock that morning, handled seven other horses before coming here (one of them her mate down the road) but above all, that I did not pose any harm to her.

I picked her right front foot up, and without any problem whatsoever, I managed to trim the hoof and the other three after that in a matter of twenty minutes.

The lady was over the moon. "Polly is so much different than last time." she said. "She was rearing up and kicking and biting, it was horrible. I think that Polly really likes you. I hope you don't mind coming back next time?"

I watched her give the fresh washed baby carrots to Polly and said, "I don't mind coming back next time; she is a really well behaved pony. I suspect the other farriers were a bit in a hurry or their personalities clashed with that of Polly, I don't know. She is a nice pony." After a few more pleasantries I made an appointment for the next time and left to see another customer.

For a long time I tried to work out what really happened with the last two farriers. Were they really in a hurry and did Polly take offence to that? Did they try to lift Polly's legs up too high? Or did they simply have no patience, understanding, or a little respect for Polly and how she would like to be treated?

But maybe Polly decided for herself that she would play up for the last two farriers for reasons only known to her. It sure is possible as horses have their good and bad days, sometimes due to the weather, or too much, or not enough feed, or simply a different time of the day to upset their normal routine.

Then of course the lady herself might be part or cause of the problem without even knowing it. What if she was not feeling very well that day or took an instant dislike to the farrier for whatever reason, her mood change would be instantly picked up by Polly who would not like the farrier either.

All in all, there are too many variables.

With some understanding and a bit of patience I managed to trim Polly's feet and had to conclude that she was a very well behaved pony.

"Very simple," she said. "It is impossible to lift his near hind leg up, so don't even bother. I will pay you for trimming four anyway."

I simply trimmed three feet, accepted the money and busy as I was, I went to the next customer.

The next visit, though, I did have a bit more time, so I decided to try lifting up the near hind leg. The pony was not that big, but a bit chubby. It was amazing how much weight he could put on one foot. It was just as if he was lifting the other three feet at the same time to put all the weight on the near hind.

I guess she said it right; it was impossible.

The third time was my lucky time. I was a bit early and caught the pony in his small paddock behind the shed. I walked him over to the gate, carefully watching how he was walking, and I was surprised that he was walking very well. See, before watching his gait, I had the impression that he must have had an injury or something physically stopping him from lifting his leg. But for an old pony he was very free moving. By the time the lady got there, I had finished the three feet and reported on my findings. I asked if I could give it one more go. I made sure that the lady was in the right place in front of the pony, the pony nice and relaxed on the flattest piece in the paddock and myself, in what I hoped to be the right spot, with the tools in my right hand. If this was going to happen, I probably only had one chance, so it better be a good one. With my back to the lady and hunched to the pony's level, focused on the hind leg, I asked the lady to move the pony one step forward. She pulled a little bit on the lead rope and the pony started moving. My biggest worry was that the pony would move too quickly, but this one was in no hurry.

As he lifted his near hind leg, I grabbed it with my left hand. The plan was just to hold it at any height the pony was happy with and hang on to it if he was going to move off.

At the moment I got hold of the hoof, the poor pony got such a fright that he moved sideways in a flurry of steps, but I managed to hang on and follow the pony so as not to put any extra strain on the leg. When he stood still, I released my pressure, just enough to hold on, and started stroking his leg to give him a bit more reassurance that all was well. The pony was caught, physically but more importantly emotionally. He was as good as gold to have his foot trimmed.

The next time we did the same, waiting until he took a step, and then quickly picking his hoof up. He has been good ever since.

She did warn me, I must say that. But it still came as a big shock.

The Pinto horse had an offside back leg that she did not like to pick up. Whether the horse was three or four or five years old was of no significance, because it was simply ready to start being ridden.

The first time I was there, just before Christmas, the partner of the lady owner was holding the horse with one hand and a cold beer the other. It was that time of the day.

I finished the offside front leg, and almost with a sweeping motion I started lifting the hind leg on the same side, dreaming of being home in a couple of hours to enjoy a nice cold beer myself.

As often happens when your mind is wandering off, things went wrong. The horse did lift its foot up for me, but lifted it too high, making it hard to hold on to, and a little higher again, so I let go. When the foot managed to touch its belly, the horse appeared wobbly, suddenly lost her balance and slammed the foot on the ground, causing the rest of her body to follow the leg and all the weight of the whole back end of the horse came slamming into me. Because of its momentum, the horse had to take another step before she could stand still again.

It gives me a hell of a fright when the horse shunts towards me. Almost a hundred percent of the horses I handle go away from me in the case of a fright of any kind. When the horse can't hold its own weight anymore, and this two or three hundred kilogram back end comes towards you as if falling over, it is a rather unnerving experience. You have to get your footing perfect to get out of the way quick enough before the horse lands on you.

Recovering from this near mishap, I turned to the handler, who happily took another sip of his beer.

"I don't think I am going to lift this one up," I said to him.

He merely replied, "I don't think so either," with a tone as if he really did not care one way or another.

But for good measure, I had to try again, if only to see whether this was a 'one off' instance or if the horse was always going to do it. I was a little more prepared this time, but the result was almost the same; however, the crushing force came at me even faster this time.

Two frights within five minutes were enough for me, thank you, so I tried the other back leg. Expecting the same response, I was surprised to find the horse well behaved. It was almost unbelievable. The front one was also very good.

The owner came back and said she was not surprised and not too worried. The horse did this to her as well, and the last farrier could only trim three feet as well.

The next time was exactly the same. I just could not resist trying, just to make sure that it was not a one-off episode.

On the third time I asked if I could rope the leg up a bit, and the owner did not mind, so I found myself a nice soft rope and put it around the leg. Before it was in the right place, the horse told me in no uncertain terms that I had gone way too far, and she started to lash out at the rope and anything that came too close. After she settled down, I tried again to put the rope on, and this time it took a bit longer as the horse was on the top of her nerves.

I managed to get one end of the rope between the hind legs and managed to retrieve it with my rasp. Quietly I gathered the rope so that it rested just above the hoof and started to apply a bit of pressure. After a while, the horse finally started to lift the leg, and I held it there for a little while just above the ground while stroking the top of her leg. Then I lifted the leg a little bit higher, and the horse still let me carry on, so I took the hoof in my hand, relaxed, and slowly put it on my lap. I could not believe it, it felt so good.

The lady passed me my nippers, and in a record time I managed to trim the hoof, all the while making sure that any movement and change of position was done as slowly and fluently as could be. The end result was rewarding—this was no longer a three-legged horse.

She was almost a head taller than I was, and maybe twice as heavy. She looked a bit heavier than Valery Adams, and like her, she was as strong as an ox. Wherever they organised strong man and woman competitions, she would be there, throwing hay bales around or carrying beer kegs a certain distance, never making a fool of herself.

Hillary was the giant's name and she had a lovely darling old giant Clydesdale-cross horse, which used to be as strong as her, but was lately showing her age a little bit.

Today, the mare was as lame as could be, very reluctant to put any weight on the sore right front hoof. Hillary had heard a lot about stone bruises, abscesses and lame horses in general, but in the few years she had owned horses, none of them ever got lame. So I told her she was lucky. While cleaning the hoof, she took a keen interest, watching every move I made as I progressed into this overgrown hoof. When I was happy with the look of the bottom of the hoof, I dressed the front of the hoof as well, in case I might have not gotten around to doing it for some reason. That finished, it was time to put the hoof in between my thighs and put the hoof testers to work, to hopefully show me where the hoof was sore by applying pressure on a small part of the hoof at a time. It was pretty obvious that the infected area was in the toe, five centimetres left from the middle as the horse flinched from the pressure put on the spot.

It was time to put my freshly sharpened hoof knife to work. While she watched intently from very close by, I cut a sliver from the sole. The horse reacted with a flinch again as it must have hurt. My observation told me I was in the right spot as I could see a bit of black in the sole where no black should have been. All it needed was another sliver to be taken off the sole in the same spot, which I did.

Bingo. The abscess must have been brewing and ready to pop, because the creamy brown puss was forced out in a nice little arc and landed directly on the face of poor Hillary. The horse let out a sigh of pure relief. It took a split second for Hillary to become aware of an incredible horrible and nasty smell coating her face. The smell was so bad that she involuntarily vomited, right there and then, not even having time to turn around. The smell of the puss was rotten, but together with the smell of Heather's vomit I had to declare the place unfit to work in and walked away. The horse was happy just to stand there for a while, glad that the feverish pressure in her hoof was released.

Hillary was slowly coming to terms with what just happened and started cleaning her face using water from the nearby trough, slowly regaining all her senses. "That was absolutely horrible," she said, "Disgusting. And the smell was so bad; I would not wish it on anybody."

I said, "Sorry about that, you were just a little bit too close."

"But what a force behind that stream, it was like a water pistol, and there was a lot of it too," she said.

"It could have been as much as a tablespoon full, one of the worst ones I have had to deal with. If you like, we can have a look at the foot and see what the hole looks like," I replied. "But instead of me going to the horse, you better bring him here, please. It's a little bit smelly over there."

She brought the horse over, and with my hoof knife I carved the hole a bit bigger to reveal a big cavity next to the wall. It was maybe 20 millimetres deep and extended underneath the outer sole towards the toe, as well as towards the heel. In time the hoof would shred a lot of the sole.

As could be expected, the whole area was very sensitive, but now the pressure was relieved, the inflammation in the hoof would disappear, and everything would start to heal again.

Tomorrow the horse would be walking around just fine again.

Hillary would be able to tell her horsey mates a story of how she witnessed the farrier open up a stone bruise.

"That is really good that you will travel this far to trim my donkey's feet. I just need to know a few days in advance, so that I can book the vet in to sedate him," she said over the phone. This sounded very interesting, to say the very least. It could be very dangerous too.

"I am willing to come and have a look," I said "but I would not call the vet. It sounds a bit extreme, it costs a lot of money and do you do that every time?"

"Yes I did, as the farrier would not do him without sedation," she said.

We arranged a date and a time right there and then, and when

I got there a few days later, on time, the donkey was tied up in a small pen. That made me happy from the start. Two positives: a pen and a donkey tied up. At least we would not have to catch him in a 10-acre paddock or something.

While I walked over to the donkey, the owner tried to tell me all about him. He was a rescue donkey, and she'd had him for a couple of years now. She did not do anything with him except tie him up now and then to give him a brush. There was no way she would lift the feet up or anything like that. But the donkey just enjoyed his life here, really. The last farrier was getting a bit old and short tempered, and he really did not want to do him anymore. She had heard through the grapevine that I had a lot of patience and was very quiet with donkeys.

So there I was, starting by spending some time letting the donkey smell me. I rubbed the left side of the neck, then his shoulder, all with the back of my left hand. I kept on rubbing it all the way to the hoof. There was still no reaction, so I shifted my hand so that the fetlock was covered by my palm. Since nothing continued to happen, I moved my hand up a little bit and put the big tendon in between my thumb and forefinger. Still, nothing happened, so I gently started squeezing it. I put more and more pressure on and would not let go until something happened. It did not take long before the donkey lifted his foot up and I started doing my work. It was obvious the donkey had had this done to him a lot of times, so he was well used to it, really.

The front feet were so good to handle that I knew they did not warrant a visit from the vet, so the trouble must have been with the back ones. After finishing the front one, I put all my attention on the hind left. I started rubbing his neck again with my left hand, to the shoulder, along the side towards his bum; all good. Now all I had to do was maintain contact all the way to the hoof, and then lift it up.

It is incredibly important where your own feet are in relation to the donkey's legs. It is not too hard to visualise that when you bend your back, your head will also go down, and if you are not careful, your head will be in the firing line of the donkey's hooves. That is a nasty experience, which I had already found out the (very) hard way.

There was nothing left to do but lower my hand slowly down the leg… I came to the widest part of the hip when the donkey kicked—not a kick to kill a fly, but a kick to break bones—so quickly it was incredible.

Though these reactions are always bad for my nerves, I had to do it again, unfortunately with the same response: a massive kick.

"So that is what you think of it," I said with as much conviction and experience as I could muster, as it did give me a bit more confidence, and it showed to the owner that I was a relaxed professional who knew what he was doing. All I knew for sure is that I did not want to be kicked, so I had to find a way around the problem. I needed a stick, one as long as a walking stick. The owner looked a bit alarmed, so I smiled and said, "Rest assured, I won't hit your donkey."

I stepped beside the donkey again, and using the lead rope, I put the donkey exactly where I wanted him. My left hand loosely held the rope while my right hand rested the stick gently on the donkeys back at the shoulder. I slowly moved it towards his tail. At the hip I would veer down towards the leg and got the anticipated result—a quick kick. The hoof smacked a solid rail of the pen with considerable noise, but there was not the slightest expression on the donkey's face. If my hand or leg were between the hoof and the rail, there would be nothing left of it.

I just repeated the action endlessly. I knew the donkey would give up. I just did not know when. But I was prepared and had allowed plenty of time for this customer.

It seemed like a long time, but it was probably only ten minutes or so. After every kick, I would put the stick back on the bum and lower it down the leg. I managed to reach all the way to the hoof before he kicked. A few more times and there would be no more kicks. There were a lot of marks on the rail but it would not break.

With the stick I touched the outside of the hoof, and I touched the inside of the hoof, and there was no more kick. I had desensitised the donkey. Using the stick as an extension of my arm was much safer and easier than using my arm at the expense of all my back, shoulder and neck muscles.

Still, I had to pick the leg up somehow. The easiest way was to lift the front leg like before but hold it in my right hand extended in front of my own legs. My left hand touched the left side of the donkey, going from hip to hoof. As there was no kick, I let the front leg go and ever so gently squeeze the tendon of the back leg and to see what happened.

What happened was exactly what was supposed to happen: the donkey lifted his foot up. So I quietly proceeded to trim his hoof without any hassle.

He had a few kicks with the other back leg but gave in very easily, and the other front one was all right.

The owner was extremely happy, and so was I. Mission accomplished. But even better was how over the next three visits, the kicking went down to zero. He made a full turnaround from being a very nasty kicker to a very pleasant likeable donkey.

I turned into Kaipara Flats Rd only to be stopped by Roger MacKenzie from Warkworth Horse Riding. His indicator lights were flashing and an arm was signalling out of the window, begging me to stop. Luckily there was just enough room for my Ute to move over.

WARKWORTH

"I have been trying to get hold of you for some time," he said.

"You succeeded. What can I do for you?" I asked, knowing what he wanted anyway. "Well, my farrier is leaving for Australia, and now I am in the s#*!. I don't know what to do and who to turn to or who to ask.

"You know, first I had Jared Polwarth shoeing for me, and that was good as he just lives down the road. Then Roland Johnson came, and he was good. He was coming twice a week, and we knew exactly what we were up to. Like I said, he left for Australia, but we were lucky as James Downer took over. He is good too, but he can't come for a little while, and we are still very busy with our trekking business."

"Sounds a bit like me," I said, "still very busy. But if you are stuck for a little while, I will help you. I hate to think that these Japanese tourists can't enjoy the horse riding and the scenery because the horses don't have any shoes on. As a matter of fact, I shod a couple of your horses quite a few years ago when you were stuck as well." Come to think of it, he still looked the same after all these years, but that was probably because he was still wearing the same old blue bib front overalls.

Roger probably could not remember I had helped him out before as he did not reply to that, but he thanked me sincerely for the offer. He would let me know. He started talking about the farriers again, who were still here and who had left him and how many horses he had with shoes on, how many customers were coming through and about this and about that as the time was marching on.

"Look here Roger, I am back here again on Friday. If you want some horses done, let me know Thursday night. Leave a message on Sunday if you want me next week." I hoped this would focus his mind on the future and enable me to move on to the next customers. Roger was over the moon, as if all his prayers were answered.

He was, in fact, a very religious man. Yes, yes, he would let me know and thanks and more thanks and see you later.

He rang the land line on Thursday morning just after I left, waking my wife who did not really appreciate this phone call just after seven in the morning. He left a voice message on my cell phone a little later as I must have been out of reach. I rang him back and got his answer phone... musical chairs. A few more times we missed each other, but finally at night I texted him to let him know I would be there tomorrow, Friday, from two until four p.m.

I arrived, and I was in a little bit of a hurry, or focused, I suppose. I had two, maybe three hours left to do whatever I could do for these people who momentarily did not have a farrier. So it was that I drove the wrong way around the tanker loop, just as Roger's wife Heather was leaving on horseback with a group of Asians for a horse trek. She told me off for driving the wrong way around and if I could please stop the engine so the group could leave. She had no trouble hopping on her horse even though she must be close to retirement age, and she had no trouble closing the gate behind her while mounted either.

Then Roger came, and he also told me off for driving the wrong way around the tanker loop.

"Shall I back my Ute up to the horse there?" indicating a horse, tied up in what looked like a nice shoeing bay, with its concrete pad and nice solid rails in a U-shape.

"No, no, we have got a system going here," Roger said.

"Well, let's hear it, time is marching on," I replied.

"Whenever you come," Roger began, "you drive that way around the tanker loop, stop there, and back up in here," his arms going all directions before they disappeared between two sheds, his body following, me too. Behind this alleyway was a courtyard where five horses were tied up, all on concrete, too... beautiful.

"I will get the Ute," I said, and was soon backing the Ute up. It only just fitted in between the two sheds. On Roger's say so, I went forward a little, as it seemed to matter exactly where the Ute was.

I was ready to do some work, so I put my apron on, took my shoeing box out and grabbed the tripod. "Just give me a horse, please," I felt like saying. But this introduction, or was it induction... was not over yet.

"These are the horses, and this is where we shoe them. We have got a system going here, and it works," Roger said, very much in his element.

Opening a little door in the wall, he pointed to an old nail box, full of horse shoes, mainly new ones. "That's probably all you need for the moment. Roland Johnson at times sold us a whole lot of shoes, so we always got some in stock. And over here, supposedly hanging on this nail, see on this nail, right here sticking out of the corrugated iron wall, is supposed to hang a clipboard. Before we go any further, I better go and get it for you, otherwise we don't know what we are doing and our whole system will turn to custard."

That is the last thing I wanted, but time was marching on, as ever. I was a bit worried about these five horses tied up before me, compared to the two or three horses that Roger booked in. It was Friday afternoon, and I was in a hurry because I had to go out that night to someone's birthday party. Yet nothing could be done until the clipboard arrived so we could see what we were dealing with.

Roger came back with his clipboard, on which was a sheet of paper with the names of five horses and what each of them needed doing:

Torpy: shoe 2 F, trim 2 B; (F is for Front, B is for back)
Star: shoe 2 F, shoe 2 B.
Comanche: shoe LB, lost (L is for left)
Harry: shoe 2 B,
Silver: shoe LF, RB (R is for right)
A wonderful system really... foolproof.

With every horse's name, Roger pointed to a certain horse, and found himself surprised that one of the horses on the list was not in the yard, until he realised that his wife was riding that one on the trek.

"Before we go any further, how much do you charge?" he asked. I told him how much, and he replied that the other two farriers charged twenty dollars less per horse.

"My price is GST inclusive," I added, to which he replied that he did not know if the others were GST inclusive, but he would find out. It was time now to get started.

Roger had one look at the list and concluded that we might as well start with Star, the name clearly inspired by the nice white star on his forehead. I might have even recognised this horse from the list when no one was here.

This horse could have been finished already if we were a bit more on the ball, I was thinking, but tried to feel relieved that we were finally working.

"Frans is just starting on Star," Roger said. Not quite knowing who he was talking to, it was time to keep my mind on my job.

"That's good," came a reply, sounding a bit metallic. "Remember when you do Torpy to tell Frans not to nail the front while the foot is in between his thighs." Then I got it, it was Heather talking through a walkie talkie. Well, who would have thought?

"Will tell him," Roger said to the walkie talkie. "First shoe off and foot dressed. He is starting on the back one now."

This promised to be a lengthy shoeing session if the commentary kept going like this "We are very lucky to have him, Heather," Roger said, quickly followed by his wife's reply:

"We are."

For an instant I had to think about those Asians on their horse ride. They might be getting annoyed with all this walkie talkie stuff, maybe they just wanted to get away from it all and have a good old quiet time in nature.

Strangely enough, the shoes did not fit as they were too small. The last farrier had a different way of shoeing, in my mind the heels of the hoof were way too long, which would make the hoof stand very upright. I lowered the heels, and suddenly the shoe was too small. There were no suitable shoes in the box, but I had plenty in mine. Without too much effort the horse was nicely shod and the horse had a natural stance about him. Roger could not quite believe that they did not fit.

When Heather came back a little while later, he had to show her the shoe that came off and the new one, just put on. Heather was not too worried.

Her horse had a little problem too; she told me all about it as I was just about to start nailing the shoe on.

"Whatever you do, don't put the hoof in between your thighs when you are nailing. She just does not like it, and everything takes twice as long, and the horse gets very upset," she said.

I told her that I would follow her advice and nail the shoe on holding the front hoof in my hand. All went well, although a bit awkwardly.

After that horse it was time to look at the clock and see what else I could do. I told Heather that I had time for another two shoes to replace, front or back, it did not matter. Heather picked another horse, and soon it was time for me to go. I said I was sorry I could not do any more, but if need be, I could be back Tuesday next week. When I was done, Roger was back as well, and they both thanked me very much and promised that if they needed me, they would let me know early next week.

I came back the next week, drove the right way around the tanker loop, backed the Ute up in between the sheds, looked on the clipboard and knew exactly what needed to be done. Roger and Heather could not run their business without the expert help from

Lily and Lara, two very capable young ladies. They were very good with horses and customers and kept on supplying me with horses to be shod, always making sure the feet were clean. I came back the week after that as well. Weeks turned into months and they turned into years.

Roger and Heather always appreciated the work I did and thanked me over and over again. But the biggest satisfaction I got was just looking out of the shoeing bay to where the customers were coming and going. From little schoolgirls to mature Japanese people, they got a real thrill out of their horse riding. For some of them it would be a lifelong dream to finally ride a horse, and the smiles of all these happy people I will never forget as it sure makes my job all the more fulfilling.

There was a horse in the yard. I turned the Ute around, so that my anvil was a couple of meters away from the gate. I had been there before and knew that the gate opened towards me. But unluckily for me, the horse in the yard was the wrong one. We have all got our own way of remembering horses, and to me, the horse in the yard was the big one, and the one in the paddock was the small one who had lost a shoe. It was just a five-minute job. I grabbed my halter and lead rope and jumped the fence. I walked over to the horse, put the halter on and wandered back to the yard where the horse in the yard clumsily rubbed against the gate.

To my horror the gate swung open against the Ute: it was not latched!

The horse slowly wandered through the open gate, and I still had to go around the yard to enter from the other side, which I did very quickly before tying my horse up on some bailing twine.

The escaped horse stood still, looked at us, then laughed at his mate, "Look at you! You are tied up in the yard, ha-ha, look at me, I am free."

With the neck arched very high, the horse started walking away from us, lifting its legs higher than the nicest dressage horse, changing its gait to a prize-winning trot past the house. At the corner in the drive the horse slowed down a bit to take the sharp corner. Then in front of him was a fifty-metre tree-lined driveway, going downhill most of the way, flattening out where it met a busy tar-sealed country road.

That is the moment you start praying, that point of no return, the start of something terrible happening. Scenes of horrible accidents start flashing in front of your eyes. Twenty metres before the road, the horse slowed down, turned around and started cantering back.

My prayers must have been heard.

It came right back past the house again towards the Ute. In a horse's mind I must look like an interesting entity sometimes, and a bogey man at other times. That day I must have looked like the spookiest thing in the whole wild world, as the horse had one look at me, and then turned around at great speed.

Disappointed to say the least, I stood there for a second with the piece of bailing twine in my hand I found for catching him again.

No finesse anymore, the horse decided, it's rip s#*! and bust time. Great lumps of dirt were flying around as the horse galloped on the side of the driveway where it was still very wet from winter.

I walked to the house, which was a bit elevated, where I would have a good look of the terrible things which could happen very soon. I was taken by the sheer idea of being witness to some terrible accident I had no control over, still wishing I could have done something. Standing on the well-kept lawn, high enough to see for bloody miles, I could see the horse galloping on the downward slope towards the road. There was not a car in sight on the left or on the right. We mere humans are conditioned, by the time we grow up, to think at an intersection... do we go left, right or straight ahead? The horse, although highly intelligent, thought (I think) that straight ahead was the quickest way to get away from that nasty man. In three strides it crossed the road and entered the neighbour's driveway; talking about being lucky. Words just can't describe how lucky it was that there was a driveway opposite this one in the first place.

At this point I got a hell of a fright.

There was supposed to be no one home, but someone was nudging the top of my shoulder next to my neck. What the hell was going on here? The other horse, not really happy being on her own, had decided to pull very hard on the bailing twine until it broke, and without making any sound, walked out of the yard, up towards and behind the house to give me a gentle nudge.

How good does it feel to be loved?

As I took the lead rope, we watched together what was happening across the road.

The horse had come to a sudden stop at the end of the far driveway, which turned into the garage, and took notice of his new environment—a parked car and a boat on a trailer... *"There is no way out, what the hell am I doing here?"*

Once again, a human is faced with three options when coming out of such a driveway: left, right or straight ahead. The horse needed three strides to get to the road, and I think that the speed he gained from these strides combined with his desire to be home, made him cross the road before any more cars or trucks passed. It was a busy road really, with a lot of cars going very fast on this rather straight and flat piece.

Like me, the small horse let out a big sigh of relief as it watched the horse come back up the hill at a 'Sunday morning canter'. With the friendly horse in tow, it was time for me to turn around and see if I could catch the horse this time. Indeed, nothing seemed to be a problem. The horse had shaken off all of its cobwebs so it stood as quietly as a lamb. I quickly tied my horse up in the yard, got my bailing twine, looped it around the neck of the escape artist, led the horse into the yard, latched the gate closed and finally relaxed. It was such a relief that all went well, and to celebrate, I decided it must have been time for a freshly made cuppa coffee. With one heaped teaspoon of Pam's instant coffee, one teaspoon of sugar, and the cup filled with hot water from my thermos flask, I could enjoy a celebratory, and what I sometimes call a lifesaving, cup of coffee. All I could think of is how lucky we were.

It took me only a few minutes to put the shoe back on. Right, you fellas, you can go back in your paddock now and eat some grass, I ushered them out.

How could I explain the deep hoof prints on the side of the drive to the owner? How was I to tell her what happened? I did check the horse, and there did not seem to be any injuries of any kind, so that was all covered. As it would involve a relatively big explanation, too big to text, I decided to leave it for now, as there were a few other horses needing attention at the moment.

As there were no inquiring or angry phone calls or text messages about the holes in the driveway, I decided to leave doing something about it for another day. As that day turned into another, and days into a week, it seemed to lose its importance. I resolved the problem in my mind by promising myself to tell her what and how it happened when I saw her next.

But there would be no next time. She left a very nice and polite, (just as she was) voice message on my mobile phone, thanking me for my services, but stating that she had had a change of plan and decided to let her regular farrier, who shod her own horse, to shoe her granddaughters horses as well.

I texted her back to confirm all was fine by me, as it made sense really for one farrier to shoe all the horses, and thanked her for her custom over the years. As she did not mention the holes in the driveway or ask what the hell happened, I did not either. She and her granddaughters would never know what happened that day.

Puhoi is at the southern end of my shoeing territory, an hour and twenty minutes' drive from home. For a few years I used to have heaps of customers there and I often carried on over the hill to Ahuroa to shoe a few more horses there.

It was a midsummer Friday afternoon, and I was shoeing a horse at one of those stables where there were a lot of horses from different owners who all seemed to have different farriers. Here I met Gregg and his apprentice, who were shoeing three horses there. Brendan called in as well, as he had just run out of horseshoe nails and came to borrow some nails from Gregg. It is always good to see fellow farriers, especially when they were working. I always seem to learn a bit more about the art of horseshoeing.

It was a hot day, one of the hottest of the summer, and that proved an interesting topic to start the conversation.

John the apprentice had it in for the weatherman on TV1. "For the last few weeks, Don the weatherman, with that big smile on his face, predicts the weather as nice and warm. Obviously, he never had to do an extremely physical job outside in the bloody burning sun. I would like to wipe that smile off his face one day."

"Even when he predicts the most horrible tropical cyclone, he got that smile on his face," Gregg added. "Just the way he is."

"There are not enough shady spots for us to hide in. Not too many customers of mine have got sheds or stables. Still hot in the shade, but that burning sun is a killer I am telling you," Brendan said.

I said, "Once I had a customer who had a loop road in front of her house, and in the middle, she had planted a beautiful tree with big leaves she called the Farrier Tree, especially for you fellas, she said. Mind you, she planted it twenty years ago, but there always seems to be a bit of a draught underneath a tree."

"Don't do that," Brendan said. "Just don't say that word 'draught'. Draught beer, I have been brought up on that stuff. You hear it less and less, but for me it always seems to wake me up."

"And the pub is not far away, probably the best one in a fifty-kilometre radius," John said.

"As if you would know where the good pubs are when you only just turned twenty. And do not even think about having a beer when we might stop there for a little while, as it happens to be your turn to drive us home," Gregg said.

But when the jobs were done, it was off to the pub. How could we resist when it was so hot and the pub was so close by. The Puhoi Pub was so rich in history that probably many a book has been written about it. I know of two couples who met there for the very first time. I don't know any couples who broke up there, but I don't go there very often, as I said, it is at the far end of my little world.

For Aucklanders, it is the first pub north out of town on State Highway 1 in a nice little rural village. For Northlanders, it is the last decent country pub before you hit Auckland. Puhoi itself was founded many years ago by people from Bohemia, a part of old Germany. They came by boat from Auckland and turned into the Wangaroa Bay, around fifty kilometres north of Auckland, and followed the river until they could go no further. The wharf is only a hundred metres from the pub.

These early settlers prided themselves incredibly lucky in finding this beautiful spot and immediately started converting the bush into farms suitable for beef and sheep. They did very well and soon built themselves homes, after which the school, church and pub were built. But in the local folklore they still argue that the pub was built first.

Driving around the countryside surrounding Puhoi, I always wonder why these people were so happy here, as the land in most places seemed too steep to do anything with. Surveying the hills around my favourite cup-of-coffee place, I could visualise those pioneers climbing these steep hills after the bush was cleared, with as many posts as they could carry on their backs as well as a spade. They would dig a hole, two feet deep, probably into limestone capped with a bit of clay. Then the post would go in, and the dirt would be rammed as solidly as it could around the post to make it stay tight for hopefully a very long time. After three or four posts it would have been time to go downhill again, have something to eat and drink and then climb uphill with a few more posts to complete the cycle.

There are quite a few pleasure horses around Puhoi nowadays, and there must have been workhorses there ages ago, but from where I was having my coffee, it seemed almost impossible for any workhorse to climb these hills with any load, whether on its back or on a sledge.

If these Bohemians thought they were in Heaven in Puhoi, I could not help but wonder what their home environment looked like.

Entering the pub was like entering a museum, or more to the fact, a place where time had stood still since a bygone era. The walls of the rectangular room were covered in all kinds of artefacts, tools, and photos from the pioneering days.

The bar itself was big, bold and made out of native timber. Plenty of signs touted beers and spirits no longer available. Unmistakable were some of the earliest Coca Cola advertisements. It was a place to get carried away by nostalgia.

But we were on serious business here... we came to quell our thirst and have a moan and a groan about the relentless summer in general and the day's burning sun. Presently being served at the bar was a couple of shearers, probably on the same mission as we were.

There were plenty of tables around, most of them still empty as it was early afternoon. The tables were not wide, but rather long, and the funny thing was that they stood rather high, so you needed a bar stool to feel comfortable if you wanted to sit. But on every table available there were only two or three bar stools. People were as happy to stand and lean on these tables as on the bar to have a yarn with their neighbour. In the old days, before I came here, the pubs used to close at six p.m., so you did not need to sit down after work as the pub closed soon, and when on your feet you could easily get another drink.

We took our drinks to a table next to the shearers and let it wet our tongue and slide down our throat.

"Wow, that is so nice. After three litres of water, this sure tastes like magic," one of the shearers said.

"Must have been hot in the shearing shed," Gregg said, "but at least you are lucky you had a roof over your head to shelter from the sun. Us fellows had to endure the fierce direct sun rays on our backs all day."

"No breeze today either," Brendan added.

The second shearer had to put in his bit by agreeing with Brendan, "No bloody breeze today indeed. It was the hottest day today in my whole career, I bet you. It might just force me into early retirement. And look who is coming in now... Neil and his fencing crew. I bet you, they can feel the heat too, they look even more sunburnt than you fellas," indicating us farriers.

Indeed, the fencers looked beat. They probably climbed up and down hills where none would dare drive a tractor, and work had not changed in one hundred and fifty years. They probably had been digging holes since seven this morning on the steepest hills imaginable. Apart from the motorised shearing piece, the handling of the sheep to be shorn had not changed either. And the same counted for the farriers.

Apart from our common centuries-old workmanship, we had the mercy and the wrath of the weather in common. And today, like the last three weeks, it was the relentless sun that tended to work us up a bit.

The first ones were heading back to the bar to refill their glasses. We all seemed to have a common reason to quell our thirst: the sun, the very hot and burning sun. Dragging posts up the hill, digging holes and putting in posts, going back for more, while the sun is literally burning your back.

Dragging the sheep out of the holding pen, and then putting it on its backside; shearing the wool. Don't think about the heat... the sheep is thirty-seven degrees hot, and so is the shearer, but there is no breeze coming through all the open doors and windows. The sun is burning on the roof. How hot is it here? Forty degrees? Fifty? The sheep finished, off down the chute they go. Don't look how many are left in the yard. Don't, it might kill you. Don't look at the clock; it will really upset you to see how long until the next break. Keep going, pace yourself, someone will tell you when it is time for a break. "Did we have lunch yet, or is it afternoon tea?" It is just too hot to think properly. Tonight, I will think about nice things, but first, another sheep.

"Oh why? Honestly, I don't want much, I only want to lift up your leg and have a look at your foot. Why don't you like it, what did I do to you? I don't even know you. But your boss wants me to put some shoes on your feet, so why make misery in this unforgiving relentless burning environment. I don't want to be here. I want to be home with my wife and kids, and above all, sit in the shade. To have some shade, now that would be a blessing. No! No way! Don't even think about it, no kicking, not today, not ever.

Why oh why does your owner think you are a good girl? Beats me, but she keeps on saying it all the time. According to me you are a little s#*! who always wants to have your own way.

Why do I persevere? Why don't I just walk away and tell your boss to find someone else to put the shoes on you? Is it pride or simply just not wanting to fail in the job I love? I don't love it today, you know; too hot, no shade. Life would be nice underneath a tree. A lush green one with a huge canopy. I like trees.

Now, stand still will you, I have not even started yet. The way we are going it will be three hours before the shoes are on. Why doesn't the owner tell you off? Why doesn't she discipline you and set some boundaries about what is acceptable and what is not?

It seems that the big difference between the fencer, shearer and the farrier is that the latter normally has an extra dimension to deal with, the contact with the boss, which can be stressful at times. Not just the one boss either, some days it could be eight or ten different directors. While most of them will be a pleasure to be around, there are still some who are away with the fairies when it comes to what acceptable horse behaviour is.

Being Friday afternoon, it would get busy very soon as it was the time to celebrate the end of the working week and the start of the weekend. There would be a lot of townies arriving for their weekly get-together with friends. Above all, the Puhoi Pub was a meeting place from way back where they would have a few drinks and have a good time. They would make plans about what to do that weekend while the weather was so glorious.

For our group it would be obvious that we would spend the whole weekend trying to stay out of the sun, recharge our batteries, and get ready to do it all over again come Monday morning.

Most of us were ready to leave for home when a man approached us. It was busy at the bar, and as there seemed to be a lull in our conversation he thought he would connect a bit with these men working on the land. His deduction would have been obvious by any standard: workmen dressed in singlets, jeans and boots only, their skin brown if not sunburnt red. He was obviously an office worker with some nice pants, bright shirt and polished shoes. He was only trying to be nice and strike a conversation while he was waiting for the bar to clear. All our eyes were on him as he ceremoniously wiped a bit of sweat from his forehead and said "That was a hot burning sun today, wasn't it?"

He did sum it up, all right. We looked at each other to see who would respond. We all seemed to be down in the dumps.

It was Gregg who seemed to be the brightest. "You should try working in it. Twelve hours a day. Only then will you know how burning hot that sun was today."

Gregg said it well, and he said it right, but instantly we felt sorry for the man who only wanted to strike a conversation as we all do at times.

But Gregg stood up and said to the man, "It will be my pleasure to buy you a drink, and I will tell you how hot it was today and you can tell me if the air-conditioning in your office was working well."

Gregg just had a way with people; the office worker was made to feel welcome, and it proved to be a wonderful few hours at the Puhoi Pub with a few more friends added to the list.

WARKWORTH

realequine

100% positive feedback(2275)

ADDRESS VERIFIED   IN TRADE

Northland
AROHA
Buy Now
$39.00

Northland
Hope
Buy Now
$30.00

Northland
WELCOME sign Red
Buy Now
$79.00

Northland
CROSS Rasp with Heart
Buy Now
$31.00

Northland
4 Hook Coat Hanger GREEN
Buy Now
$38.00

Northland
Kitchen Paper Hanger (left)
Buy Now
$26.00

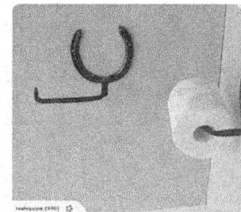
Northland
Toilet Paper Hanger (Left)
Buy Now
$19.00

Northland
WELCOME horse shoe sign black
Buy Now
$79.00

Northland
"STABLES" horse shoe sign
Buy Now
$49.00

Northland
LOVE horse shoe sign
Buy Now
$35.00

Northland
HORSE SHOE FRUIT BOWL
Buy Now
$59.00

FRANS JANSEN FARRIER PUTS A SHOE ON A HORSE

www.ingramcontent.com/pod-product-compliance
Lightning Source LLC
Chambersburg PA
CBHW071347290426
44108CB00014B/1468